ALSO BY ANGELA F. MURPHY

American Slavery, Irish Freedom: Abolition, Immigrant Citizenship, and the Transatlantic Movement for Irish Repeal (Louisiana State University Press, 2010)

The Jerry Rescue: The Fugitive Slave Law, Northern Rights, and the American Sectional Crisis (Oxford University Press, 2014)

Jermain Wesley Loguen

BLACK LIVES

Yale University Press's Black Lives series seeks to tell the fullest range of stories about notable and overlooked Black figures who profoundly shaped world history. Each book is intended to add a chapter to our larger understanding of the breadth of Black people's experiences as these have unfolded through time. Using a variety of approaches, the books in this series trace the indelible contributions that individuals of African descent have made to their worlds, exploring how their lives embodied and shaped the changing conditions of modernity and challenged definitions of race and practices of racism in their societies.

Jermain Wesley Loguen

DEFIANT FUGITIVE

Angela F. Murphy

Black Lives

Yale University Press | New Haven and London

Published with assistance from
The Office of the President, Yale University.

Published with assistance from the Mary Cady Tew Memorial Fund.

Yale University Press books may be purchased in quantity for educational, business, or promotional use. For information, please e-mail sales.press@yale.edu (US office) or sales@yaleup.co.uk (UK office).

Set in Freight Text Pro type by Integrated Publishing Solutions.
Printed in the United States of America.

Library of Congress Control Number: 2025934818
ISBN 978-0-300-27957-3 (hardcover)

A catalogue record for this book is available from the British Library.

Authorized Representative in the EU: Easy Access System Europe,
Mustamäe tee 50, 10621 Tallinn, Estonia,
gpsr.requests@easproject.com

10 9 8 7 6 5 4 3 2 1

CONTENTS

Jermain Wesley Loguen

INTRODUCTION

In February 1860, Syracuse resident Jermain Wesley Loguen received a disturbing letter from Maury County, Tennessee. It was from Sarah Logue, the woman who claimed him as her property. Loguen had escaped bondage at the Logue plantation twenty-five years earlier and settled in central New York, where he had established his reputation as a prominent minister, educator, reformer, and agitator in the quarter century since his escape. Throughout his adult life, the threat of reenslavement hung over his head, but he had not heard from the Logues in all that time. Now, however, Sarah found herself in dire economic straits and wrote to demand compensation from Loguen for the theft of his person. Loguen considered himself a free man. Sarah, and indeed the laws of the United States government, did not.

Sarah's letter opened casually enough. Addressing him as "Jarm," the name the Logue family had given him as a child, she said she wrote to let him know how the Logue household was faring. She was disabled but "still able to get about," and his mother, who remained on the Logue plantation, was "as well as common." She did not mention her husband, Manasseh Logue, the cruel enslaver who had abused Loguen in his youth, for he had passed away in 1852.

The letter then took a turn. Sarah told Loguen that the family was suffering financially and that she blamed the situation "partly in consequence of your running away and stealing Old Rock, our fine mare." She informed him that she had received an offer from a potential buyer to purchase her claim on Loguen. She needed the money, but she wished to present an alternative: "If you will send me one thousand dollars and pay for the old mare, I will give up all claim I have to you."

Sarah then proceeded to elaborate on the situation. "In consequence of your running away," she told him, the family had sold his siblings, Abe and Ann, as well as twelve acres of the Logue estate. She wanted money to reacquire the land. If he refused to send her the funds, she would arrange for someone else to purchase him, and, she said, "you may rest assured that the time is not far distant when things will be changed with you."

She also took issue with what she felt were lies Loguen had spread about his experiences with her family. The year before, Loguen published a narrative that detailed the hardships of his time enslaved by the Logues, an act that was likely what had drawn her attention to him as a source of financial relief. Sarah admonished Loguen for his depiction of the cruelty he experienced in slavery. "You know that we reared you as we reared our own children," she declared. She felt Loguen owed a debt to the family for the injustices he had committed against it, and she demanded: "You had better comply with my request."[1]

Since his escape from their plantation as a young man, Loguen had wondered when the Logues might try to assert their claim on him. He had fled from their Maury County property in his early twenties and, after a brief sojourn in Canada, settled in upstate New York, where he established himself not only as a minister but also as an educator and an outspoken reformer who agitated for racial justice. He had married, and he and his wife, Caroline, had six children in their Syracuse household, which served as a significant hub in the Underground Railroad network that aided other fugitives from slavery. Their operation was decidedly public, for the Loguens advertised their home address as a refuge for those fleeing slavery in city newspapers and made regular reports in the press of their actions. Since the passage of the Fugitive Slave Law of 1850, which pledged federal support to slaveholders who sought the return of those they enslaved from the free states, Loguen had become one of its most outspoken critics. He helped plan the rescue of a fugitive arrested under the terms of that law in Syracuse in 1851, following which he gained much attention for his advocacy for fellow freedom seekers. By the decade's end, he was known among his contemporaries in New York and beyond as the King of the Underground Railroad, for his household assisted more fugitives than any other station in that state. Loguen published a narrative of his enslavement, flight, and freedom, *The Rev. J. W. Loguen, as a Slave and as a Freeman,* in 1859 with the aid of abolitionist friends to raise money to finance the operation he ran out of his home.[2]

As Loguen gained attention throughout the North for his reform efforts, he and his colleagues knew he was ever more vulnerable to reenslavement. Abolitionist friends made numerous offers to purchase Loguen's freedom over the years so that the Logues would release their claim on him. Each time they offered to do so, however, Loguen refused. He believed that self-purchase was a compromise that would damage his reputation as a minister, a man, and an advocate for other fugitives such as himself. He was determined to use his position "as a defiant fugitive from slavery" to call attention to the wrongs of slavery so long as he, and so many others, remained exposed to them.[3]

Loguen was consistent with this position in his response to Sarah Logue, written on March 28, 1860. He told her he was glad to know his mother was alive and "as well as common," though he said, "What that means I don't know." He then wasted no time addressing her demands: "You sold my brother and sister, Abe and Ann, you say, because I ran away. Now you have the unutterable meanness to ask me to return and be your miserable chattel, or in lieu therof send you $1000 to enable you to redeem the *land*, but not to redeem my poor brother and sister!" He expressed pity for the disability she mentioned. Still, he told her he was "indignant beyond the power of words" that she should complain about her condition while informing him of the fate of his siblings and asserting her claim on his own life: "Wretched woman! Be it known to you that I value my freedom, to say nothing of my mother, brothers and sisters, more than your whole body; more indeed, than my own life; more than all the lives of all the slaveholders and tyrants under heaven."

He noted the irony of the threat to sell him if he did not send her money while "in the same breath and almost in the same sentence" claiming that the Logues had brought him up as they had their own children: "Did you raise your *own children* for the market? Did you raise them for the whipping post? . . . Where are my poor bleeding brothers and sisters? Can you tell?" If she was not responsible for selling them "into sugar and cotton fields, to be kicked, and cuffed, and whipped, and to groan and die," then her husband was, and she was complicit. "The very letter you sent me shows that your heart approves it all," he wrote. "Shame on you."

He closed the letter with an unequivocal rejection of her demand for compensation: "Did you think to terrify me by presenting the alternative to give my money to you or give my body to Slavery? Then let me say to you, that I meet the position with unutterable scorn and contempt." He lived among people who recognized his rights, he told her, and he assured Logue that he trusted them to "be my rescuers and avengers" should anyone threaten them.[4]

Jermain Wesley Loguen
(Courtesy of the Onondaga Historical Association)

After sending off his response, Loguen publicized the correspondence in sympathetic newspapers in Syracuse. The letters were then reprinted in the abolitionist press and, eventually, included as an appendix in a new edition of his freedom narrative. The exchange between Loguen and his former enslaver vividly drew attention to the shameless claims of slaveholders, his determination to reject them, and his expectation that his family, friends, and neighbors would support his resistance to reenslavement. Each of these had been recurring themes that textured Loguen's life's work. It was not the first time that Loguen had emphasized his fugitive status to draw attention to the injustices of American slave laws—but published at the height of the American sectional crisis over slavery, it was the last.[5]

Within a year of Loguen's airing of the letters, a civil war over slavery began in the nation, and a few years after that, emancipation would come. Loguen and those like him played no small part in this turn of events, for the stories of slavery told by fugitives from the South, their work to aid others who fled from enslavement, and their efforts to promote racial justice after relocating to the free states of the North had helped bolster northern sympathy for the twin causes of Black freedom and equality throughout the antebellum years. The aid that men and women like Loguen provided to freedom seekers, and their elevation of the cause of the slave among northern reformers, helped to provoke a defensive reaction in the South and a counterreaction in the North to southern demands for the protection of slavery, leading to the great sectional crisis that brought war and eventually the abolition of slavery in the nation.

For his part, Loguen worked tirelessly to highlight the injustices of slavery, but his focus was primarily on the needs of Black Americans who sought to establish lives in freedom. Loguen knew firsthand the devastation that those who seized their liberty felt at leaving behind friends and family in the only homes they ever knew, however tainted those places had been by the slaveholder. He knew also the importance of promoting security and opportunity for freedom seekers in the society into which they settled once they liberated themselves from slavery and established new homes. Even after emancipation came, Loguen would rely on his long-held identity as a defiant fugitive to guide his work. His own experiences of slavery, of carving out a new life in freedom, and of assisting others in doing the same informed his continued efforts on behalf of Black Americans during the first years of Reconstruction. Both before and after the fissure of the Civil War, Loguen advocated for their material, educational, and spiritual uplift, and he promoted social, economic, and political equality for all, regardless of race. The twin causes of his life's work were thus to provide aid to those who ran from slavery and to foster a virtuous society in which to live and prosper once liberty was secured. Through these efforts, Loguen's life is a compelling testament to the power of resilience, defiance, and the enduring quest for justice and equality in a nation that provided neither for Black Americans.

Although he labored alongside other notable reformers in upstate New York who are more familiar to most Americans—men and women such as Frederick Douglass, Harriet Tubman, and John Brown—Loguen is less well known to modern audiences. This is largely due to his desire to concentrate on the needs of the Black community at the local level and his tendency to take on essential administrative roles in the reform societies to which he belonged. He was at times, however, forced into the limelight by his desire to speak out against slavery and the laws that supported the institution, especially after the passage of the Fugitive Slave Law of 1850 made Black men and women in the northern states more vulnerable to enslavement. Indeed, he lectured forcefully against that law and actively resisted its execution. But Loguen was more comfortable ministering to the small Black congregations he circulated among in the towns surrounding his home base in Syracuse. He once explained to his friend Frederick Douglass that he felt writing was "not his *forte*" and that he had to work to overcome his tendency to speak "in the style of an untutored slave." He knew that he must raise his voice against injustice, nevertheless. "Had I not been horribly wronged, as you and all our race, I think I should have been a very still, quiet man," he told him, but "oppression has made me mad; it has waked up all my intellectual and physical energies."[6]

And so, Loguen spoke out publicly against slave laws, and he did so effectively. He was increasingly thrust into leadership roles within the activist community due to his growing stature among upstate New York reformers, Black and white. He worked closely with the leaders of the New York antislavery crusade, which included men such as Douglass, Samuel J. May, Gerrit Smith, and Samuel Ringgold Ward. He also rose to prominence as a religious leader in the African Methodist Episcopal Zion (AME Zion) Church, eventually becoming one of its bishops. Through all this, however, Loguen always prioritized Black uplift at the grassroots level. Although he would gain widespread contemporary attention through his protests of the Fugitive Slave Law and his Underground Railroad work during the 1850s, and later as a bishop in his church, he viewed himself as a community organizer and religious leader rather than a national figure, especially in the years before the Civil War.

It is time more people knew of the accomplishments of Black reformers like Loguen who contributed to the freedom struggle on the ground in their local communities. There were many such men and women, and historians are beginning more frequently to give them their due. Together, accounts of these lesser-known reformers—often, like Loguen, quite well known in their time—flesh out our understanding of Black activism by painting a picture of a vibrant Black community working together toward social justice rather than one of singular, exceptional figures who brought the needs of this community to the forefront of the American conscience on their own. Among these studies of nineteenth-century Black activists, scholars in recent years have given particular attention to the importance of those, like Loguen, who aided fugitives from slavery. This attention has come with the increasing recognition of the historical significance of the impact of the Fugitive Slave Law, the self-liberation of the enslaved, and the Underground Railroad in the larger story of the abolition of slavery in the American Republic. Loguen's life is an important part of this history, for his work fused the need to attack the oppressive system of slavery that defined the society *from* which fugitives fled with the need to elevate the Black condition in the society *to* which they ran. And after emancipation, Loguen's work for racial justice in New York informed the broader effort to aid the freedpeople of the South and attack racial subjugation throughout the newly reconstituted American nation. A lifespan does not honor the traditional chronological divisions that we erect in the study of history, and so Loguen's life story, as well as that of other nineteenth-century Black activists, naturally highlights the continuities in the Black freedom struggle over time.[7]

Loguen was a remarkable man. He was complicated and full of contradictions. He was outspoken but also full of humility; he was a nurturer but also a fighter; and above all he was a family man, even as he had to abandon family members left behind in slavery. Loguen's unique life experiences allowed him to connect with fellow fugitives and needy members of the northern Black population in an especially effective way as he clung to his fugitive identity and ministered to their needs. At the same time, Loguen recognized that his work was part of a larger collective effort, and he was not shy about crediting the support of his family and the larger community in which he lived as he carried out his mission. Loguen's story is thus not only his own; it sheds light on the goals and tactics of Black reformers of his era writ large. His emphasis on Black self-help, the claims Black Americans had to the fruits of American freedom, the need for equal rights and economic opportunities, and the importance of Black political solidarity were all characteristic of this community of reformers. This biography is thus not only about Loguen's personal transformation in his journey from slavery to freedom to leadership in the reform circles of upstate New York and later the nation; it also provides a window on the larger nineteenth-century Black American experience.

The following pages bring the story of Jermain Wesley Loguen and his life's work for racial justice to the broad audience he deserves. Highlighted throughout is Loguen's conception of himself as a man, a minister, a fugitive, and a freeman. Equally significant are his roles as a son, husband, and father and his engagement with a broader community of activists. These relationships underscore the pivotal roles that home, family, and community played in his endeavors. All these dimensions of his identity collectively propelled his trajectory as an important voice for a generation of Black Americans.

As a fugitive who had been able to elevate his own position in society, Loguen saw his life as a testament to God and an example for others. He believed that those who, like himself, had escaped slavery and achieved a measure of success in freedom had an obligation to aid other members of the Black community to do the same. His life bore witness to this conviction.

CHAPTER 1

Slavery

IN JUNE 1865, Jermain Wesley Loguen visited his old home in Tennessee, now a free man. In October of the previous year, the military governor of the state, Andrew Johnson, had declared all its enslaved population free, and in February 1865, an amendment to the Tennessee constitution codified emancipation within the state's borders. Any previous claims his old enslavers made on Loguen's body were now nullified. It was a triumphant, yet bittersweet, return.

As Loguen approached the rough plantation on which he came of age, little of it seemed familiar to him. Situated on Little Bigby Creek near Columbia, Tennessee, the plantation and surrounding landscape had been altered by time and the devastation of war. The estate where old Manasseh Logue and his household had lived, farmed, and distilled whiskey was nearly unrecognizable. Manasseh had since died, but his wife, Sarah—she who had written the letter five years before, threatening his freedom—survived. Loguen sought out the old woman when he arrived but found that he no longer recognized her nor she him. His brothers and sisters had either been sold away or perished. Everyone was a stranger. "The land of my childhood," Loguen wrote to a friend at home in Syracuse, New York, "was like a strange land."

There was one familiar face, however—the face he had come to see. Though she had become "aged and infirm," Loguen recognized his mother. The years had done their work on the woman, whose birth name was Jane but who was known on the Logue plantation as Cherry. The jet-black skin he remembered from childhood was now wrinkled, and her hair, worn short and curled to the head, was now gray. Her body, which he remembered as "large, symmetrical, round, and muscular" and "a model of health and strength," was infirm and bent with age. Nevertheless, to him she was unmistakable.

Jane recognized her son as well. The tall, broad, middle-aged man with a mane of hair neatly parted on the side held little resemblance to the wiry youth who had fled from the plantation nearly thirty-five years before; still, she knew him immediately. He asked her how she was able to recognize her child in the man he had become after so many years had passed. She said that she knew him by his walk.[1]

Loguen had spent most of his adulthood in New York State, away from his mother, but she had never been far from his mind. He was free, and she had remained in slavery in Tennessee. His life's regret was that he failed to deliver her from that condition. After his own flight from the Logue plantation, he had been cut off from family members by the border between slavery and freedom in the United States. As long as his home state sanctioned slavery, it had been too dangerous for him to travel there. Now, in 1865, emancipation had finally made it safe for Loguen to venture back to see his loved ones.

And so Loguen returned to the place where his life's story had begun. To understand his early life of enslavement, as well as his development into the defiant man he would become, we rely heavily on Loguen's later reminiscences. In 1859, Loguen joined the ranks of fugitives who published their experiences of slavery and escape with *The Rev. J. W. Loguen, as a Slave and as a Freeman: A Narrative of Real Life.* Written in the third person, his account reads like a novel, but as the title indicates, the work is the "real life" personal narrative of his early years in slavery and freedom. In many ways Loguen's memoir follows a template common among the numerous freedom narratives published during the 1850s. It recounts the horrors of slavery, giving particular emphasis to the administration of cruel corporal punishment, the threat of separation that loomed over slave families, and the special victimization of enslaved women. It emphasizes the importance of literacy, education, and temperance. And it highlights the hypocrisy of the Christian slaveholder. Throughout it all, Loguen recounted the evolution of his sense of himself as a man, which was what led to his quest to assert his independence, gain his freedom, and help others do the same. Following a rousing story of escape, it then explores the beginning of Loguen's life as an activist.[2]

In addition to these familiar themes found in most freedom narratives, one that is central in Loguen's account is the profound significance of home and family. Loguen's narrative is replete with references to his sense of homelessness and his relentless pursuit of what social critic bell hooks has called a "homeplace." In Loguen's life, the concept of home was not merely a physical space but a sanctuary of resistance and resilience. Loguen's search for home thus was not just about finding a safe place for himself and others but also about establishing a sense of belonging and stability that had been denied by racial oppression and the institution of slavery. And even as he was able to do so, Loguen also suffered a sense of loss. Following his flight from Tennessee, as he worked to establish a homeplace for himself and others, Loguen was haunted by thoughts of his mother and siblings left behind when he seized his own freedom. As he tells the story of his past, Loguen thus chronicles his experiences with a poignant emphasis on the instability of the home in slavery and the desire to create a society where all Black Americans could establish a stable and nurturing homeplace for themselves in freedom. And so, informed by the narrative he published in 1859, we begin his story at his "old slave home" in Tennessee.[3]

Jermain Loguen's mother remembered almost nothing of her life before she was kidnapped from her home in Ohio at the age of seven. In discussions with her son, she indicated that she had lived under the guardianship of a man named McCoy and that her given name was Jane. The trauma of her abduction and later enslavement wiped out all other memories of her birthplace. She knew nothing of her kin or the details of her first years of life beyond a "distinct remembrance" that "she was once free." When she spoke to him of her past, she expressed regret that she had only a "flickering recollection of happy days in early childhood."[4]

She did remember in vivid detail the day she was seized by kidnappers, sometime around 1802. She had been out of sight and hearing of her home when a man approached her from a covered wagon. He grabbed her and placed his hand over her mouth to prevent her from screaming, pulling her into his lap in the front of the vehicle. As the man told the teamster to drive on, Jane saw that there were other children of her dark skin-tone in the back. All were around her own age. All were sobbing, their captors issuing threats to silence them. "For long and weary days and nights," Loguen later said of her story, "not a joyous look or laugh varied their depression and wretchedness" as they undertook the journey across the Ohio River into the slave state of Kentucky. Once in Kentucky, the kidnappers sold the children one by one to purchasers found along the road as they traveled south.[5]

Jane's journey ended in Davidson County, Tennessee, on a small plantation on Mansker's Creek, about sixteen miles from

Nashville in the central part of the state. She was purchased by Elinor Logue, a widow who lived there with her three sons and two daughters. Elinor was looking to add to the small force of enslaved laborers who had been left to her after the death of her husband, John, and children like Jane who could be purchased from illicit slave traders were affordable.[6]

When Jane arrived at the rough log home on what Loguen later called a "miserably cultivated plantation," the widow and her family at first received her with warmth and concern, reassuring a child scared and weary from travel. But when Jane began to tell them that she was born free in Ohio and had been stolen by those who sold her to Elinor, their friendly expressions were replaced by angry frowns. They whipped her and threatened her with greater violence until she promised she would "never again repeat the offensive fact of her freedom." Once she capitulated to this demand, the Logues told her that she was to go by the name of Cherry from that moment on. Jane felt that not just her freedom but her very identity had been stolen from her. "Thus was this innocent child," Loguen stated in his retelling of the story, "metamorphosed from a human being into chattel."[7]

Jane's transportation south across the Ohio River indeed signaled a change in her status. In 1787, the Northwest Ordinance had prohibited slavery in the Northwest Territory, the land above the Ohio River that later would become the states of Ohio, Indiana, and Illinois. Below the river, the Southwest Territory remained open to slavery. In 1802, around the time that Jane was abducted, the state of Ohio was formed with a constitution that made slavery illegal, while south of the Ohio River the new states of Kentucky and Tennessee allowed the enslavement of human beings.

It is important to note that this does not mean that all Black Americans in Ohio were free at the time of Jane's kidnapping. Although chattel slavery—which defined a person as a piece of property that could be bought and sold—was barred in Ohio's state constitution, other forms of bondage existed there. In particular, it was common for white settlers in the region to hold Black indentured servants, for although Ohio law prohibited slavery, it allowed for those who brought enslaved people into the state to hold them for a period of time before they were considered free. These servants worked without wages for room and board. In addition, many children were bound to indenture in Ohio due to the economic hardship faced by Black families. Parents hoped that such a contract would not only provide for their children's material needs but also allow them to gain skills that might set them up for independence later in life. By law, female children who were indentured gained their freedom at age eighteen and males at age twenty-one. Although Jane did not remember the circumstances of her childhood before her kidnapping, her reference to McCoy as a guardian indicates that this may have been her situation. Whatever her status in Ohio, however, there is no question that her transport across the river through Kentucky and into Tennessee robbed her of a future in freedom.[8]

Sadly, Jane's situation was not unique. The kidnapping of Black Americans from free territories to sell in the slave states happened regularly in early US history. Children such as Jane were especially vulnerable because they had little power to challenge their new situation and because it was easier to erase a young child's memory of his or her origins. Although kidnapping was illegal throughout the young republic, there was an absence of effective legal protection for free Black Americans that would ensure their independence. Most southern whites assumed a Black person was a slave unless they could prove their freedom, and most were dismissive of an enslaved person's claims to free status. Without the presence of freedom papers, which kidnappers would be careful to remove if found on those they abducted, only a white witness could attest to assertions of freedom. What's more, most southerners would not be disposed to validate a freedom claim even if they had no vested interest in the situation.

White Americans did little to prevent the illegal practice of kidnapping and selling free people into slavery, and because the practice carried few risks, its easy profits rapidly drew disreputable men into the business. In time, free states would institute stronger antikidnapping laws to protect their vulnerable Black populations, but these were often ineffective in the face of federal legislation that supported slaveholders' right to claim their human property when an enslaved person fled. Kidnappers seized many free Black people under the guise of upholding federal fugitive slave legislation. In his recounting of his family background, Loguen commented on this situation in reference to his mother. The status of "colored orphans" such as herself, he said, "illustrate[s] the helplessness of the whole colored race, in a country where slavery is guarded and sacred; [for] in proportion as slavery has the protection of law, do the persons of all colored men, women and children, lose the protection of the law." There was no place in the United States that a Black person could feel truly free from the threat of bondage.[9]

Jane was thus enslaved and absorbed into the Logue household with the new name of Cherry. She begrudgingly accepted the name and obediently refrained from speaking of her origins publicly, but according to Loguen, she never made peace with her condition. She submitted to the demands of the Logue family out of self-preservation, but her submission was "with the same contentment that the young Leopard feels under the restraints that cages and tames him."[10]

The Logues settled Jane in a small cabin in the slave quarters near the main house, itself a rustic log home where Elinor lived with her children. Jane was charged with many responsibilities on the small plantation, including domestic work in the main house, fieldwork, and, eventually, oversight of the family's distillery, the Logues' most profitable operation.

The Logue plantation was typical of the small frontier operations found in central Tennessee. In addition to the production of whiskey, the family grew crops, including corn for their distillery, and raised livestock on Mansker's Creek. Elinor had settled on the land bordering the creek with her husband, a Scotch Irish Presbyterian named John Logue Jr., in 1789, a year before North Carolina ceded this frontier area to the federal government. The Logue family had left their home in Orange County, North Carolina, after the state gave John a thousand-acre military grant on its frontier in recognition of his Revolutionary War service. The land grant was on Sugg's Creek on the south side of the Cumberland River in what was then Davidson County. John would later deed this land to his three sons, but he and Elinor never settled on it. Instead, they carved out their homestead on Mansker's Creek for safety reasons. At the time they arrived in the area, hostilities between white settlers and the Cherokee population in the Cumberland region were rampant. Many white families moving into the backcountry during this period chose to set up their homes near American forts, which they felt offered a measure of security. There was such a fort on Mansker's Creek.[11]

John died in 1793, and soon after, hostilities with the Cherokee population abated, leaving Elinor and her children to live in relative peace. Her daughters married and set up households elsewhere, but her three unmarried sons lived with Elinor well into adulthood. Eventually the older sons, Manasseh and Carnes, would move away to establish their own homesteads—Carnes settling on the land left to him by his father on Sugg's Creek, and Manasseh selling his share and establishing a small plantation near Columbia in Maury County, Tennessee, around sixty miles to the southwest. The youngest son, David, also sold his share of the Sugg's Creek property, and in exchange he acquired the deed to the eighty acres his mother lived on at Mansker's Creek, becoming the head of that household. By the time he took charge of the place, David had fathered three children with Jane.[12]

Loguen stated that "it is rarely possible for a slave to identify his father with so much certainty" as he could, for Jane had been the "admitted mistress" of David Logue since she came of age. And Loguen bore a strong resemblance to him: "his size and form—his walk and motions, everything but his hair and complexion, was a striking expression of him" as he grew older.[13]

Sexual connections between white male slave owners and enslaved Black women were accepted, yet generally concealed, throughout much of the slave-owning South; but in frontier societies such as Mansker's Creek, these relationships often took place out in the open. Because there were few white, marriageable women in the region, white men often chose to have open relationships with those over whom they claimed ownership, and few questioned these associations. Thus, according to Loguen, Jane and David Logue's connection was "confessed and allowed, not by the parties only, but by the family and the neighborhood." By the time she was twenty-eight years old, Jane had given birth to the three children fathered by David Logue, and among them was the child who would eventually take the name Jermain Loguen. She called him Jarm. Her other two children were girls, one of whom she rebelliously named Jane. The other's name was Ann. They all went by the surname of Logue.[14]

Loguen's paternal connection to the man who claimed him as a slave was a common one throughout the South. Although many in Mansker's Creek referred to Jane as David's "mistress," implying a consensual relationship, it must be remembered that the men who held bondspeople had control over the bodies of those they claimed as property. Varying degrees of force were involved in the relationships that took place between white slave owners and enslaved Black women, but all relied on the oppressive arrangements that gave one person power over another. None of these relationships could be truly consensual.

Still, although she had little choice in her part of it, Jane's relationship with David Logue offered her a modicum of security and protection within the institution of slavery—at least for as long as Jane remained in David's favor. "Ignorant and brutal as were her masters," Loguen remembered, the family respected both Jane's "natural loveliness" and her "indomitable impulses under wrongs"; and although Jane had to accept "violence from her masters" and remain cautious in her resistance of their brutality, according to Loguen "she never endured it from others."

Loguen's narrative contains a story that illustrates his mother's situation. Because Jane was attractive and because she spent long hours working in a distillery, she was often surrounded by white men who were hard drinkers. These men frequently harassed her with drunken advances, all of which she "promptly repelled." Because of the Logue family's standing and the recognition of her relationship with David, most of these men retreated in the face of her rejection. On one occasion, however, a white neighbor tried to force himself on Jane violently, and Jane, "careless of caste and slave laws . . . grasped the heavy stick used to stir the malt, and dealt him a blow." Her attacker was not dissuaded. He retrieved a knife and continued to advance on her. Jane was able to knock the knife from his hand with the stick she still held, but he continued his approach. Making use of the stick once again, Jane "plied a blow upon his temple," knocking the man unconscious.

Jane believed she had killed her assailant, but she did not flee. Instead, she went to the main house to inform the Logue family what had happened. The entire family ran to the distillery, where they found their neighbor "laying in his gore," near death but not deceased. They cleaned his wounds and sent him home, where after many weeks he recovered. Although she acted in self-defense, Jane and the rest of the slave quarters prepared themselves for harsh punishment, for Jane had laid her hands on a white man. Instead, she faced no consequences. Her relationship with David Logue offered her protection.

Loguen was around six years old when this attack took place, and he said that he remembered it well because it became the stuff of legend in Mansker's Creek—a story often told among the Black residents of the area. When Loguen recounted this story in later years, he expressed pride in his mother's willingness to defend herself and to hold "her own estimate of her rights and wrongs." Although as he grew older he had to witness her "knocked down with clubs, stripped and bound, and flogged with sticks, ox whips and rawhide until the blood streamed down the gashes upon her body," his grief and pity was replaced with pride after these attacks as "when released from the place of torture, she never retired with a subdued spirit." She returned to her work—"a sullen tigress." Loguen considered his mother to be a role model, and throughout his life he adopted a similar spirit of resistance in the face of great wrongs.[15]

Despite the sentiments Loguen later expressed for his mother in his remembrances, Jarm did not witness the brutality of her situation in his earliest years. As a young child he was ignorant of her, and his own, subservient place within the Logue family, and he felt great affection for and admiration of his father. Dave, as family and friends called him, was a commanding presence, a "full six feet high" and "sprightly in the issue of abundant muscle"; and Loguen described him as a man who had inherent generosity and nobility. Although he was an "impulsive, drinking, and chivalrous rowdy" who was "unscrupulous in his pleasures," Loguen noted that he was always ready to help a friend. Later in life, Loguen would say that he believed that if Dave had been raised in the northern states of the union, he would have been someone to admire. He blamed the corrupting environment of frontier Tennessee for his father's shortcomings.[16]

Dave had lavished affection on Loguen when he was a child, for he was, according to Loguen, his father's "pet." He had at times allowed Jarm to sleep in his bed and throughout his childhood treated him with "many little favors and kindnesses which won his young heart." In return, Jarm had "loved and revered him as a father." This blind reverence would end abruptly, however, once he was confronted with knowledge of his mother's, and his own, tenuous status within the Logue household.

Loguen would later muse that his early youth was "an exception to the general rule" of most of those born into slavery. He experienced "multitudes of kindnesses, partialities, and unquestionable loves" as he grew up, and he had been free to range around the Logue property, playing by the bank of Mansker's Creek, hunting mice and chipmunks, fishing, playing with ducks and geese, and napping in the sun or shade. Wearing a "single loose, coarse cotton garment" that "covered his burly body" in the winter as well as the summer, he helped to feed livestock on the farm, and he was at times allowed to "ride on Dave's back or trot by his side" to the main house, where he would play with Elinor, whom he called "Granny." At times, Jarm spent the night at the main house. Of his early years, Loguen professed that "personally, he suffered no treatment from his masters which hinted to him he was a slave."[17]

He would, however, gradually come to understand the nature of slavery. He witnessed the abuse of other Black children on the property for actions "which he knew would not attract censure had he been the subject," and the inconsistency puzzled him. He also saw men taking children away, never to return. He had memories of Granny telling him that he would be free someday, unlike these other children, but he did not fully realize what her words meant at the time. His real awakening to slavery came, however, when he encountered his mother by Mansker's Creek one summer evening when he was around seven years old. Not knowing of her son's presence, Jane had approached the creek, crying in distress and bleeding. She had intended to wash herself in its waters before seeing anyone, but as she began her task, Jarm interrupted her grief, approaching to ask her what was wrong.

She broke down when she saw him. She had hoped to shield him from the truth of their position in the Logue household longer, but she worried that her son might endanger his own favored position with the Logues if he went to them with questions about her distress. She also feared that as Jarm grew, he would assert his independence and manhood in a way that the family would find threatening and that this would put him in danger. So, Jane explained to Jarm what had happened to her. It would be his introduction to the conditions of their enslavement.

Jane told Jarm that she had angered Carnes Logue and that he had whipped her. She made Jarm promise not to let Carnes, Manasseh, "or even Dave" know that he was aware of what happened. "If you should speak to them about it," she warned him, "they will not treat you so well as they have done." She told him that Carnes and Manasseh often beat her, "and even Dave had lately treated her roughly" as their romantic connection had waned. She then explained fully to him their "helpless condition" in the household and related the story of how slave traders stole her as a child and sold her to "Granny" and the "white Logues." She warned him that, although he was now loved by Granny, Dave, and the other members of the family, he must be cautious with them and take care to maintain their goodwill. She feared that if "his unrestrained spirit should be an inconvenience to her oppressors . . . Dave would consent to the breaking of it, by the same brutal treatment that other little colored children on the plantation suffered." Worse, she feared that they would sell him to slave traders, and they would never see each other again.

This conversation forever changed Jarm's feelings about his white family members. He continued to have free run of the property in the immediate years that followed, but he felt increasingly distant from his father and grandmother. Even so, Jarm heeded Jane's warnings to hide his growing sense of resentment of the power dynamics within the household.[18]

Jarm's education on slavery advanced further when he was around ten years old. One spring day, as he was taking a walk, he witnessed a horrific incident on the bank across Mansker's Creek. Loguen later remembered that he had been lost in the beauty of his surroundings when he heard a "howl of agony" from the opposite bank. He quickly took shelter. From his hiding place he had a clear view of the owner of the land on the other side of the creek, "a savage man" and "habitual drunkard" named Zachariah Betts, known for his cruelty to the men and women he held in bondage. Jarm witnessed Betts murder one of his enslaved laborers—a young man named Sam whom he knew as "a good-feeling, kind-hearted fellow." Just a few weeks earlier, Sam had scooped Jarm out of the creek when it began to flood with rain, keeping him from drowning. Now he watched with horror as Betts beat Sam, whom he had strapped to a whiskey barrel on the bank above the stream of Mansker's Creek, in front of a group of bondspeople. After Sam took his last breath, Betts simply rolled the barrel into the river, Sam still attached. He then instructed the enslaved onlookers to retrieve the body and bury it. In shock, Jarm stealthily removed himself from his hiding place and made his way home. "Any more teachings on the subject of the slave's helplessness, and hard fate," Loguen said of the event, "were now superfluous."[19]

But it was not only Jarm's expanding understanding of enslavement that changed his perception of the Logues from family to enslavers. His relationships were also shifting because of his father's loss of affection for his mother. In 1816 or 1817, Dave brought into the home a white woman, Polly Gascoe, to become his wife. In preparation for her arrival, Dave distanced himself from Jane and their offspring. Jarm at first felt relief at the turn of attention away from his mother, for he had grown disgusted by the "forced and unnatural" nature of the relationship. What he did not realize, however, was that the arrival of Polly also made Jane and her children more vulnerable to the vagaries of the slaveholding system.[20]

By the time that Dave married Polly, his brothers had moved on to set up their own households, and Dave had become the sole owner of the Mansker's Creek property and its enslaved labor force. With his impending marriage, Dave for the first time was feeling "the delicacy of his condition as father of the colored Logues." He and Elinor decided that the best way to keep Jane and her children on the plantation while avoiding "disturbing domestic influences" that would upset his new wife was to arrange for a new relationship for Jane. Although Tennessee law did not recognize slave marriages, the Logues felt that an informal union, such as those that were often formed within and between the slave quarters in slaveholding communities, would be their solution to the continued presence of Dave's children and former mistress. They wanted to find someone to "represent a husband and father" to Jane and her children as Dave pursued a life with Polly.

The Logues found this man in Henry, "a kind, warm-hearted fellow" around the age of thirty, who was enslaved on a neighboring plantation and who held affection for Jane. Although he was fond of the woman he knew as Cherry, Henry was initially reluctant to marry. He had witnessed the heartbreak of many families broken up by sales to slave traders and did not wish to make himself vulnerable to such grief. In response to these concerns, both Dave and Henry's enslaver promised the couple that they would never be separated by more than ten miles if they united as a family.[21]

With this promise, Jane and Henry happily consented to the proposed relationship, and Loguen remembered the years immediately following their union as a time of relative contentment. For Jane, the bond with Henry had brought a feeling of hope and belonging that made her daily workday bearable. After one year, they had a son, Henry Jr., expanding their family. It was a happy time for Jane and her children. Within two years, however, Dave Logue's financial affairs would cause him to destroy this family that he had helped to create.[22]

The Logues had never been particularly good businessmen, but Jarm noticed that his father had become more attentive to his work and serious in demeanor since taking a new wife. The plantation seemed to thrive as it had not before, and there was a general sense of "more order, peace, and profit" in its affairs. The improved situation, however, was a result of Dave's attempt to avoid losing the plantation to creditors who were starting to demand payment. An eleven-year-old Jarm became alarmed when he overheard one of Dave's friends offer to purchase Jarm to help Dave out financially. Dave refused, but he then confided to his friend that unless he could stave off his creditors, he would have to give up some of his people. He said he knew this "will break their hearts" and "almost break" his own, but he must do something to avoid bankruptcy.[23]

If Dave had not had so many creditors, he might have been able to salvage his situation; but as they became aware of one another, they all filed against him quickly to have priority over any lien placed on his property. They were not willing to wait for profits to begin to roll in from his improvements at Mansker's Creek. Soon Dave realized that to remain solvent he would have to sell his land and all his bondspeople, including Jane, Jarm, and Jarm's siblings. Although he had promised Jane that he would eventually grant freedom to their children, and although he also had promised never to separate Jane and Henry, Dave concluded that he could not keep his promises and avoid financial ruin. In telling the story of Dave's actions in later years, Loguen acknowledged that the decision to "convert his slaves, and even his own flesh and blood, into money to pay his debts" pained his father. Ultimately, though, "his interest overbalanced his sympathies and good intents," and Dave decided to sell everything off as quickly and for as much money as possible.[24]

Dave was careful to keep the sale a secret from everyone until the deed was done. He found a buyer for the acreage on Mansker's Creek and then went to Nashville, where he found a trader who was willing to purchase all his enslaved laborers. The purchaser told Dave that he planned to transport them to Alabama. Dave's brother Manasseh lived on a plantation to the southwest of Mansker's Creek, along the path the trader would travel, and so as part of the bargain, Dave insisted that the trader sell Jane and her children to his brother. With this provision, Dave was able to alleviate some of his feelings of guilt in his belief that he had made better arrangements for his offspring than for the rest of the laborers. They would remain within the Logue family, at least for a time.[25]

On the day that Dave finalized the sale, Henry had come to Mansker's Creek for a visit. He, Jane, and the children had joined "the whole circle of slaves" who were "seated around their cabins, in the same social and happy contentment they enjoyed since Dave was the separate owner of the estate." They had no hint that this would be the last time they would all be together.

At the end of the evening, Henry returned home; and that night, when all the enslaved people on the Logue plantation were asleep, slave traders entered the cabins and began to place the strongest men and women in chains. When Jane awoke to her situation, she called out for Dave, and then she called out for Henry; but the only responses she received were from strangers that "stood over her and the rest, armed with whips and pistols." After subduing them, the intruders chained all the bondspeople together in an extensive line known as a coffle. The next morning, attached to a wagon and with men on horseback at its front and back, the coffle was marched southwest, away from the only home Jarm had ever known.

Following the sale, Jarm would not encounter Dave Logue again. Tennessee records indicate that after he liquidated his landholdings, Dave remained in Davidson County in his mother's home until her death in 1831. He and Polly divorced after just a few years of marriage, and in 1830, Dave married a woman named Susan Winchester. After 1830, David Logue no longer appears in Tennessee census reports, but in 1854, he emerges in records for the state of Missouri. In that year, at the age of sixty, he applied for bounty land in return for earlier service as a member of a Tennessee regiment of volunteers in the War of 1812. In his application, Dave listed his place of residence as St. Louis County.[26]

Despite his disappointment with his father and his feelings of betrayal and abandonment, Loguen never completely lost his care or concern for Dave Logue. In 1859, when he recounted the story of his childhood, Loguen expressed his regret that after he seized his freedom and became a man of moderate means, he could not "contribute to his father's necessities—and help the infirmities of his sin-smitten and rapidly declining age." Loguen's legal status as chattel prevented him from being able to do so, for to aid his father might call attention to his location and make him a target for reenslavement. And the conditions he experienced after he was sold to Dave's brother would build within him a resolve, once he escaped them, never to make himself vulnerable to such treatment again.[27]

After several days of travel, Jarm and his enslaved family members arrived at Manasseh's place on Bigby Creek in Maury County, near the town of Columbia. There Dave's brother lived with his wife, Sarah, and their children, most of whom were older than Jarm. On this plantation, the Logues grew wheat and corn, and, following the Mansker's Creek model, Manasseh erected a distillery for the manufacture of whiskey. It was here, Loguen recalled, that young Jarm truly "felt, for the first time, what it was to be a slave."[28]

Because of his favored position in his father's home, Jarm had never learned how to do fieldwork, but at Manasseh's plantation he was immediately sent out to labor in the corn and wheat fields with the other enslaved hands. Jarm was in his preteen years at this time, but he looked old for his age. The overseer thus expected the productivity of a man from him. He was thankful for his mother's presence alongside him, for she helped him to learn to keep up with the work and avoid punishment.

And there were serious punishments imposed when work fell short of expectations. Jarm saw many of his friends from the slave quarters "maimed and bruised shockingly, and sometimes left almost dead" after angering one of the Logues. During his second year on the Maury County plantation, Jarm himself felt the wrath of Manasseh's anger. As he was working in the fields one day, the iron wedge of his hoe slipped from its handle as Manasseh watched. An inebriated Manasseh punished him by shoving the wedge into Jarm's mouth and pounding on it. When Jarm resisted and was able to remove the iron from his mouth, Manasseh picked up the discarded iron and began to strike the boy on his head and face with its sharp end, leaving bloody gashes. After the beating, Manasseh then ordered Jarm to get up "and learn how to wedge a hoe." Loguen later said that after this experience, he "saw there was no other way for him, but to bear his trials with all possible discretion—and if an opportunity occurred to escape, to embrace it at whatever peril."[29]

Although Loguen recognized that slaveholding was in its very nature inhumane, in later accountings of his time on Bigby Creek, he also blamed the intemperance of the Logues for the brutality of Black life on their plantation. Manasseh and Sarah were mean drunks, and violence toward those they enslaved was especially common when they had partaken of liquor, something they did frequently. A temperance man later in his life, Loguen highlighted in his remembrances what he saw as the corrupting power of alcohol as well as of slavery. Not only did whiskey from their distillery cause the Logues to behave like "beasts," but their frequent drunkenness also robbed any sense of security from those they enslaved. "The slave must fit himself to the will of his master," Loguen said, and "this they can never do if his master is a drunkard." No one on the Logue plantation felt safe around Manasseh or Sarah "except those rare times when their tormentors were not in liquor."[30]

A year after Jarm's violent encounter with Manasseh over the hoe, however, an event took place that gave the Black residents on the Logue plantation a measure of hope for an improvement of their condition. The Logues' distillery caught fire and burned to the ground. The cause was not known. The Logues speculated that someone had accidentally left the fires burning overnight in the building, but it must also have occurred to them that one or more of their bondspeople may have been responsible. Arson was a common form of slave resistance in the American South—one of the few tools available to enslaved workers to help to regulate their experience of slavery. Whatever the fire's origin, it is notable that at the sight of the distillery's destruction, Loguen remembered that "the negroes were delighted," for they saw it "as the cause of their daily peril, terror, and suffering."[31]

When Manasseh, Sarah, and their children witnessed the distillery burning, Loguen said that their first thought was for their "aching appetites and failing revenues." Despite the economic value of the distillery, however, Manasseh and Sarah eventually came to see its destruction as a blessing in disguise. As whiskey consumption had increased throughout the region, so did concern for the problems it created, and religious reformers had begun to encourage settlers to abandon habits of drink. The Logues would soon be swept up in the religious revivalism that spread through Tennessee, and this led them to a pledge to change their ways.[32]

The evangelical spirit that had spread through the countryside became known as the Second Great Awakening, and it affected both the Black and white residents of the Logue plantation. In the first half of the nineteenth century, this surge of religious sentiment shook all parts of the United States: urban and rural, northern and southern, along the East Coast and into the rugged Appalachian backcountry. The revivalist spirit of the Second Great Awakening grew from concerns that Americans had lost a sense of piety and devotion to God as the nation expanded, and it was characterized by ministers who emphasized the innate sinfulness of man. These men preached emotional, hellfire-and-brimstone sermons meant to bring the wayward back into the religious fold, and they placed strong emphasis on the conversion experience and the idea that salvation was an individual choice rather than predestined by God. The evangelical tide brought with it a more democratic approach to religion than had existed before. Many of the ministers who participated in the revivals, especially those who rose in the rapidly expanding Baptist and Methodist Churches, were not formally educated, and their conversion efforts were aimed at all Americans regardless of their status. Very large camp meetings attended by hundreds—even thousands—of people characterized the Second Great Awakening. At these meetings, itinerant ministers promoted mass conversions and encouraged the converted to make or join churches in their communities when they returned home. Their work led to the proliferation of new churches and the growth of evangelical denominations throughout the nation.[33]

The Second Great Awakening came later to the backcountry South than it did to the northern states because it challenged its racial and gender hierarchies. There was some resistance to the evangelical movement in its early years, particularly among southern men who resented the sense of agency ministers gave to women and African Americans. Evangelical missionaries, however, learned to adapt their message to southern mores, accepting notions about slavery, race, and patriarchy. By the early 1830s—around the time the Logues' distillery had burned—revivalism had gained momentum in the region.[34]

In central Tennessee, the religious reawakening was largely facilitated by the Methodists, who had for years held camp meetings in the backcountry. There was a campground near Manasseh's plantation where Methodist preachers held annual revivals, attracting people dressed in their finest clothes from all the neighboring counties. These were a great social occasion for all parts of the Tennessee social order—wealthy and poor, male and female, Black and white. Enslaved laborers attended, as their enslavers often brought them to the gatherings to serve their needs, have a little holiday, or perhaps sell some of the produce that they may have been able to grow on the small patches of ground designated to them as personal gardens.[35]

At the camp meeting that followed the burning of the Logue

distillery, the evangelical impulse was particularly high, and there were many conversions. According to Loguen, his mother was among those who felt the revivalist spirit, as were Manasseh and Sarah, who "melted into penitence" as they "trembled and groaned together, in view of the eternal and awful Hell the preachers hung out before them." Baptisms proliferated after this meeting; and Jane was baptized together with Manasseh and Sarah at the nearby Methodist church after their return home. The Logue family from that time on incorporated daily Bible readings and prayers for all members of their household into their routine. Unfortunately, despite the hopefulness it engendered, the Logues' status as church members did not markedly improve the situation of those they enslaved.[36]

Although the loss of the distillery had seemed like a blessing to those in the slave quarters of the Logue plantation, it meant a significant loss of income for Manasseh; and financial crises on southern plantations usually spelled trouble for those that labored on them. Such was the case for Jane and Jarm.

To raise money, Manasseh decided to mortgage the two of them out, sending them off to work for a neighboring planter in exchange for an infusion of funds. Their work would stand in for interest until Manasseh could raise enough money to pay back the amount of the mortgage. This type of arrangement usually put those mortgaged out in a brutal situation. Slave owners were invested in their enslaved laborers as a financial asset, and therefore there existed at least some incentive for them to maintain the health and fitness of their bondspeople. But for persons holding enslaved workers as part of a mortgage, their interest was in extracting as much labor out of them as possible before the mortgage was paid off, and so the laborers' work was usually relentless and backbreaking. This was the situation in which both Jane and Jarm found themselves.[37]

Their stay on the neighbor's farm did not last long, however. Two months into the arrangement an incident put an abrupt end to it. Jarm had been hoeing corn, Jane alongside him, while the overseer drove the workers, whip in hand. The overseer singled out Jarm and began to lash him with the whip to speed up his work. When Jane saw this happen, she intervened, hoe in hand, and told him to stop whipping the boy. When the overseer continued, she threw her hoe at him, issuing threats and chasing him away from her son. Although she had become a Christian woman, Loguen notes, "her religion was not of the passive sort" when dealing with "tyrants." Following the incident, Jarm and Jane were immediately returned to Manasseh's place. Presumably, Manasseh was forced to pay off his mortgage early and with interest.

Loguen remembered later that the Logues seemed agreeable after his return to the plantation on Bigby Creek. The following Sunday, Jane attended church with the family, and all of them took communion together. That night after supper, Black and white residents of the household assembled, as had become practice, to hear Manasseh read from the Bible, following which Jane and her children joined the Logues in prayer. There was no sign of the heartbreak that was to come.[38]

In his narrative, Loguen told the story of the events that followed with great emotion. The next morning, he remembered, Manasseh sent all the enslaved adults into the field while he kept the children behind at the house. Soon after the parents had departed for their work, while the children played in the yard, several men rode up on horseback. After conversing with them, Manasseh ordered the older children "to stand perfectly still, and say not one word unless spoken to, while the strangers examined them." He then turned to the men and told them they could make their choice for purchase from among them.

The men proceeded "to examine the bodies and limbs of the

children," after which they selected two of Jarm's younger siblings—a brother who was around thirteen and a sister who was age eight. Decades later, Loguen would vividly remember how his sister, "not daring to move, on hearing the fatal decision, turned one imploring look at Jarm, and then broke into tears and sobbed aloud." The slave dealers took no note, and they immediately fastened the children together by their wrists with a sturdy cord. Hearing their children crying, the mothers came running from the field. As they arrived, they saw in the distance "a long coffle of little children"—around seventy-three of them. The slave traders marched these children toward the house so that Jarm's brother and sister could be added to their number.

Manasseh had just completed the sale, and one of the traders was astride his horse holding the rope fastened to the children's hands when Jane arrived. Immediately, she threw her arms around her son and daughter, demanding that they not be taken away. Screaming commenced all around as Jane continued her cries for the release of her children and the trader refused them. The slave dealer employed a heavy lash to whip Jane, but it had little effect on her. Eventually, "fearing that his most valuable chattel would be disabled, and perhaps destroyed," Manasseh intervened and ordered two of his bondsmen to pull Jane away. Fearing punishment, they reluctantly complied.

Jane then "fell into a frenzy of grief and passion" as the boy and girl were dragged away from her. Manasseh locked Jane away, chaining her in the slave quarters to a loom used for weaving the coarse "negro cloth" worn by the plantation's Black workers, until the next morning. After this event, Jane gradually recovered from the beating and returned to physical health, but, Loguen said, following the loss of her children there remained "a perpetual wound upon her spirit, which time could not heal."[39]

In addition to the hardships brought on them by Manasseh's

financial choices, Jarm's family also had to endure episodes in which the Logues abandoned their pledge to abstain from drink. When they were able to procure whiskey, they partook. This led to a resumption of occasional violence on the plantation, and teenage Jarm, who "was now approaching manhood," had come to a dangerous age, "when the slave is subjected to the severest process of being subdued by hard service and cruel discipline."

One fall morning, when Jarm was feeding the hogs on the plantation, he once again faced Manasseh's wrath. Manasseh took exception to the place that Jarm decided to pour the corn for the swine, and he fell into a rage. He attacked Jarm with a hominy pestle, "a thick, solid, heavy wooden instrument, used to pound the corn into a mortar." Manasseh hit him on the head with it and knocked him to the ground. After he fell, Manasseh continued to strike his head with the pestle "until he was helpless and insensible."

When Jarm awakened, he was lying in the same loom room where his mother had earlier been imprisoned, and she was there tending to his wounds. She implored him to be silent so as not to catch the attention of Manasseh, and she stayed with him until evening and time for family worship in the main house. As Jane retired from Jarm to join in the Bible reading, she hoped that he would not attract attention, but to her dismay, as Manasseh began to pray following the Bible reading, Jarm's increasingly loud moans were heard clearly in the main house. As the sounds punctuated Manasseh's calls out to God, the slaveholder became frustrated and angry. He rushed through his prayer and then stalked through the night to the slave quarters where Jarm lay. Cursing at him, he began to kick Jarm repeatedly until a commotion outside interrupted him. Numerous voices were crying out in alarm: "Fire! Fire!"

Manasseh left Jarm and ran outside, where he saw the flames rising next to the opposite side of the main house; and there he also saw Jane, who "stood most conspicuous" near the blazing fire with several fellow laborers, a pail of water in her hand. Jarm was forgotten as Manasseh dealt with the emergency, coordinating an effort to contain the fire and limit its damage.

Jane, of course, had set it. Fearing for her son's life she had lit up a bundle of straw that lay near the other side of the house as a diversion. It had worked.

As Loguen later related, after they extinguished the fire, Manasseh and Sarah speculated on how it might have been set. They did suspect that their Black residents had started it intentionally. They did not know for sure, though, and Sarah pressed on Manasseh that it had been a message from God. They had quit drinking in the wake of a fire, and now God was angry that they had broken their promise to abstain. It was a sign that they must repent.

Jarm continued to moan loudly from his room after the emergency passed, but Manasseh's attitude toward him changed. He sent for a doctor to tend to the young man's wounds, and he and Sarah renewed their pledge to "never again drink a drop of liquor, and to love and obey . . . [their] Savior."

Loguen reported later that, although they continued to drink at times, the Logues' behavior improved with this new pledge. He lamented, however, that the Logues did not understand the true "depths of their selfishness" as slave owners, "much less . . . look it in the face and overcome it." Their sin did not stop with drink as they believed. The real sin was that "they had not begun to think that their slaves were equally entitled to life, liberty and happiness with themselves."[40]

CHAPTER 2

Freedom

As Jarm entered adulthood, his experience of slavery shifted once again, for when he was around nineteen or twenty, Manasseh mortgaged him out for a second time. The slaveholder took a loan of $550 from a neighbor who lived fifteen miles away, and he sent Jarm to live and do work for the man until Manasseh could repay the money. On hearing this news, Jarm brooded, worrying that he might never again see his family, and his thoughts turned once again to escape. "His eye was ever open in that direction," Loguen remembered, "but all was dark around him now." He knew there were opportunities for freedom to the north, but he did not know how to make such a journey.[1]

When Loguen arrived at his assignment, however, he found himself in a far better place than he had left. The members of the family for whom he had come to work were deeply religious and had qualms about slavery. They also held more liberal ideas about racial equality than most southerners. In his narrative, Loguen gave the family a pseudonym, referring to them as the Prestons, because their relatively enlightened views would put them in danger with their fellow white Tennessee neighbors if publicized. In Loguen's remembrances, he presented his time with the Prestons as his first small step toward self-emancipation. The family's treatment of him helped him to develop a sense of self-worth, nurtured a recognition of the spiritual dimension of his existence, and sparked in him a new hope for his future. The Prestons did not save him from slavery, for despite holding antislavery ideals, they were not prepared to challenge entrenched proslavery sentiment in their society. They did, however, encourage Jarm to develop the personal tools necessary for him to save himself.

Mr. Preston was "a red-haired gentleman, of middling stature, and about fifty years of age" who lived with his wife and his five children—young adults with whom Jarm would develop close friendships. Religion was at the center of life for the Prestons. They were nominally Methodists, but they attended evangelical meetings of all stripes. While he lived with them, Jarm was introduced to a Christianity grounded in a plain folk work ethic common among yeoman farmers in the Old South. Central to the Prestons' approach to religion, Loguen said, was the idea of "use—use to others, and use to self for the benefit of others." This, he said, "was the beginning and end of their creed."[2]

This idea of usefulness was an important element of the nineteenth-century Protestant work ethic ideal. As the evangelical fires of the Second Great Awakening spread through the nation, so too did the expansion of American markets, which provided new economic opportunities and encouraged upward mobility through hard work. Many Americans combined the economic and religious values that were emerging in the early 1800s, and the idea of this work ethic became widespread in the nation. Four key ideas were associated with this ideology: "the doctrine of usefulness," a "fear of idleness," a "dream of success," and a "faith in work as a creative act." All of these values were part of the Prestons' moral code. All of them became part of Loguen's.[3]

The orderly surroundings in which Jarm found himself at the Prestons' made an impression on him. In his narrative, Loguen's descriptions of the Preston farm were highlighted almost to the same extent as the people who surrounded him in his new environment. Throughout his remembrances, Loguen drew frequent parallels between the living conditions of those he encountered and their character. The Logue farm was depicted as shoddy and ill cared for, a reflection of Manasseh and his family's character. The Prestons' tidy and comfortable farm, in contrast, reflected their respectability. "The farm was a sunny spot in the dark woods," Loguen remembered, a metaphor for the Prestons' existence within the larger slaveholding society in Tennessee.[4]

Jarm was thankful for the betterment of his living conditions at the Prestons', but he found that he was frequently embarrassed by his inexperience in dealing with the relatively egalitarian views they held and the way this affected their treatment of him. During meals, he ate with the family. Although he sat at his own table set apart from its members, he ate the same food, the two eldest sisters serving it to him. When he realized that "they were in fact waiting upon him," he felt an awkwardness about "this inversion of the rule of his life." Loguen also remembered feeling great discomfort when the Preston siblings initiated a game of blind man's bluff. He was mortified by the proposal that he play this game, for he had been taught that "so humble and degraded a thing as he" should not put his hand on a white woman. As the Preston children encouraged him to participate, he said, "his condition as a slave came upon his nerves like a heavy hand upon a stringed instrument." When he explained his discomfort to the Preston siblings, one of the sisters wondered why. Her brother answered her, "His life explains it; life is not natural with him yet."[5]

Although according to the law of slavery, Jarm was for the Prestons merely "a thing for their uses," they treated him as an essential member of their household—almost as a member of the family. In his narrative Loguen pinpointed an early episode at the

Prestons' that provoked in him a new sense of self-worth. When Mr. Preston assigned him his first task—to build himself a log cabin in which to live—Preston urged him to take his time and make the house as refined and pleasant as possible, a suggestion that seemed utterly foreign to Jarm, given his experiences at the Logue plantation. When Jarm protested that he didn't need much, Preston impressed on him the importance of doing work for himself "as nice and as well" as he did for others. Jarm was struck by these words. The idea that a Black man had as much right to comfort as a white man "set him to reasoning in a way that awakened and encouraged his self-respect." Loguen later remembered that the "concession to his manhood" inherent in Preston's instructions helped to awaken in him a "consciousness of his individuality." Embracing a work ethic that would support that individuality became one of his core values from that point on.[6]

As he settled into a routine on the Preston farm, Jarm's sense of "servitude and danger" faded away. He accompanied the Prestons to religious services. He began to take pride in his dress and speech, taking care that he presented himself to others in a dignified manner. He developed an expertise in managing agricultural pursuits on the plantation, and he began to learn his letters. All these activities elevated his sense of self-worth. As Jarm adapted to life in the Preston household, he shed any acceptance of the idea that he must submit to a slavish existence. He spent each day at the Prestons' in "a regular succession of industry, amusement and instruction."[7]

Jarm spent two and a half to three years with the Prestons before his time there was cut short. Manasseh had waited so long to pay off his mortgage and reclaim Jarm that both Jarm and Mr. Preston had begun to believe that the slaveholder had decided to forfeit his claim and that Jarm had become a permanent part of the Preston household. They were, however, mistaken. One spring morning, three men arrived at the family farm on horses to repay Manasseh's debt. Preston offered to forgive the debt and to pay "any reasonable sum" to retain Jarm, but the men refused his proposal. Jarm's time with the Prestons had ended.

Although he did not want to return to the Logue plantation, Jarm saw no alternative. The Prestons had given him a taste of a different kind of life than the drudgery, violence, and oppression he had experienced in Manasseh's household, but despite the elevation of his circumstances with them, he still was considered chattel in Tennessee. He had no rights. At the Prestons' home he had thought he had found a new way of living, but now he was forced to leave it behind. As he made his way back to Bigby Creek, Jarm realized that if he truly wanted a new life, he would have to create one himself—this time on his own terms.[8]

When Jarm arrived back at the Logue plantation, he made a show of contentment, a trick that soon paid off. Jarm had learned much from Mr. Preston about farming, and Manasseh made use of his new knowledge by putting him in charge of managing the plantation. Jarm was successful in this new role. He worked to put the farm in order, repairing fences and preparing the fields, which, following the larger southern trend, were now primarily dedicated to profitable cotton crops. Jarm treated the work as if he were doing it for himself. In doing so, he "obtained from his master the greatest confidence, kindness, and indulgence that a surly, selfish, drunken man can feel or allow to a cherished and valued chattel." The status that Jarm cultivated with his work and seeming dedication to the plantation allowed him the space to develop a plan for flight and collect resources to ensure success.[9]

It would take more than a year for Jarm to make the necessary preparations. His first task was to gather knowledge about the geography of freedom from a young neighbor who had spent time in Illinois. From the neighbor, he learned that he would have to travel north through the state of Kentucky to the Ohio River, which was about a week's horseback ride away. After he crossed that river, he would be in one of the free states. Vague though the information was, he made up his mind that he would travel north as soon as he gathered enough resources for the journey.

Around eighteen months after his return to the Logue plantation, Jarm reached out to two nearby bondsmen named Jerry and John. They began to plan their escape from slavery at a cave in the woods just over a mile away from the Logue plantation.

John was an enthusiastic coconspirator. As was true of Manasseh Logue, John's enslaver, John Farney, struggled with his consumption of whiskey. His wife realized that her husband had a drinking problem, so she made sure she kept the title to the enslaved laborers that she inherited from her father in a separate trust that would pass ownership to her children rather than her husband on her own death. When she died, Farney, as she had expected, descended further into alcoholism and hit hard economic times. In 1834, he began to talk about moving to "the Indian nation" and taking with him the family's enslaved, who were now the property of his children. His declarations of these intentions coincided with the timing of Jarm's suggestion of flight.[10]

For his part, Jerry was more cautious about their plans, for he felt he owed his life to the man who claimed him as a slave. The slaveholder had saved Jerry from punishment when he physically resisted a sale away from his nearby wife and children, and he had also told him he could purchase his freedom once he saved enough money to do so. Flight was a costlier proposition for Jerry. He nevertheless joined in with his two friends as they made their plans. At their first meeting, the three men talked about the provisions they would need—a good horse for each of them with saddle and bridle, saddlebags of food and clothing, money, and counterfeit passes for travel. They realized that gathering such supplies would take time, and they thought that they would need around a year to prepare for their escape.

The three men agreed that they would steal horses and saddles for their journey. To gain passes that would allow them to travel freely, they approached a white man named Mr. Ross whom they knew had fallen into poverty and would provide a pass for each of them in return for payment. Although the divide between white and Black was the norm throughout the southern states, men like Ross sometimes aided the enslaved due to their own economic hardship and resentment of the slaveholding class. Jarm and his enslaved allies agreed that they would take bread and bacon from their own plantations to provide Ross with six months' worth of meals for his family in return for the documentation that would allow them to travel. Jarm did not have any problem stealing from the slaveholders to facilitate his journey. He explained his position to Ross as they made their arrangements: "We have no scruples to take property which our masters call theirs, because it ain't theirs," he said, "it has been earned by us and our kindred, and not by him or his."[11]

Obtaining money was the most difficult part of completing their plans, and it was this hurdle that proved most problematic for Jarm. He was able to raise some funds by selling cotton grown on a one-acre patch that Manasseh had allowed him for his own use. He had to work this land during the night after the regular workday was over, but he expected to bring in fifty dollars that year by selling the cotton. He supplemented his yields with cotton taken from Manasseh's land. Manasseh's son John gave some of his father's cotton to Jarm in return for tasks that he would do for him, and Jarm also made deals with fellow bondspeople who stole cotton for him to add to his amount for sale.[12]

Jarm knew he would need more money than the amount he

could raise selling cotton. He thus hatched a plan to buy a barrel of whiskey from a distillery that he could then sell at a profit. He set out to complete this task one day when Manasseh was away from home, taking oxen and a cart to the distillery to procure the product. He planned to hide it and portion it off for retail. His plan went awry, however, when Manasseh returned home before Jarm and witnessed Jarm arriving back to the plantation with his team and cart, loaded up with the whiskey. Crossing Manasseh in this way placed Jarm's plans in jeopardy.

Manasseh, determined to punish Jarm for stealing away from the plantation with his property on personal business, retrieved his whip for a lashing. Jarm, however, had resolved that he would not submit. He had just been through an ordeal due to a conflict with a laborer on a neighboring plantation. In defense of himself, Loguen had beaten the bondsman badly. The man's enslaver had complained about Jarm to the justice of the peace, and Jarm was sentenced to receive thirty-five lashes for his assault on another man's property. His back was still raw from this beating as Manasseh confronted him.

Although Manasseh was aware of the bloodied state of Jarm's back, he nevertheless ordered him to remove his shirt so that he might administer more lashes. Jarm refused to obey. At his resistance, Manasseh rushed to tackle Jarm, but Jarm fought back, picking his enslaver up off his feet and throwing him to the ground. He then fled to his cave hideout in the woods. He was without a change of clothes and supplies, and he knew he must eventually go back to the Logue farm to conduct his plan of escape. He also knew that it would be wise to wait for things to calm down before his return.

Jarm's strategy of hiding out for a few days was a common one among enslaved laborers in the Old South. Truancy—short-term "lying out" from the plantation—was the most common form of flight. Enslaved laborers often would hide away from the plantation for a limited time in response to overwork, abuse, or the need to connect with friends and family outside their own quarters, returning home after a cooling-off period. At times truants might be hunted down, but often slaveholders chose only a mild punishment, or none altogether, when the fugitive returned, for they valued their labor. Truancy, though risky, was a way that an enslaved laborer could negotiate their circumstances with a slave owner.[13]

His time lying out worked according to plan. After a few days, Jarm returned to the Logue farm. As he did so, he approached Manasseh "for the first time . . . with his hat on his head." He touched it and bowed, as one would greet an equal, and asked Manasseh if he had work for him to do. Manasseh inquired if he had already had breakfast and, with Jarm's affirmative response, told him about a fence that needed repair. With that exchange, the two put the matter to rest. "Jarm was peaceable as a war measure," Loguen would later muse, "and his master was peaceable as a measure of economy and policy." Although it was "a forced, hypocritical and false position" on both their parts, it served each other's ends for the time being.[14]

During Jarm's period of preparation for flight, there was one last heartbreak of slavery to come. His sister Maria, who by this time had a husband and three children, one of them an infant, was sold away to slave traders. Once again Jarm witnessed a female family member wail at the loss of her children. As the traders tied Maria's hands with rope, Loguen remembered, "she resisted screaming and praying" and calling for her children. She was ignored and forced into a wagon. She then began to beg at least for her newborn if she could not take all her children with her. Again, her plea was refused, and the wagon carried her away, leaving her family members in grief. Her last words as she rode away were to Jarm: "Tell my children they had a mother."[15]

Despite his new assertiveness with Manasseh, Jarm remained powerless to help his sister. The rest of his life he grieved that he "was obliged to look on, riveted in his tracks by a sense of impotence and a desire of vengeance." Following Maria's sale, he resolved to expedite his plans for escape. He knew he would miss his mother and his other family members once he left the Logue farm, but he also knew that there were no guarantees that he would be able to remain with them if he stayed. The threat of sale hung over all their heads.[16]

That fall, Jarm, Jerry, and John met up at the Methodist camp meeting, sneaking away to their cave hideaway to make their final plans to flee from Tennessee. They decided they would be ready with all their supplies by Christmas Eve so that they could start their journey during the holidays when everyone was distracted with merrymaking. Ross joined them at the cave and provided each of them with an appropriately dated pass for travel. Ross advised them that if anyone asked to see their papers, they should request a magistrate before producing them. They should not look for a fight, but if anyone who was not a proper official delayed them or pressed them about their status, they should "knock them down" and "fight like lions." In addition to the passes, Ross had procured pistols, warning that these were to be used only as a last resort. No one could ever know he had given them weapons, or his own life would be in danger.[17]

In preparation for his journey, Jarm, who oversaw Manasseh's horses, began to give special attention to one of the best ones on the Logue farm, Old Rock, feeding the horse extra food and making sure they were well acquainted with one another. Jarm was able to steal a new saddle, finer than any owned by the Logues, off the back of a neighboring slaveholder's horse. On Christmas Eve, Jarm awakened his half-brother, Henry, to tell him that he was leaving. He was too afraid to tell his mother what he was doing. He feared she might react in such a way to the news as to expose his plans inadvertently to Manasseh.

Jarm could not make himself leave, however, without visiting the room where Jane slept. He agonized at their separation as he looked on her, crying as he kissed her on her forehead. When she began to stir, Jarm turned and left the room. He met his traveling companion John outside, both men dressed in a cap, gloves, and an overcoat to withstand the freezing weather. Together, they rode to meet up with Jerry, who told them when they arrived that he was not prepared to go with them. "They all felt this as a misfortune," Loguen later remembered, "but agreed that John and Jarm had best go on."[18]

And so Jarm and John headed north. For the first few days of their travels, the two men had luck following the advice of Mr. Ross, who had urged them to carry themselves with confidence. They stuck to the main roads, stayed in private homes, and rested in public taverns, holding themselves out to be free brothers who were traveling together to see their mother in Kentucky. The first three nights passed without incident. On the fourth day, however, as they traveled through "thinly settled and uncultivated country," John and Jarm encountered three white men on foot. "In half shabby dress," Loguen later wrote, "they resembled a set of men known only in the south, who are most dreaded by black men, and despised by white men." They were slave catchers—men who made a living off capturing and returning fugitives for a bounty.[19]

The men stopped them on the road and demanded to see their travel passes. As advised, John and Jarm informed the men that they would produce them only before a magistrate. At these words, the men attacked the two travelers, and Jarm and John were forced to fight for their freedom. Jarm knocked one of the men unconscious, and when his companions saw this, they turned and fled.

From this point on, the two fugitives had to abandon their plan to act boldly and instead "be fugitives in earnest." They left the main road, and they sped up their pace as they traveled along back roads. They fed from hay and corn stacks found in fields and slept outside at night. "Their policy now," Loguen wrote, "was, to be as private and expeditious as possible to get out of the slave states."[20]

Several days after their encounter, Jarm and John crossed into the slave state of Kentucky. They rode toward the Ohio River, on the other side of which was the free state of Indiana. They understood that the closer they traveled toward the river, the greater the danger of capture, for the region to its south was filled with slave-catching gangs. It was not long before the travelers encountered such individuals for a second time. Again, the men accosted them, and they had to fight for their freedom; again, their attackers fled as Jarm and John showed their strength.[21]

The next traveler they encountered was a Black man walking alone. He told them about a little-known path off the main road that would take them to the river. Should any pursuers come after them, the path would provide many places for them to hide in the woods. Jarm and John spent one night along their hidden route and arrived at the river the next day without any more encounters, but there they found that it was iced over. They talked with a ferryman near the river, who demanded money to help them cross the ice, but the two fugitives, seeing fresh horse tracks visible, decided to make their own way across.

Jarm and John carefully led their horses on foot in single file along the tracks. As they approached the shore of the other side, they saw a group of men who watched them with morbid interest. They knew what Jarm and John did not, that despite the tracks, the ice was weak and could cave in on them at any point. There had only been a lightweight horse or two with no gear that had made the crossing recently. Jarm and John nevertheless made it safely to shore, and when they arrived on free soil, they both removed their pistols and fired into the air in celebration.

The white men who had watched their crossing disappeared following these rounds, leaving a lone Black man behind. This man approached Jarm and John and issued them words of warning. He told them that the group of men who watched had thought they were fugitives and had been preparing, should they make it across the river alive, to capture them and return them to the slave states for a bounty. But when Jarm and John fired into the air so openly, the spectators concluded that they were free Black men who had been in Kentucky for the holidays, for slaves would not so casually wield pistols. Having come to this conclusion, the white men had left the scene, as the two men crossing the river were no longer objects of interest to them.

Jarm and John expressed shock at the man's words. They had believed that once they were in a free state, they would be safe. Was not Indiana free?

"It is called a free State," the man informed them, "but the laws allow slaveholders to hunt their slaves here, and hold them, to take them back." He told them that although some would sympathize with them as fugitives from slavery, many would not, and they could never truly be safe unless they made their way farther north to British Canada, which did not recognize American slave laws. "There is no place in the States where you can be safe," he said. This was the first time that Loguen would become aware of the American laws concerning fugitives from slavery, laws that he would spend most of the rest of his life resisting.

Jarm and John sought advice from their friendly acquaintance. They had never heard of Canada. They asked how they should navigate there. The man told them they should make their way north, following the North Star. There were people who would help them along their way, but there was also a constant danger of capture and return to slavery. For their initial destination, he sent them along a road from the river to a town called Corydon, about twenty miles away. There, they would find a friend who would provide shelter and send them to their next safe destination.

Loguen later remembered that as the man gave Jarm and John advice, the two fugitives felt a wave of "great sadness and disappointment." Instead of becoming true freemen, they remained slaves in the eyes of American law. Jarm and John would have to "track their way from point to point, and from abolitionist to abolitionist, by the aid of the Star, through the dreary wilderness to Canada" before they would truly be free.[22]

And so, although it wasn't yet widely called an Underground Railroad, and although it wasn't as fully developed as the enterprise in which Loguen participated later in his life, after they crossed the Ohio River in 1835, Jarm and John became dependent on a loose network of individuals who gave shelter, sustenance, and advice to freedom seekers as they undertook their journey to Canada. The backbone of this network of aid was the Black population, who took in refugees from the South, advised and cared for them, and then sent them to contacts farther north who could do the same. But although Black northerners were the primary movers in this work, sympathetic whites often collaborated with them and formed links in the chain of acquaintances on which fugitives would rely. Many of these white helpers were Quakers. Since the 1770s in the United States, Quakers, members of the Society of Friends, had barred slave owning among adherents and been important voices in the antislavery movement. As antislavery sentiment grew among the group, many living in slave states sought to relocate to free soil to disassociate themselves from the sin of slaveholding. Some migrated to the Northwest Territory and later to states, such as Indiana, carved out of that territory. Quaker settlements throughout Indiana became active in the state's burgeoning Underground Railroad. Jarm and John would depend on this biracial network, relying on aid from Black residents and white men and women whose religious sentiment encouraged sympathy for their plight as they made their journey to Canada.[23]

Corydon, the village that was to serve as their entry into this web of aid, was an important base of Underground Railroad activity in Indiana because of its proximity to the Ohio River. It was located less than thirty miles from Louisville, Kentucky, and was an early stop on a central route through the state. From Corydon, fugitives would move north toward Indianapolis, around a hundred miles away, from which they would be sent into Michigan. In Michigan, many made their way to Detroit, where they would eventually cross over the Detroit River into present-day Ontario. This was the route Jarm and John would follow.

The two travelers arrived in Corydon the day after their river crossing, and they easily found their contact there. He was a Black man who said that he had, despite the prejudice that surrounded him, been able to raise himself out of poverty and become a man of enough substance that he could provide aid to others. He told the weary travelers that he was "ready to advise and assist them to the best of his means."[24]

Loguen does not give the name of this contact in his account of their meeting, but it is possible that Jarm and John's new acquaintance was Oswald Wright, a Black resident of Corydon who later would achieve fame for his aid to fugitives. In 1857, twenty-two years after Jarm and John passed through the town, a Kentucky posse seized Wright from a friend's house and transported him across the river, where he was tried for aiding a fugitive who had fled across the Ohio River. As a Black man, living on free soil had provided him with little protection from the Kentucky men when they invaded Indiana. He did not have his freedom papers on him when they confronted him, and under state and federal laws, they were legally able to take him over the border under the suspicion that he was a fugitive. Once he was in Kentucky, state officials charged Wright with aiding in a fugitive's escape. He was found guilty and jailed for five years in the Kentucky penitentiary for this crime, after which he finally was able to return home. Some accounts indicate that Wright settled in Corydon as early as 1820, and so he very well could have been the contact that Jarm and John made in 1835. Whatever the case, Wright's story illustrates the risks assumed by Black operatives along the slave-free state border. Providing aid to fugitives so close to a slave state, the man with whom Jarm and John met placed his own freedom in jeopardy.[25]

Although the practice of hunting down fugitives from slavery along the Ohio River was certainly more active at the time of Wright's arrest in the 1850s than it was in the 1830s, it had a long-standing presence in the area. Violent clashes surrounding fugitive escapes occurred along the border between slavery and freedom in the United States beginning in the 1780s, when northern spaces began to define themselves as "free," and steadily heightened over time, eventually contributing to disunion and civil war. Historian Stanley Harrold has referred to this drawn-out conflict as a "Border War."[26]

Jarm and John were lucky to have found their way to an important hub of Underground Railroad activity, but because Corydon was also an active hunting ground for slave catchers, they were in great danger. As they visited with their contact there, the man explained their vulnerability to them and assured them that, indeed, it was safest to make their way to Canada. Their new ally sent them on their way to Indianapolis. There, he told them, they would find another Black friend, a man named Mr. Overall, who would assist them. Overall had lived in Corydon for some time but had moved to Indianapolis in 1830, providing an important connection between the two towns in the early development of Indiana's Underground Railroad. Fearful of staying longer near the border, Jarm and John set out late that same night on what they expected would be a long and difficult journey to Indianapolis.[27]

Hardship came more quickly than expected, for Jarm and John promptly became lost. They wandered with their horses through the snowy and heavily wooded forest, freezing and without food. Their directions became confused while they were in the thick woods, and when they emerged from the trees, they found that they had turned back to the Ohio River rather than advancing toward Indianapolis. But fate intervened on their behalf once again. The weary men had traveled into an area with settlers, and when they approached a log house to seek food, Jarm and John met a kind, religious white couple who took them in for breakfast and directed them to the nearby village of Salem, where they could stop at a tavern for further aid. There, a friend would give them more provisions and instructions on how to make their way to Indianapolis. As Jarm and John continued their odyssey, they were struck by how vulnerable they were and how much they had come to rely on the kindness of strangers. They had never heard of Canada until they arrived in Indiana, and they had no knowledge of the surrounding geography. "These facts show[ed] how utterly unfit they were to be cross questioned," they realized, "or even to respond to accidental enquiries in regard to themselves" should they encounter hostile strangers on the road.[28]

Nevertheless, they made their way safely to the tavern in Salem, where they were well treated by a Black man who took them in. The man sent them from there to a settlement that was a day's ride away on the road to Indianapolis. There they found a Black colony of fifteen to twenty farmers, each with small plots on which they lived with their families. They were as happy, Loguen later said, as people "could be, surrounded by those who despise and disfranchise them." This community was one of dozens of rural Black communities that existed in Indiana before the Civil War. Hoping to find security and comfort in the free state, Black families who had gained their freedom colonized fertile areas in Indiana, establishing agricultural settlements. They usually chose sites near sympathetic Quaker communities where they would find some white support for their independence. Many such settlements existed on the free side of the Ohio River, and these small communities were important sanctuaries and conduit points for fugitives from slavery.[29]

Jarm and John stayed in the Black colony for three weeks, where they were received warmly and given much-needed time to rest. They became popular with the settlers, especially the young people, who no doubt would have welcomed them had they decided to stay. Unlike the other residents, however, they were not legally free from slavery. All Black men and women in the state were vulnerable to slave catchers, but without legitimate freedom papers, Jarm and John were especially at risk. They were determined to find their way to true freedom and believed they could not rest until they were in Canada.[30]

Thus they continued their journey to find Mr. Overall in Indianapolis. Their progress remained slow. They rode in the rain all day and forded several rivers on their horses with some risk. There were close calls as they crossed deep and rapid waters, but each time, their luck held.

It was not only nature that provided difficulties for the two men; they continued to remain on guard against kidnappers who would return them to enslavement. In his narrative, Loguen relates a memory of stopping at a tavern on this leg of the journey. He was determined to act like a free man, and so he picked up a newspaper and pretended to read it as he sat at his table. Soon after, he realized that he had made an error. He had only learned the first letters of the alphabet during his time at the Prestons', but it was enough for him to recognize, when he saw the letter "A" on the page, that he was holding the newspaper upside down. Luckily, no one had noticed this. He threw the paper away from him, he remembered, and "firmly resolved to let newspapers alone, until he reached a land where it was safe to handle them."[31]

Eventually, the two men were successful and reached Indianapolis, where they found their contact. James Overall was a property owner and well respected among both white and Black citizens of the town. He was a fixture in Indianapolis, a leader of its Black community. In the 1840s he would become a trustee in the Black-led African Methodist Episcopal (AME Bethel) Church, which itself became known for its Underground Railroad activity. That same decade he would help found the Indiana Colored Convention Movement, formed to agitate for Black rights and uplift. Overall was an early model for the man Jarm would become.[32]

Overall inspired the two men's trust, and he was the first person since their stop in Corydon with whom Jarm and John explicitly shared information about their flight from slavery. Overall warned them that keeping this fact a secret from those who aided them had been a mistake. They would be more likely to receive aid from the white men and women they encountered in Indiana as fugitives than they would as freemen. He advised them not to conceal who they were if the matter came up in the future because, although many in the state had sympathy for the plight of those fleeing from slavery, they had less warm regard for Black settlers in the region.[33]

Indeed, although Indiana had established itself as a free-soil state, its laws reflected the marginalized position of Black settlers within its borders. At the time that Jarm and John traveled through Indiana, Black residents could not testify in court, vote, or marry a white person. In 1831, a law was passed requiring new Black residents to post a five-hundred-dollar bond to the state as security against becoming a criminal or a dependent on others, foreshadowing more stringent provisions against Black settlers that were to come. The Indiana Colonization Society, which urged the relocation of all free Black people to Africa, was established in 1829 and attracted a significant following. In 1851, a revision of the Indiana constitution would bar new Black settlers from the state. The majority of white Indiana residents may not have wanted slavery in their state, but neither did they want to have Black neighbors. As fugitives heading to Canada, Jarm and John were objects of sympathy to such residents; as settlers, they would have been objects of derision.[34]

For the next leg of their journey, Overall directed them to travel from Indianapolis to a Quaker settlement forty miles away. On their arrival, their Quaker contacts gave the two men a valuable geography lesson, telling them that, although it meant that they would have to traverse a large wilderness area, they must head directly north or northwest through the rest of the state and not attempt to navigate around the undeveloped area. Southern and eastern Indiana both were unsafe, as there were many emigrants from the South, allies of slaveholders, who had settled there. If they made their way through the wilderness to the north, they would find on the other side emigrants from the northeastern states. These settlers were not immune from color prejudice, but they would be more likely than those living elsewhere to help them on to Canada. The Quakers warned them that they were likely to encounter Native American inhabitants and white hunters as they traveled through the wilderness, but they assured them that they would be more secure traveling among them than in areas with Indiana settlers from the southern states.

As a final piece of advice, the Quakers urged the two men to stay put and wait until the warmer weather of spring came before continuing their journey. Jarm and John, however, were impatient. The reminders of southern influence in Indiana had struck a chord, and they decided that they would rather endure the cold than remain at risk of return to enslavement. Armed with provisions from their Quaker helpers, they set out to ride north through the vast forest.[35]

As they traveled, the two men indeed encountered Native American peoples. None were hostile, and in fact, Jarm and John came to depend on them for aid and shelter. They also came across white hunters, whom Loguen sarcastically described later as "less reliable than the savages." Although they were less helpful, Jarm and John did learn from them that they should look out for bears, wolves, cougars, and wild boars as they traveled. They noted the tracks of these animals as they made their way north but luckily had no encounters with any of them.

As the Quakers had warned, weather provided another challenge as they crossed through the forested region. At one point they encountered a blizzard that caused snow blindness. "They foundered among the trees," Loguen remembered, "to the peril of the riders," but they were able to shelter themselves at the base of a large hill, feeding from frozen provisions and staying active to avoid "sleep and frost" until morning. The next day they became lost as they traveled through the snow, but eventually they came to a cabin where they found shelter, food, and sympathy among its Native American inhabitants. After the storm broke, Jarm and John were able to make their way out of the wilderness, entering the white settlements that existed to its north. Loguen noticed that the "talk and manners, houses and fields" were all unfamiliar, indicating that they were in a new type of society. More important, the northern settlers were willing to receive the two Black men, never turning them away. Jarm's and John's fears of kidnappers dissipated, but still they pressed on toward Canada.

They met with additional hardships along the way. They had begun to run low on funds, and Jarm swapped horses with "a benevolent looking Quaker" for "boot money," a practice that he would use multiple times on the road at need. The man, however, cheated him, giving him far less money than his superior horse was worth during this exchange. They also encountered more winter storms, causing them once again to become lost. Their destination was Detroit, from whence they planned to cross the border into Canada, but they had lost sight of the North Star in the snowy weather and wandered off course to the west. Finding themselves near Lake Michigan and far from any settlements, again they relied on Native American peoples for aid and shelter as they made their way back toward Detroit. When they finally arrived, they were, according to Loguen, "nearly frozen" and "nearly starved."

They felt vulnerable in Detroit, for cities on the border between the United States and Canada, like those on the boundaries of slave and free states, were prime hunting grounds for slave catchers. Jarm and John decided to separate so that they would attract less attention. Each on his own, the two men crossed over the Detroit River, meeting up on the other side in the Canadian village of Windsor.[36]

Loguen sent up a prayer of thanks once he reached Canadian soil. In Windsor, however, he also reflected on "how different the scene before him" was from the idealized place he had held in his mind. In Canada, Jarm and John had to confront the fact that they were both "nearly penniless" in the "cold raging winter" of a new land where they knew no one. Making matters more difficult, in Windsor many of the people spoke only French, and they could not easily communicate with strangers there. John's disappointment was exacerbated by his lack of a horse and saddle, for the owners of the lodging he had procured in Detroit had appropriated them. When he confronted his situation in Canada, John decided to go back to Detroit to lay claim to his property. Jarm never saw him again. Loguen grieved at the loss of his friend. Later in life, he would attempt to find John, whom he thought of as a brother, but he was never successful.[37]

Jarm thus found himself alone in a strange, cold land. Unable to find work in Windsor, he traveled northeast looking for an amenable place to settle. In village after village, he met with little luck. Along the way, he made another horse trade for boot money and was eventually forced to sell his final horse outright for room and board. He caught rides with strangers, and he eventually found himself in Hamilton, a village on the western shore of Lake Ontario, close to the Canada–New York State border. It was here that Jarm made his first home in freedom.

Jarm was around twenty-one years old when he arrived in Hamilton. He was "penniless, ragged, lonely, homeless, helpless, hungry, and forlorn," but he found the town to be a beautiful place, situated in a valley running east to west, with the lake on the north side and a "perpendicular mountain" to the south that "hangs its brow over the village." Even so, he had no contacts in the area from whom he could seek aid. Years later, Hamilton would become a refuge for fugitives from slavery, and Loguen would be central in helping freedom seekers make their way to the village from the state of New York. There, they would find a vibrant community of Black men and women that would take them in and help them start new lives. Jarm found no such community as a young man. Loguen later reflected on his feelings on arrival in Hamilton in a letter that he wrote to his friend Frederick Douglass in 1856. "I had freedom," he told him, but he felt that "nature and man were against me."[38]

Still, he soon found a place to settle down. He met a white

couple who took him in, agreeing to provide room and board for his labor if he would cut cordwood and split rails for them. They paid him more than he asked for the work, and, Loguen remembered fondly, they taught him "many lessons of religion and life." With them, he learned all his letters, and they took him to the Sabbath school in Hamilton during his first summer in Canada. A year later, he graduated as a Bible reader in nearby Ancaster.

Loguen became close with the couple, and he was grateful that he had gained their confidence and affection. "My story attached them to me," he told Douglass. This was a valuable lesson that Loguen took with him later in life as he sought other white allies to aid in his work with fellow fugitives. His story of enslavement and escape inspired them to connect with him and his cause, and he used it to profound effect throughout his career.

In addition to the labor he provided in exchange for room and board, Loguen worked for a farmer in Hamilton, making ten dollars a month helping him clear his land. He was self-supporting and would have been happy, he wrote to Douglass, "but for the thought that ever torments the fugitive," that his loved ones remained in "cruel bondage" and he "could never embrace them again."

Even so, Hamilton would always remain a place Loguen would treasure. "It was my first resting place from slavery," he wrote, "and I love it the more because it has been, and will continue to be, a city of refuge for my poor countrymen." Living as a free man was transformative. After two years in Hamilton working, learning to read, and saving his wages, he decided to take "the name he now bears." The paternal name of "Logue" did not fit with his new station in life. He added the letter "n" to the name "to suit his taste." The diminutive "Jarm," a name he associated with his enslavement, was transformed into the more formal "Jermain."

He adopted the middle name "Wesley" in honor of the founder of the church of "his Methodist friends" from whom he had learned so much in Hamilton. From that moment on, he said, he "was known only by the name of JERMAIN WESLEY LOGUEN." He had become his own man.[39]

CHAPTER 3

Mission

LOGUEN WAS OPTIMISTIC initially about making a home in Canada, but he lived there for only a few years. Once he had established himself in Hamilton, he made a sharecropping arrangement with the owner of two hundred acres of land, farming it and using his portion of the profits to purchase implements and animals for himself. Encouraged by his success, in his second year he decided to take on a partner to maximize yields. This turned out to be a mistake. Unbeknownst to Loguen, his new colleague had debts before their arrangement. Although they did well farming together, his partner's creditors seized their crops as well as most of the assets Loguen had worked so hard to accumulate. Loguen, who had no knowledge of the legal system or idea about how to advocate for his rights, found himself left with only his personal goods, a little money, and a horse and wagon, all of which together he estimated to be worth about three hundred dollars.

Upset about his financial setback, he went to the nearby town of St. Catharines in the Niagara region and invested his remaining funds in a house on a small lot. He then immediately crossed the international border, traveling into the United States to Rochester, New York, where he was able to find employment. It was the fall of 1837, and he was around twenty-four years old.[1]

Situated near the southern shore of Lake Ontario, Rochester was a burgeoning town when Loguen arrived. Early settlers of the eighteenth century had focused on lumbering and farming, but in the nineteenth century, industry began to take hold as settlers learned to harness the waterpower of the rivers that ran through the area to produce textiles, shoes, flour, and other products. Also facilitating the growth of Rochester was the construction of the Erie Canal, which brought to western New York greater settlement and trade with the East Coast. The canal opened in Rochester in 1825, and by 1830, the town had grown substantially from several thousand people to a population of around ten thousand. By 1850, it would hold around thirty-five thousand people. It was a prototypical frontier boomtown, earning the nickname the Young Lion of the West.[2]

Loguen did not give the reason for his decision to move to Rochester in his narrative, but it is likely that his experience in Hamilton prompted a distaste for farming—he never returned to the vocation—and he felt that there was more opportunity to find work in Rochester than in St. Catharines. His move coincided with the Panic of 1837, which plunged both Canada and the United States into an economic depression. One went to where one could find work, and despite the downturn, there were opportunities in Rochester.

Indeed, Loguen found a lucrative position in that town as a porter and "confidential servant" at the city's finest hotel, Rochester House. The hotel had been erected in downtown Rochester on the south side of the Erie Canal on Exchange Street in 1827. It was a grand building that signaled Rochester's coming of age as a city. Like other inns and hotels constructed in the settlements that arose along the Erie Canal, Rochester House catered to travelers and new arrivals looking for room and board in addition to being a social spot for town residents and a place to conduct business, hold government meetings, and host other activities. Rochester House was a public space, with bars and parlors for gathering and common rooms that provided newspapers and pamphlets to read. Visitors there found plenty of opportunities for conversation and gossip. Until the hotel fell on hard times in the 1840s due to the construction of an aqueduct on the canal that made it less accessible, it was one of the most prestigious gathering places in western New York. Remembering its "richly furnished drawing rooms and chambers, from the bridal chamber to the inviting family rooms," one Rochester resident later recalled that "when Rochester House was in its glory," it made Exchange Street "*the street* of Rochester."[3]

Once Loguen secured his position at the hotel, he sold his property in St. Catharines and took up permanent residence in Rochester. He held his position at Rochester House for two years, and the work was fruitful. He was able to rebuild his wealth, earning between three and six dollars each day.[4]

The enhanced economic opportunity that the Erie Canal brought to upstate New York also promoted cultural and religious exchange, and the revivalism of the era especially transformed the area along its path. The fires of evangelical religion burned so hot there, in fact, that it became known as the Burned Over District. Along with the spread of this religious sentiment came a commitment to reform, for northern evangelical Christians, especially those who resided in the Burned Over District, believed that their job was to purify not only their own souls but those of the community surrounding them and, indeed, the nation. During this time, upstate New York became home to many new church communities and a base for reformers dedicated to social movements including the abolition of slavery, temperance, and women's rights. Loguen moved into the region amid this change, the spiritual awakening in the region giving him a sense of security as he moved across the border into the United States. He soon would ally himself with those in the region who were dedicated to reforming American society.

It was at Rochester House that Loguen first became familiar with the abolitionist crusade. By the time of Loguen's arrival in New York, the movement, which promoted Black equality and the immediate, unconditional end to slavery in the nation, had grown into a phenomenon in the North under the leadership of William Lloyd Garrison and the American Anti-Slavery Society (AASS). Loguen had little previous knowledge of public affairs when he arrived at Rochester House, but once there, he was privy to "boisterous" conversations in the bar room and "more quiet considerate ones" in the parlors as he went about his work, awakening him to the escalating debate in the United States over slavery. He felt called to learn all he could about the subject.[5]

Loguen also worked to further his more formal education in Rochester. The overheard conversations at the hotel, as well as his experiences on the road and in Canada, had shown him how important it was to be knowledgeable about the world around him. And so, during his spare time, he attended a public school for African Americans in the city to build on his early educational endeavors in Hamilton. It was at this school that his world really began to expand. One of his teachers was Elymas P. Rogers, a Black student on his winter break from the biracial Oneida Institute, a college in Whitesboro, New York. Like many of the Oneida students, Rogers spent his vacation from classes teaching, and as he interacted with Loguen, he sensed in him a kindred spirit. When Rogers explained the educational opportunities available to Black men at Oneida and told him of the institution's commitment to racial equality and the antislavery movement, Loguen was eager to enroll. With Rogers's encouragement, he put his earnings from

Rochester House in the bank and moved to Whitesboro, returning to the hotel porter position in Rochester during his first two winter breaks from school, the work allowing him to earn enough to defray his college expenses and still save a little for the future.[6]

The Oneida Institute was itself a child of the revivalist spirit of the age. In 1827, its founding president, George Washington Gale, established the school to foster the spread of evangelical Christianity and provide an outlet for education that operated on the manual labor principle—the idea that physical and intellectual labor should go hand in hand to create healthy, well-rounded individuals. By the time Loguen attended, it was under the leadership of the abolitionist Beriah Green, who had become the school's president in 1833. Green's vision for the institute was as a training ground not just for evangelical ministers and educators but also for social activists and abolitionists. A member of the AASS, Green accepted the post at the school with two conditions: first, that he could freely promote the antislavery movement; and second, that he could accept students without regard to race. Once the trustees agreed to these conditions, Green took the job and transformed Oneida into an abolitionist institution where young men prepared themselves for participation in the movement for racial justice.[7]

Along with Loguen, other prominent Black abolitionists attended Oneida, including Alexander Crummell, James Forten, Henry Highland Garnet, William Allen, and Loguen's friend who had introduced him to the school, E. P. Rogers. Loguen would later collaborate with these men in churches, within the Colored Conventions Movement, and in abolitionist organizations such as the New York Antislavery Society, the Liberty Party, and the American Missionary Association (AMA). He also would nurture connections with white students who became reformers, such as Hiram Wilson, who later worked with Loguen to aid fugitives from slavery who settled in Canada.

Loguen's narrative does not go into detail about his time at Oneida, but in it, he stated that it was while he was in school that he "began to feel the delight of living for use—the only real delight that God allows to man." He made his first "public profession of religion" after he enrolled. Although he had felt connected to God since he was a younger man in Tennessee, Loguen said that until he found a Black church to attend, he had been disgusted with the hypocrisy of organized religion and churches that failed to attack the sin of slavery. This changed when he found a "colored church" in nearby Utica while he attended Oneida.[8]

Loguen immediately became involved with the Utica church on his arrival at the institute, serving as a vice president for its First of August Celebration to celebrate British West Indian emancipation, held in 1838. He participated in this event along with E. P. Rogers, who served as the meeting secretary. Other students from the Oneida Institute, Henry Highland Garnet and Alexander Crummell, gave speeches for the occasion. All of those attending the meeting passed resolutions that praised British emancipation and promoted the end of slavery in the United States.[9]

In addition to such celebrations, Loguen taught Black students to read at a Sabbath school in the Utica church, and in 1840, Loguen organized Utica's first school for Black students. In Utica, as in many other northern towns, Black youth were barred from attending public schools, even though their parents paid taxes that supported them. Loguen, who had become familiar with the condition of the Utica Black community through his church, saw a need. He rented a room on Post Street, where many of the Black residents lived, and he started to hold classes for young African Americans in the city. Beginning with just a few students, the school quickly gained attention, and soon Loguen was teaching a class of forty. At the close of the school term, he hosted a public exhibition of his students' work to display their progress to parents and city residents. It was the first such exhibition in central or western New York.[10]

The time spent at the Oneida Institute and nearby Utica proved to be important in Loguen's development. It was there that he became educated and involved with a community of fellow activists with whom he would work for the rest of his life, and it was there that he was introduced to the Black church. His time in Utica proved to be a milestone in another way as well, for it was also where he met his future wife.

Caroline Storum was a freeborn mixed-race woman from Busti, New York, a Chautauqua County town around seventy-five miles south of Buffalo. She was slender and of medium height, with olive skin, dark eyes, and a mild-mannered temperament. Loguen became acquainted with her at the Utica Sabbath school, where he taught when she was visiting friends in the city. She and Jermain became fast friends, and "an intimacy commenced . . . which ripened into a mutual attachment." They married in 1840, when Loguen was around twenty-seven years of age. Caroline was herself around twenty and, according to Loguen, "of pleasing person and address, amiable, and of the best breeding which undervalues the shining and superficial, and highly esteems the intellectual and substantial, the useful and the good." In Caroline, Loguen found someone with values similar to his own, and she became Loguen's partner not only in raising six children but also in his work for social justice. Like Loguen, Caroline's background led her to an interest in aiding fellow members of the Black community, but from a quite different angle, for she was raised with opportunities that Loguen, enslaved for the first part of his life, never had. Loguen often commented that he wished he were as well educated as his wife, whom he admired and in whom he expressed much pride.[11]

Caroline was the daughter of William and Sarah Storum, a couple whom Loguen describes as "slightly tinged" with African blood. They owned a 140-acre farm in Busti and maintained a high social status in their community, comfortably providing for their family and giving their children the best educational opportunities available. According to Loguen, "The standing and respectability of the family always protected her from color prejudice." Even so, Caroline was raised in a household that was gravely concerned about slavery and racial injustice. Her father and mother's home served as an Underground Railroad station, and two of her father's brothers aided fugitives in their own homes.[12]

In 1841, soon after their marriage, Caroline and Jermain moved to Syracuse, around fifty-five miles east of Utica, in Onondaga County, where Loguen hoped to build on the foundation he had established during his first years in New York. On arrival, Loguen could not help but notice that the situation of the city's small Black community of around two hundred was severely lacking in resources and opportunities. Utica's Black residents also had clearly needed aid and uplift, but those of his new home, he said, were "comparatively uncared for." In Syracuse, then, Loguen found a calling. He would dedicate himself to bettering the lives of these forgotten residents. By his side, Caroline supported her husband's work as they built a family together in what would become their permanent home.[13]

Loguen's resolve led him to the ministry. He became a pastor in the AME Zion Church, a predominantly Black church that placed a high value on social justice and on developing structures that would improve the material and spiritual conditions of its Black congregation. As he became increasingly involved with a Zion congregation in Syracuse during the 1840s, Loguen worked not only to strengthen the town's Black religious community but also to build a Black school. From the beginning, though, Loguen's ministry expanded outward from his new home. He ministered to congregations in surrounding towns, helping to grow churches and promote education for Black students. Like many Black religious leaders, Loguen considered that his ministry and his exertions for education went hand in hand, for both were necessary levers for racial justice, social change, and personal elevation.

Syracuse was a burgeoning town when Loguen arrived in 1841. Its population stood at around 11,000 at the time, but by 1850, the total would double to a white population of 21,901 and a Black population of 370. As an Erie Canal town, Syracuse bore many of the same markers as Rochester, Utica, and other settlements that lay along the canal's axis, experiencing not only an economic and population boom after it was built but also the evangelical awakening and growth of a spirit of reform that affected all the Burned Over District. Syracuse's particular location facilitated these developments, for it was in the center of New York State between Albany and Buffalo, and it lay at the junction of several transportation arteries: the Erie and Oswego Canals, a few rivers, turnpikes, and, by the 1840s, railroad lines in every direction. Because of the ease of travel to Syracuse, it became a popular location for meetings and conventions during the antebellum era, earning it the nickname Convention City. Syracuse thus became a town that opened itself up to an influx of new ideas—political, spiritual, radical, and humanitarian. Although its Black residents were generally relegated to the bottom of the economic and social ladder, as the city grew, Syracuse attracted Black and white reformers who, like Loguen, were concerned with Black rights.[14]

When Loguen arrived in 1841, however, Syracuse had yet to develop its reputation for reform, and Loguen felt that the Black residents of the town needed his aid. "Syracuse has its philanthropists, and those who can feel for the colored man," Loguen wrote in a letter to the *Colored American* in May 1841, "but candor compels me to acknowledge that there prevails a most reprehensible apathy in regard to education" for these residents. And education, Loguen believed, was key to Black uplift. "It seems to me that we are more in want of education than any other people on the globe," he said. It was "the only means whereby we shall be able to efficiently contend for our rights or to enjoy them when secured."[15]

One of his first tasks on arrival in Syracuse was therefore to set up a school for Black youth, as he had successfully done in Utica. In 1841, Loguen rented a room to teach reading and writing, and he quickly attracted a group of forty-four students. As in Utica, he hosted a public exhibition of his students' work at the end of the term, inviting both the Black and white residents of Syracuse to gather at the Congregational church, where he taught Sunday school during his first years in the city. There they would bear witness to his students' accomplishments.[16]

There was a great need for Black schools such as the ones Loguen helped to establish in Utica, in Syracuse, and, soon after, in other New York towns and villages. In 1841, the same year that Loguen became involved in building a school in Syracuse, the New York legislature passed a law that guaranteed public education for all children in the state, leaving it up to individual districts to decide whether to set up integrated schools or separate schools for Black and white students. Most districts chose to set up separate schools, but many areas had a small Black population and so provided no public schools that were open to African Americans, despite the state law. Most small private schools for Black pupils, such as the ones Loguen helped to create, emerged in the 1840s under the wing of Black churches. At times these Black schools faced hostility from the communities surrounding them. Loguen, for example, initially chose a site for his school in Syracuse in the central part of town, but the neighborhood where he established it protested. He then used oxen to move the school building from its position on Church Street to a new location on the far edge of the city. He knew that Black colleagues in other towns had experienced similar protests. In one case in Canaan, New Hampshire, hostile residents demanded that a racially integrated school founded by abolitionists, the Noyes Academy, be removed. When their demands were refused, they made similar use of oxen to drag the building from the neighborhood. In Syracuse, Loguen wanted to keep the focus on the needs of his charges rather than battles with white neighbors, and so he moved the school voluntarily.[17]

In addition to a school in Syracuse, Loguen also helped raise funds to construct a church building for Black residents, a project undertaken soon after his arrival. Members of the city's Black community had already come together to establish a congregation associated with the AME Zion Church before Loguen moved to town, but they did not yet have a formal meeting place. Loguen saw an opportunity to serve in helping to create one.

The AME Zion Church arose as an offshoot of the Methodist Episcopal Church in New York City and had grown since its formation in 1820 with congregations spreading throughout New York State and beyond. It became a center of activism for African Americans and others wishing not only for a place of worship but for an outlet to support the abolition movement and the elevation of Black people's condition. According to AME Zion historian William J. Walls, the "Underground Railroad was practically a church movement," with many of its leaders serving as conductors who used their churches as Underground Railroad stations. It was an attractive spiritual home for Loguen.[18]

In many ways like the African Methodist Episcopal (AME Bethel) Church, founded by Richard Allen in 1816 in Philadelphia, the AME Zion Church arose out of a frustration among Black church members at the racial discrimination they suffered within the Methodist Episcopal Church. African Americans were attracted to the denomination when it took hold in the United States in the eighteenth century, for its founder, John Wesley, and Francis Asbury, who facilitated the spread of the church in the United States, both expressed strong opposition to slavery. The structure of the church, emphasizing class meetings that provided a nurturing community of support for church members, also drew members of the Black community to it. By the turn of the century, however, racism had made its mark among the Methodists, and white members became more ambivalent on the slavery issue, a situation that eventually would lead to a church schism. In addition to the move away from its antislavery origins, the church's unequal treatment of African American members led to their increasing frustration. In New York City, Black worshippers were denied access to the main floor during regular church services and were relegated to sitting in the gallery. And although the Methodists allowed for Black lay preachers, official church positions were held exclusively by white ministers, and Black spiritual leaders were not able to participate in church governance.[19]

The Zionites first came together in 1796 in New York City after Black members of the Methodists' Wesley Chapel on John Street successfully petitioned Bishop Asbury to allow them to establish separate worship services at Zion Chapel. Oversight of their meetings, however, remained under white control. The original intent of the Zionites was not to form a separate congregation, for they remained satisfied with the official tenets and structure of the Methodist Church; but in 1820, frustrated at increasing control by white leaders and bolstered by their success at raising funds to support their own meetings, members of the Zion Chapel severed ties with the white Methodists, elected their own elders, and established an independent church. They modeled their church discipline on that of the Methodist Episcopal Church, but, unlike the white church, the Zionites took a strong, official stance opposing slavery, and they fashioned their church not only as a place of worship but also as an instrument for promoting abolition and Black rights. In its early years, the Zionites simply called themselves the AME Church, but in 1848, they officially took the name AME Zion in order to differentiate themselves from Richard Allen's AME Bethel Church, founded concurrently in Philadelphia. There were attempts to bring the two congregations together into one African church after their creation, but these attempts were not successful.[20]

In 1841, when he saw the condition of the Black congregation in Syracuse, Loguen applied for a license to preach from the Geneseo Conference of what would become the AME Zion Church. This license would not give him a church or full ecclesiastical privileges, but it meant that Loguen could freely preach at the request of a pastor, and it allowed him to assume a position of spiritual leadership. Although Loguen did not take on a formal ministerial position at the Syracuse church in the 1840s, from the moment he arrived in town, he considered its AME Zion church his spiritual home, and he was a central figure in its growth.[21]

Syracuse's Black worshippers had already come together in a community, if a somewhat disorganized one, by the time Loguen appeared on the scene in 1841. This community had been nurtured by a Zion missionary named Thomas James, himself a fugitive from slavery, who traveled around upstate New York during the 1830s setting up churches. In 1835, Zion church leaders sent him from a previous assignment in Rochester to Syracuse to form a Black church. Once there, James gathered a small congregation of worshippers who met in private homes. In 1837, they purchased a structure in the city on Salina Street to serve as a meeting place, but when Loguen arrived in town four years later, he noted that although a religious spirit had spread among the village's Black community, their house of worship was "enclosed, but not finished." Loguen, therefore, set about the difficult task of raising money to help complete a structure where they could meet, traveling to surrounding counties to solicit funding in 1842 and 1843.[22]

In 1842, soon after Loguen joined up with these Black worshippers, the Syracuse church was organized formally under James's leadership as "The First African Methodist Episcopal Church of the Village of Syracuse." Its members, however, continued to meet in private homes until a church building was finally finished on South Crouse Avenue in 1848. During his first years in Syracuse, Loguen worked closely with Reverend James until the end of James's tenure as minister in 1844, and later he collaborated with James's successor, Rev. John Lyles, who led the church until 1851. Loguen assumed the spiritual leadership of the church after Lyles's departure. Although he took a break from the ministry during the mid-1850s to concentrate on his work with fugitives from slavery, during that decade the church became known to Syracuse residents as "Mr. Loguen's Church."[23]

During the years that he worked in an informal capacity for his home church, Loguen quickly rose through the Zion ranks. In 1843, he became a deacon, which allowed him to preach as a probationary minister and assist in administering sacraments, and in 1844, he was ordained as a church elder with full ecclesiastical privileges. As an elder, he often was called away from Syracuse as church leaders sent him on assignments to help establish and nurture churches in nearby towns, a model that it used to spread its reach. Although Loguen maintained a permanent residence for his family in Syracuse, he spent much of his time away from home in the 1840s, serving for three years as a minister in the village of Bath in Steuben County and for two in the town of Ithaca in Tompkins County. In both locations, Loguen also set up Black schools as he had done in Utica and Syracuse, and in Ithaca he became involved in the church's effort to aid fugitives from slavery, for it was an established hub in New York's expanding Underground

Railroad network. He also spent time traveling throughout the state, preaching, teaching, and helping to set up schools in other counties.[24]

Although his work was rewarding, the travel required by his church came with a cost, for the years in which he established his ministry were also those in which he and Caroline began to build their family. Their first daughter, Elizabeth Letitia, was born in 1842, and their second, Helen Amelia, in 1843. Loguen not only missed his young children and wife when he was away from home; he knew that his long absences were a hardship for Caroline. He also knew, however, that itineracy was integral to the growth of his church and its efforts to better the lives of Black New Yorkers. He felt called to fulfill the duties of his ministry.

Historically, Black pastors in the United States wore multiple hats, serving not only as spiritual leaders but as educators, activists, politicians, businessmen, and role models for members of their community; and Loguen's activities as he was drawn into the church reflected the multifaceted nature of this work. In just a few short years after his arrival in New York State, he had become the quintessential preacher-politician, marrying his concern for spiritual development with a strong reformist spirit. As the decade progressed, he would become even more involved with the reform movements of upstate New York, involving himself especially in antislavery and Black politics.[25]

The presidential election of 1844 was a turning point for Loguen, leading him into a more formal connection with New York State reformers. That year, while he was stationed in Bath, he undertook a tour of New York's Tompkins and Cortland Counties to raise funds for his church. It was during the height of the campaign for the nation's upcoming fifteenth presidential election. Democrat James K. Polk ran against Whig Henry Clay, and the contest proved to be a particularly controversial one, for the annexation of Texas, which would bring a large slaveholding state into the nation, was at stake. Polk supported the annexation, while Clay, knowing the issue to be especially divisive within his party, refused to take a stand. Slavery became a key issue in the campaign, and the recently formed Liberty Party complicated the election by presenting an abolitionist alternative to voters in northern states, nominating James G. Birney in a third-party challenge to the Whigs and Democrats. Its members rejected not just the expansion of slavery in the nation but the legitimacy of the institution wholesale.

The Liberty Party was a political expression of abolitionist immediatism. Its members were concerned about the unwillingness of the mainstream churches and the two major political parties to challenge the institution of slavery, and they sought moral purity in both their politics and their religion. Practicing what they called "Bible politics," they created an alternative political party that was uncompromising in upholding God's laws and willing to infuse a moral imperative in the political arena that insisted that the government follow these laws. The Liberty Party also presented an alternative to the Garrisonian abolitionism of the AASS, which called for its members to "come out" of the corrupt political parties and churches, eschew political attacks on slavery, and focus instead on ending slavery through "moral suasion." Because of their conflicting views on whether it was best to attack slavery within existing structures or outside of them, there was a growing rift within the abolitionist movement between the Garrisonian and political abolitionists in the 1840s as each sought to end slavery through different means.[26]

New York State was a center of Liberty Party activism, and the growth of the party was especially significant for the state's politics. Not only did it prove to be an important disruptor of the two mainstream parties in a swing state, but on its agenda at the state level was the elimination of New York's discriminatory $250 property requirement for suffrage placed exclusively on African American voters. The emergence of the Liberty Party was also significant in that it was the first party that welcomed African Americans into local leadership positions. Black activists who already practiced their own "parallel politics" in the independent Colored Conventions Movement—where they spoke against slavery, promoted community uplift, and organized politically behind issues important to the northern Black population—infused the Liberty Party in New York with energy and influenced its direction on issues important to Black New Yorkers, most especially that of suffrage reform. During the 1840s, Loguen increasingly became involved with both the Colored Conventions Movement and the political abolitionists of the Liberty Party in New York, helping to implement strategies put forth in both organizations to agitate for change. He became a political activist during the first half of this decade.[27]

A visit to Cortland Village amid the electoral excitement of 1844 brought Loguen into Liberty Party circles. Loguen arrived there in late September, hoping to raise funds for his church in Bath, but he had run into roadblocks, as the town's ministers refused to let him speak to their congregations. These were overcome, however, when he ran into two men on the street who were discussing their frustration with the lack of concern the Presbyterian church, of which both were members, expressed for the plight of the enslaved. One of them was John Thomas, a prominent Liberty Party man. In the midst of their conversation, they saw Loguen on the street and stopped to inquire if they could be of assistance to him. Loguen told the men of his difficulties with the churches, and they in turn, suspecting that he might be a fugitive from slavery, asked him if he could speak on the cruelties of the institution. When Loguen gave an affirmative answer, the two men said they would arrange for him to do so. That evening, Loguen found himself giving a talk in the Presbyterian church. The next day he spoke to a packed house at the Baptist church, the people of Cortland showing great interest in hearing his story of enslavement and flight.[28]

Loguen proved to be an effective advocate for his people, and the speech that he gave in Cortland's Baptist church gives one a sense of how Loguen's role as a spiritual leader mingled with his commitment to social justice. His rhetoric displayed an unusual combination of passion, approaching anger, and humility—traits that were characteristic of Loguen as a man. When he addressed the Baptist congregation, Loguen later remembered in his narrative, he "did not enter the pulpit, but fell upon his knees before the altar and the people, and poured out the passion of his soul for the redemption of the slave." He spoke on their suffering and said that although he prayed for slavery to end without bloodshed, he hoped that God would "smite" the slaveholders, if that was what it would take to end such misery. He paused his address for a public prayer that revealed his own situation and reinforced his point. "Have pity on us," he prayed to God. He continued: "How long shall our little children be torn from their parents, and our innocent sisters and daughters and mothers be given to pollution? O! Give me my mother! Thou knowest how she is robbed of her children, and flayed and tortured because she grieves for them. My little brother and sister on one occasion, and my beautiful sister Maria on another, torn from her, and driven, screaming, away, by cruel men, who lashed her body and covered it with her dear blood, because she struggled and prayed for her children!" All were in tears as he finished his prayer. Loguen rose from his knees, "adjusted his face and form as if he had come suddenly into a new presence," and apologized for his lack of education and experience. The only thing that qualified him to lecture on slavery, he said, "was his practical acquaintance with it."[29]

As he continued his lecture, he called for the audience to support antislavery politics and "vote this hated monster [of slavery] to death," telling them that otherwise, "its fangs will drive deep in the bosoms of your children." Loguen warned his listeners of God's retribution if the sin of slavery continued to corrupt the nation, and he communicated his stance on how far he would go in bringing it to an end. "Do you ask if I will fight?" he inquired of the audience. He responded, "Yes, I'll fight, if I must. We were never made to have God's image ground out of our hearts without resistance. If our rights are withheld any longer, then come war—let blood flow without measure—until our rights are acknowledged or we perish from the earth." He reminded his mostly white listeners: "White men fight—all men fight for their freedom, and we are men and will fight for ours. Nothing can stop the current of blood but justice to our poor people!"[30]

In this lecture, Loguen spoke not only for himself but for a growing portion of the Black community in New York. Frustrated by the intransigence of slaveholders, the refusal of the major political parties to address the injustices leveled at the American Black population, and the general apathy of the northern white population on slavery, Black reformers began increasingly to use revolutionary rhetoric. Unlike many of their white counterparts who adhered to principles of nonviolent resistance, Black abolitionists approached the question of resisting slavery with greater urgency and practicality, as they faced immediate and personal stakes. They were advocating not only for their freedom but also for their own survival and that of their families and communities. For Black Americans, the question of violent resistance was not theoretical; it was a matter of life and death, freedom or enslavement.[31]

But although they were willing to fight for their cause, Loguen and others hoped to avoid violence, seeing it as a last resort. And so, in the 1840s many of New York's Black reformers worked with the Liberty Party to promote political redress for Black grievances. This was a fitting home for them as the members of that party not only took a pragmatic, political approach to ending slavery but held a more nuanced position toward nonviolence than the mostly pacifist members of the AASS. They understood that slavery directly threatened the lives and freedoms of Black Americans. Loguen was attracted to the Liberty Party's pragmatic approach, and so his ministry, which focused on encouraging Black New Yorkers to advocate and provide for themselves by gaining an education, leading a spiritual life, and agitating for their rights, increasingly became fused with the work of this party and the larger political antislavery landscape.

Following his performance in Cortland, the Liberty Party men in the town were impressed. "Such a rehearsal I have never before heard, and have never heard since," John Thomas said. He convinced Loguen that he should go "on the stump" for Birney and the Liberty Party for the rest of the electoral season, and he and his colleagues set up appointments for him to speak throughout Cortland County. They also introduced him to Gerrit Smith, the acknowledged leader of the party in New York. Smith was a wealthy white philanthropist who had been instrumental in establishing the New York Antislavery Society in 1835. Since that time, he had become one of the state's most outspoken political abolitionists, taking the lead in Liberty Party affairs. As Loguen became acquainted with the Liberty men, Thomas wrote a letter of introduction to Smith, recommending Loguen as an abolitionist ally. When Smith met with Loguen at his home in Peterboro, New York, he was impressed. "What a man you sent me!" he wrote to Thomas. "I invited him to pray in my family, and he prayed so feelingly for his mother that he set us all in tears."[32]

Because it brought him into the Liberty Party, Loguen would later describe his speech in Cortland as the event that initiated his commitment to political abolitionism. Indeed, his connection to that party elevated his position in mainstream antislavery circles. Even earlier, however, Loguen had been politically active on behalf of Black liberty and equal rights—since at least 1840. The New York Colored Conventions Movement emerged that year, and Loguen attended its inaugural state convention in Albany, accepting a leadership role in the movement that would follow. Loguen's sermon of 1844 in Cortland, in fact, was reflective of many of the concerns that were addressed by the colored conventions; for at them, in addition to suffrage reform, there was discussion of the evils of slavery and how it affected families, the question of violent resistance and the right to revolution that existed among Black as well as white men who were denied their rights, and the desirability of political action against slavery to ward off such violence.

The New York conventions were part of a larger movement. Colored conventions had begun in the northern states in 1830 in response to anti-Black violence and discrimination in the free states, and meetings were held sporadically through the Civil War, with a semblance of them reemerging throughout both the North and the South in its aftermath. Although many associate the beginnings of the abolition movement with William Lloyd Garrison's establishment of his antislavery newspaper, the *Liberator*, in 1831, and the subsequent creation of the AASS in 1833, the colored conventions came first, and even as a biracial movement emerged, Black activists continued their meetings. They created what historian P. Gabrielle Foreman has called a "parallel politics" alongside the mainstream societies and political parties as Black activists developed their own avenues of "communal expression." At the colored conventions, delegates attacked the institution of slavery, promoted strategies for Black uplift and self-help, and advocated for political reforms to encourage racial equality.[33]

Loguen's activism reflected the concerns of the Colored Conventions Movement. He attended every New York convention between 1840 and 1868 as well as several of the national ones. During the 1840s, there were only three national conventions, but the state conventions in New York met annually and kept the issue of Black uplift and equal rights in the public eye. As he became involved with the conventions, Loguen agitated for the creation of a more cohesive Black community and the development of institutions for self-help like the schools and churches he worked so hard to create. Still, he also emphasized the need for the vote, and he encouraged the expansion of the Liberty Party in New York. Loguen's approach to antislavery also had a radical bent, as was evident in his Cortland speech. Since his escape from slavery, he consistently condoned violent resistance to the institution should it be required, an issue that was frequently debated at convention meetings. During the 1840s, however, most of his attention was given to third-party abolitionist politics and the effort to broaden Black rights.

Loguen was still a student at the Oneida Institute at the time of the first New York convention in 1840. He became involved with the movement as it emerged in the state, serving as a representative for Whitesboro on the corresponding committee appointed to publicize the meeting and its goals. When the convention met in August, Loguen also accepted a position on the finance committee, a role he often would fill in organizations with which he associated due to his financial aptitude. In this capacity, he collected funds from the conventioneers to pay for the publication of conference proceedings and an address of the convention "to their fellow colored citizens" in New York, which called on them to come together and demand equal voting rights. Asserting that "the possession of the franchise right is the life blood of political existence," it called on a "united, vigorous, and judicious manly effort" to "redeem ourselves." Women could participate as well, the address stated, through their "tender, gentle, and benign" influence.[34]

The Liberty Party had formed just two months before the call for the first state colored convention went out to Black New Yorkers, and from the beginning the two movements were intertwined. The new party held its inaugural meeting on April 1, 1840, in Albany, four and a half months before the colored convention met in that city. Growing side by side in upstate New York, the Liberty Party and the New York colored conventions exhibited a cross-fertilization of ideas. At the inaugural state colored convention in Albany, for example, one resolution praised the "designs and purposes" of the Constitution's "great originators," echoing the Liberty Party assertion that, based on its preamble, the Constitution was inherently an antislavery document. In later New York gatherings, conventioneers would formally endorse that party. At Liberty Party meetings, suffrage reform, a central concern of New York's Colored Conventions Movement, became a major plank of the party platform. In addition, several of the most prominent Black leaders involved in the conventions held leadership positions in the Liberty Party by 1843, among them Samuel Ringgold Ward, Charles B. Ray, Henry Highland Garnet, and William Wells Brown. Loguen would join their ranks after the election of 1844.[35]

As the presidential election of 1844 approached, the Liberty Party had grown in strength in New York. It tightened its bonds with the Black leaders of the state's colored conventions, many of whom helped to direct Birney's campaign. Loguen was an effective advocate for Birney, and his influence was credited with helping to bring in six to seven hundred Liberty Party votes in Cortland County. Although Birney did not come close to win-ning the presidential election, his bid demonstrated the increasing influence of political abolitionists in New York, for the party attracted significantly more voters than it had in the election of 1840, and the party's appeal to some traditionally Whig voters had a powerful impact in the swing state. Many believe that the strength of the New York State vote for Birney caused Clay to lose the election to Polk. Although Polk was the least friendly candidate for the abolitionist cause, Liberty Party supporters were encouraged by the influence they had wielded in the election. Afterward, they sought to capitalize on their show of power by asserting themselves more actively in state politics.[36]

Following the election, suffrage reform in New York topped the agenda of both the New York Liberty Party and the state's Black reformers. In May 1845, the New York legislature scheduled a convention for the following year to revise its constitution. Hope sparked among New York's political abolitionists as they set about encouraging the election of delegates to this convention who would support measures to give equal access to the vote by eliminating the $250 property requirement imposed on Black men. Passionate about the issue, during this campaign Loguen started to take a more visible role in the parallel politics of Black New Yorkers.

As Black activists organized "Free Suffrage" conventions in the state, Loguen emerged as a leading voice. He attended the meetings, and in October 1845, he chaired a meeting in Geneva, New York. There, he was instrumental in the creation of resolutions and an "Address to the People of the State of New York" that declared Black disfranchisement to be "a shameful denial of the fundamental doctrine of genuine Republicanism" and demanded the end to the property requirement, which "draws one line of caste between blacks and whites and another between colored men."[37]

Meanwhile, leaders of the Liberty Party also organized to promote equal suffrage by supporting the election of delegates who would support it at the constitutional convention. Despite their efforts, however, representatives of the Democratic Party dominated the convention proceedings. The convention nevertheless entertained suffrage reform measures in October 1846, deciding that the best way to resolve the issue was to submit it directly to voters in a referendum. Sadly, New York voters rejected the measure for equal suffrage by close to a three-to-one margin (224,336 to 85,406). The $250 property requirement for Black voters would remain in place.[38]

The failure to achieve suffrage reform at the convention in 1846 was a devastating blow to Loguen and the other New York abolitionists who had vigorously worked to promote equal access to the vote in their home state. Their efforts nonetheless were significant. They solidified connections between Black activists and the Liberty Party in New York and led political abolitionists to articulate their position on Black rights and citizenship so that it helped provide a basis for future organizing and argument. In the years that followed, the Liberty Party, as well as the colored convention meetings in New York, continued to address the problem of unequal suffrage, reaffirming a commitment to constitutional reform. These efforts, however, made no headway during the years before the Civil War.[39]

Nevertheless, following the failed attempt to change the state constitution, Loguen remained dedicated to extending Black political rights in New York. He continued to work with the Liberty Party, giving speeches and serving on its finance committee. By the end of the decade, he had become a full-fledged politician, for in 1848, the year that Gerrit Smith ran as the Liberty Party's presidential nominee, the party nominated Loguen as the Liberty candidate for state senator from Onondaga County. Neither candidacy was successful.[40]

As Loguen became more involved with the Liberty Party, he developed a close working relationship with Gerrit Smith. His first collaboration with Smith was on a unique project concocted by the philanthropist to encourage Black economic uplift and provide a less conventional means to expand Black suffrage. On August 1, 1846, on the anniversary of British West Indian emancipation, Smith announced a land distribution plan that would grant forty-to-sixty-acre plots in the Adirondack region of the state to three thousand Black New Yorkers at a price of $1 per parcel. Smith hoped that the land parcels would set recipients on the road to fulfilling the $250 property requirement to vote, but even more so, he wanted to give impoverished Black men in his state a chance to establish economic independence and create secure homes for themselves and their families.[41]

To execute his vision, Smith engaged Black community leaders to promote the "Smith Land" project, help him vet worthy recipients of his grants, and make sure the land was distributed fairly. Involvement in Smith's land scheme thus became an explicit expression of the parallel politics that had developed in the state among Black reformers. All of Smith's Black allies in the program were members of the Liberty Party and active leaders of the state colored conventions, including Loguen. Although Loguen had himself chosen to eschew agricultural pursuits in favor of his work as a spiritual leader and reformer, the land scheme fit neatly with his focus on "usefulness" as a path to self-actualization and independence, which he had learned as a young man on the Prestons' farm and which had been reinforced by his education at the Oneida Institute. He helped Smith to promote his program, noting that settlers who chose to occupy and improve on their rural land grants could "hereafter furnish them or their children with comfortable homes, where they may be happy, and useful to the world and themselves."[42]

Smith's land grant program, however, did not proceed smoothly. Although three thousand grants eventually were made, fewer than two hundred parcels were settled, and only twenty to thirty grantees had taken possession of their acreage by 1848. Soon after the initial grants were distributed, reports filtered in that the conditions of the Adirondack parcels made them unsuitable for development. Farming the rocky, acidic soils of the region was difficult, and the harsh winters of upstate New York were an added hardship. Smith responded to the complaints about the land with a request that Loguen undertake a tour of the acreage granted in Essex and Franklin Counties and report on the conditions he witnessed.[43]

Loguen accepted this assignment, spending seven weeks traveling through the region in August and September 1847. There he found that the land granted in Essex County was "as good land as any man can need" for farming. Some of the parcels in Franklin County also were appropriate for this purpose, but many were not. Loguen felt that those grants, however, would be "very valuable for the timber upon them." In all, he determined that among the plots he toured there was "not one that is worthless." The real problem Loguen found in Franklin and Essex Counties was not related to the quality of the lands granted, he said, but was the "high-handed game" that was "played upon many of our colored brethren, who had gone there to visit the lands of which they had received deeds." Loguen reported that there were predatory men in the region who presented themselves as guides who would help the grantees locate their lands. These men played several cons on the would-be settlers. Some took them into the woods for multiple days and nights, charging them a hefty rate of up to two dollars a day for their efforts before taking them to a lot that might or might not be the one they were granted. Others might guide a would-be settler not to his designated grant but to "a very undesirable spot—perhaps a mountain peak or an irrecoverable swamp, and when he has paid well for the toil of his pilot, that has ended in bleak disappointment, he will be kindly offered four or five dollars for his estate, and be made to think himself happy to get rid of it so well."

Loguen's findings reinforced his ideas about the importance of education as a foundation for Black uplift. He advised that grantees refrain from searching for their parcels "unless they can read and write" or were "in the company of tried friends, who can do both." They should first visit the county clerk for the area where their grant was located, record their deeds, and get advice from the clerks on finding their lands. Then, he said, they should take with them the land lot number and any physical descriptions that would enable them to locate their holdings. In his report, Loguen provided names of trustworthy men who would help the settlers. He advised grantees that "they must not be surprised if they meet with many persons ready to discourage them by speaking disparagingly of the lands and the noble benefactor who has given them." Instead, they should "keep their own counsel, refrain from disputation, still more from intoxicating liquor, which they will find there in great quantity and high repute." They should "press on diligently to the end of their journey," where every lot had been surveyed and marked with deed numbers. "My last advice to our brethren," he concluded, "is not to sell their land for a song." No matter the condition of the land, "they can be no poorer for keeping it," for all the lots had some worth, and "in the course of a few years, they must rise in value."[44]

Ultimately, despite Loguen's optimism and sage advice, the Smith Land project never lived up to the potential Smith had imagined for it. Few Black grantees took up permanent residence on the lands. Still, it did provide opportunities for families to acquire property and accumulate some wealth. Small Black communities emerged in the region, the most famous of which was known as Timbuctoo, near the settlement of North Elba. In 1849, an influential white ally would settle in that community, purchasing his land from Gerrit Smith. His name was John Brown, a figure with whom Loguen eventually would become well acquainted.

Loguen was enthusiastic about his new pursuits in the late 1840s, but his ministry and expanding reform work left him little time to be with his family in Syracuse. In 1848, he reevaluated his priorities and decided to move home and dedicate himself more fully to his abolitionist activities while using Syracuse as a home base. At the end of his two-year stint in Ithaca, he gave up his position with the AME Zion Church and moved into his little house at 293 East Genesee Street with Caroline and his growing family. By this time, he and Caroline had three young children: Elizabeth Letitia, who was six; Helen Amelia, who was five; and Gerrit Smith Loguen, born in 1847 and named after Loguen's new friend and colleague. It was a bittersweet time for the couple when Loguen returned home, for they also had recently lost a child. Their infant daughter Gabriella Clorinda, born in 1846, died in September 1847 while Loguen was on his Adirondack tour on behalf of Gerrit Smith. No doubt this was one reason Loguen moved home to spend more time with his loved ones. In an apology letter he wrote to his colleague James McCune Smith for his lack of communication for an extended time, Loguen explained that he and his family had been in "a deep affliction" since one of his "dear children" had died. "This sudden bereavement," he said, "added to the cares and labors that devolved upon me, on my return to the church and the people of which I have the pastoral charge" and "took entire possession of my thoughts, and engrossed my time for several months."[45]

By giving up his AME Zion appointment, Loguen was able to settle in with his family and, at the same time, renew his efforts on behalf of the Syracuse Black community. And Syracuse would serve as a comfortable place from which he could travel to give lectures and work for Black uplift in shorter stints in surrounding towns. With his return to Syracuse, Loguen began his work as a full-time reformer in earnest. "From that time forward," Loguen said, his life was "a series of incessant activities for the freedom of his family and race."[46]

After Loguen returned to Syracuse, his first task was to find a way to support his work financially. Abolitionist colleagues in New York encouraged Loguen to enlist as a missionary with the American Missionary Association to support his reform activities. The organization had been founded in Albany in 1846 when evangelical abolitionists became frustrated with existing missionary organizations that accepted funds from slaveholders and refused to take a stand against American slavery. They sought to create an alternative abolitionist umbrella for missions at home and overseas, and the AMA especially was dedicated to supporting missionaries who would minister to members of the northern free Black community. Many of its members were affiliated with the Liberty Party. With both organizations headquartered in New York State, a natural alliance grew between the two groups, and they often worked in tandem.[47]

The organization seemed a natural fit for Loguen, so his fellow Black Liberty Party colleague Samuel Ringgold Ward contacted AMA leadership to recommend support for his work in 1849. White antislavery men from Syracuse—Ovid Miner, Charles Wheaton, and Abner Bates—also reached out to recommend Loguen. Miner, Wheaton, and Bates all spoke highly of Loguen's influence with the Black community of Syracuse and expressed confidence that he was worthy of support. Each of these white colleagues, however, also recommended a lower salary for Loguen than he required. When asked what he needed to support himself, his family, and his work, Loguen estimated that "with economy" he could get along with $500 a year. He felt he could raise around $280 from friends of the Black community, and he hoped that the AMA could help make up the difference. In his recommendation, however, Miner suggested that Loguen could make do on $400 a year, with $125 to $150 coming from the AMA. Wheaton and Bates suggested that the AMA pay Loguen $100 a year. This was quite a bit less than what the AMA provided Miner for his own work as a missionary with the organization, a sum of $750 a year.[48]

Nevertheless, on February 12, 1850, Loguen was appointed as a home missionary with the AMA for the region around Syracuse. He would receive $125 in support from the AMA for that year. Though he had hoped for more, Loguen expressed gratitude for the aid. "I must take carefully the help of the Lord," he said, "on account of my poverty and demands of wife and four little children." He and Caroline had added another child, Sarah Marinda, to their brood in 1850, and he was happy to be able to provide for his growing family and still devote himself full-time to spreading antislavery sentiment and tending to the needs of Black communities in central New York.[49]

In August, however, he wrote a less positive follow-up letter addressing the challenges he faced in his work, the most notable of which was the problem of white racism within the evangelical community. In Syracuse, he said, most of the white led evangelical churches that accepted Black people in the congregation relegated them to the so-called negro pews located in the gallery. He listed the Wesleyan Methodist church as the only exception, implicitly criticizing the town's Congregational church, which was loosely affiliated with the AMA. The churches with these discriminatory practices, Loguen said, "may save white people," but he was certain that the preaching that took place in them "will not save colored people," for "it has not God enough in it." Although white church leaders asserted that negro pews were "good enough for colored people," Loguen proclaimed: "I for one shall not consent to occupy them." Loguen ended his letter stating that should AMA leadership "think me not worthy" to continue as a home missionary due to his focus on the needs and rights of the Black community in Syracuse, "they need not give themselves any further trouble about me," for, he said, "I shall continue to labor in the field, pay or no pay." He knew God would provide for him in some way.[50]

In addition to his concerns about racism in the evangelical abolitionist community, simmering in the background of his work with the AMA were conflicts between Loguen and white leaders of the organization, not only about pay but also about how to measure his effectiveness as a home missionary and how exclusive he would be to the AMA. Looking at the numbers, which were the focus of the AMA missionary reports, leaders in the organization appear to have been worried that Loguen was concentrating too much on his efforts with the small Syracuse Black community and falling short in the number of new churches, converts, and children attending Sabbath schools throughout upstate New York that he reported to the organization. Those parts of his job that could not easily be measured—comfort to the needy, improvement in education, agitation for antislavery and equal rights, and advice provided to the Black community—were not considered. And, also problematic, in the spring of 1850, just after receiving his assignment as a home missionary for the AMA, Loguen reengaged with the AME Zion Church and began working with a congregation in Troy, New York, just outside of Albany, about 144 miles southeast of his assignment in Syracuse. Though he would miss his family, Loguen prepared to take on this new assignment out of a sense of duty and, perhaps, a need for more support than was provided by the AMA. When word traveled to AMA offices that the church had asked Loguen to move there permanently, however, AMA officers considered withdrawing their funding from Loguen. They wanted him to focus on AMA priorities.[51]

All was about to change for Loguen, however. Amid these exchanges with the AMA, on September 18, 1850, the US Congress passed a new Fugitive Slave Law, which pledged federal support for the return of fugitives from slavery to those claiming their service in the South. This placed Loguen's freedom in a precarious position. He was in Troy when news about the law's ratification broke. After consulting with his friends and family, he decided he would not accept a Troy church assignment. Instead, he returned immediately to Syracuse, where he felt he would find more security. With this decision, the AMA continued Loguen's support as he embarked on a new phase in his activism—one that was focused on calling attention to his status as "a defiant fugitive from slavery" and protesting the new law as he provided aid to others who were endangered by it.[52]

CHAPTER 4

Resistance

LOGUEN HAD ESTABLISHED himself as a prominent activist by the end of the 1840s, but he also had experienced a fair amount of heartbreak during those years. He had made a new home for himself, yet he remained a fugitive from slavery, alienated from his mother and siblings, whom he left behind in Tennessee. He gloried in the family he created with Caroline in New York but grieved over the loss of his third child. He experienced many of the benefits of freedom, but he saw the failure of suffrage reform in his adopted state and continued to battle against racial prejudice in the North. On top of those frustrations, with the passage of the Fugitive Slave Law in 1850, he felt more vulnerable than ever about his own liberty as he entered the new decade.

Loguen's continued status as a fugitive, however, was a conscious choice he made. Through the years, he was given several opportunities to free himself from the Logues' claims over him through a purchase of his liberty. He always rejected such action, however, as one that denied that freedom was his God-given right. In addition to his determination to oppose any attempt to label him as a slave to another man, Loguen's rejection of freedom purchase was a purposeful expression of his desire to embrace his identity as a "defiant fugitive" from slavery. He wanted to use his own story, and his continued vulnerability to enslavement, to create sympathy for the antislavery movement and the cause of racial justice.[1]

His first opportunity to secure his freedom through purchase began with an effort to free his mother, Jane. After he gave the Cortland lecture in 1844 recounting his family's experiences of slavery, Loguen's new Liberty Party colleagues were especially affected by his sorrow at his mother's continued plight, and they decided to raise funds to negotiate her purchase from Manasseh Logue. Loguen's new ally John Thomas corresponded with Logue soon after he met Loguen, and the old slaveholder responded, agreeing to a price of $250 for Jane's freedom. The abolitionists raised money by subscription to send an agent, Liberty Party member Nathanial Goodwin, to travel to Tennessee to finalize the agreement.[2]

When Goodwin arrived in Tennessee, however, he found that his task was not so clear-cut. Manasseh balked at following through with the sale. He told Goodwin that, as a rule, slaveholders in the region held that they would not sell a slave to a slave. As news spread of their business arrangement, everyone in the surroundings of the Logue farm became so convinced that Jarm was behind the proposed exchange that they demanded that Manasseh refuse to go through with the sale unless Jarm would agree to purchase his own as well as his mother's freedom.

Goodwin informed Logue that Jarm, who now went by the name Jermain Loguen, would never agree to these terms, for he considered himself to be a free man. When Logue pointed out that, according to federal law, he had the right to seize his former bondsman and return him to service, Goodwin scoffed at him. He warned Logue that he would never succeed at taking Loguen by force. "You can no more take him and make him a slave, than you can the Governor of New York," he said, for Loguen was "a man of property—a preacher of the Gospel, and loved and respected the country over."

The two men continued to discuss the matter over dinner, after which Goodwin was introduced to Jane. When Goodwin asked her if she would like to be reunited with her son, she was visibly emotional, struggling to fight off tears. She told Goodwin she would like to live with Jarm but could not leave Tennessee.

Goodwin recognized that she felt she could not leave her home, close to family and friends who remained enslaved. Ann, her one remaining child who had not yet been sold out of the county, tried to convince her to consider the opportunity, and hoping that Jane would agree to go with him, Goodwin returned to discuss the matter once again with Logue. Ultimately, though, because Goodwin knew that Loguen would never agree to allow a purchase of his own freedom and because Logue was unbending on this demand, the negotiation was unsuccessful. Having reached a stalemate, Goodwin left the Logue farm on horseback. Logue followed him on foot for several miles, entreating him to persuade Jarm to agree to his proposal, but Goodwin, holding back his own emotions, ignored the man and continued to ride away.[3]

When Goodwin returned to New York and told Loguen "he could not have his mother until he owned himself," Loguen was "deeply grieved and indignant." In his narrative, he explained that "he felt wronged and insulted by the proposition," and the incident cemented his "extreme of hatred against slavery." From that point on, "his whole time and talents and passions were given to war with it. Where there was excitement, there he was to inflame it—where there was none, there he was to set the fire blazing."[4]

Loguen was not the only prominent Black activist who had to consider the appropriateness of purchasing his own freedom. It was a question that many fugitives, especially those who came into the public eye, had to confront. Those who spoke openly of their fugitive status put their liberty at stake. Greater security could be found if they could find a way to purchase their freedom from those who claimed them as slaves, but also important to men such as Loguen were their antislavery principles. They did not want to give legitimacy to the idea that their freedom was a commodity. Purchasing a fugitive's freedom also presented a dilemma to northern abolitionists, Black and white, who wanted to aid freedom seekers but did not wish to be complicit in the business of buying and selling human beings.

The appropriateness of this method of procuring freedom came under special scrutiny in 1846, the same year as Goodwin's failed mission to purchase the freedom of Loguen's mother. That year, a debate broke out among antislavery reformers when news spread that famous fugitive Frederick Douglass had allowed abolitionist friends to pay for his freedom so that he could safely return home from Great Britain, where he had been living because his fame made him more vulnerable to reenslavement. When Douglass allowed his freedom to be purchased, some fellow members of the AASS criticized him. The concession, they argued, weakened Douglass as an antislavery advocate and strengthened slavery. Those who trafficked in human beings did not care whether they profited by selling to a southerner or a northerner—a fellow slaveholder or an abolitionist. Either customer, they argued, enriched enslavers and thus supported the practice of slavery.[5]

Several of Loguen's Black colleagues also denounced compensation when the question arose. William Wells Brown raised money to buy his own freedom while enslaved, but after he escaped bondage through flight, he refused to purchase rights to his own body from someone who had no claim over him. Henry Bibb, a Black activist who helped fugitives settle in Canada, argued that the practice of freedom purchase encouraged slave hunting in the North.

Even Frederick Douglass, two years after securing his own freedom, acknowledged that "every act of purchase enhances the market value of human chattels."[6]

Despite these ethical positions, freedom purchase nevertheless remained common practice, even after 1830 and even among abolitionists who made such arguments. Black churches regularly took up collections to buy the freedom of relatives of congregation members, and white abolitionists—such as the Liberty Party men who offered to help Loguen—also saw the practice as humanitarian. In defense of those who criticized Douglass for allowing for his purchase in 1846, William Lloyd Garrison himself asserted that despite the moral position the AASS took against compensation, "it is no crime sometimes to comply with even unjust demands" to aid someone in need. He preferred to call the exchange made for Douglass's freedom a ransom and argued that the sin in such circumstances rested with the kidnapper and not with those freeing a hostage. Douglass himself made peace with the transaction by arguing that only through such a ransom could he return to the United States to continue the fight against slavery. He reasoned that the monetary exchange did not legitimize the institution of slavery but freed him from its power. Even so, he always framed the purchase as a gift from friends, taking no personal responsibility for the act. Loguen was certainly aware of these debates as he was himself presented with the option to pay Logue for his own safety.[7]

Loguen's position on the matter, however, was also shaped by his religious beliefs. As a minister in the AME Zion Church, Loguen faced a dilemma on the question of purchasing his freedom, for church policy stated that church members must avoid "all traffic in slavery, in any way." Under such constraints, Loguen might reconcile himself with the proposed purchase of his mother by abolitionist subscription, for he could separate himself from the exchange. He would not, however, be able to pretend that he was not intimately involved in such traffic if he allowed the sale of his own freedom. In discussions of freedom purchase, Loguen made clear that he considered it a sin and betrayal of God, who gifted him with freedom, to pay for rights over his own body and soul. And as a religious leader, he felt it especially important to honor this gift. As Loguen entered full-time antislavery work, he felt it was his duty to raise the "social-political consciousness" of the Black community not only through his words but also through the example of his life. As one writer on Loguen's religious sensibility has summed up, "Loguen used his life as text and personal testimony." He thus felt he must be rigorously uncompromising in his refusal to sanction slavery. Throughout his career as a minister and activist, Loguen indeed seemed acutely aware that his life was an example to others, and he clung to his identity as a fugitive from slavery in order both to emphasize his position that the freedom of all men and women came from God and to spark sympathy and emotion for the cause of freedom seekers by relating his own experiences to his audiences in his sermons, speeches, and writings. All this came at great cost, though, as his mother and sister were left to languish at the Logue farm in Tennessee.[8]

It also came at a cost for Loguen personally, for in refusing to purchase his freedom, he was far from secure in his liberty in the North. After he fled from the Logues and declared himself a free man, he nevertheless remained vulnerable to reenslavement due to legislation that gave slaveholders the right to seize those who had fled from slavery and carry them back to the South. Article IV, Section 2 of the United States Constitution guaranteed the right to seize any "person held to service or labor" who had fled to another state in the Union; and in 1793, Congress had passed the Fugitive Slave Act, which outlined the process for retrieving fugitives from slavery. A slave owner or an agent for the slaveholder simply had to appear before a local, state, or federal magistrate and obtain a certificate of removal that would allow them to detain the fugitive. The law made it illegal for any person to interfere with this process. Clearly, Manasseh Logue was aware of his legal rights regarding Loguen, having threatened to exercise them if Loguen refused to pay him off. Loguen was aware of the law, too, and he used his vulnerability to great effect, cultivating his fugitive identity as he spoke and wrote against the institution of slavery.[9]

The threat of forcible return to slavery increased, however, when Congress passed the new Fugitive Slave Law in 1850. Ratified in September, it was part of the series of measures that made up what has become known as the Compromise of 1850, which brought California into the nation as a free state following the Mexican-American War. To appease slaveholders, who had hoped that California would allow slavery, Congress beefed up the existing legislation on recapturing fugitives, providing federal assistance and enacting stricter penalties for northern refusals to comply with such efforts. It gave the federal government jurisdiction over slave cases and provided for the appointment of federal commissioners and marshals to enforce the law, essentially establishing a federal bureaucracy to support slaveholder claims. It overrode laws passed by various northern states that protected free Black people from being kidnapped and returned to slavery. It also required all citizens to lend aid in the apprehension of fugitives on request and imposed fines and/or jail sentences on anyone who refused to lend such aid or who sheltered a fugitive.

On August 21 and 22, 1850, a few weeks before the law was ratified, Loguen attended an unprecedented Fugitive Slave Convention, in Cazenovia, New York, a small community twenty miles from Syracuse, where about fifty fugitives from slavery and their allies met to protest the proposed legislation. The gathering was organized by Gerrit Smith and the New York Vigilance Committee, and Loguen assumed a leadership role, chairing a committee of fugitives tasked with presenting two addresses: one to the Liberty Party and the second a "Letter to American Slaves from Those Who Have Fled from American Slavery." The second piece, drafted by Smith, urged all who were enslaved to seek their freedom. "When the insurrection of the Southern slaves shall take place," it said, "as take place it will, unless speedily prevented by voluntary emancipation, the great mass of the colored men of the North, however much to the grief of any of us, will be found by your side, with deep-seated and long-accumulated revenge in their hearts, and with death-dealing weapons in their hands." The address was a declaration of war against slavery. "You are prisoners of war in an enemy's country," it said, "and therefore, by all the rules of war you have the fullest liberty to plunder, burn, and kill, as you may have occasion to do to procure your escape." Although flight brought with it extreme risk, "if you make your way to New York or New England," the address stated, "you will be safe." This letter, though addressed to those who were enslaved, put white Americans in both the North and the South on notice that much of the free Black population was prepared to fight to preserve their own freedom and procure it for those who were enslaved.[10]

Despite their protests, the new Fugitive Slave Law was ratified a month later, on September 18, 1850. Loguen was in Troy when he received the news. Situated near Albany at the eastern terminus of the Erie Canal, Troy had, like other towns along that artery, quickly grown as an industrial center as new shipping and trading potential arose. Unlike towns farther to the west, however, Troy did not offer a sense of safety or security to Loguen. He would explain his feelings later in a letter to AMA secretary George Whipple. In March 1851, Loguen informed his New York City colleague that he preferred not to venture eastward in New York since the new law had come into effect: "I feel that my friends will protect me in this part of the state, while I feel that it would not be safe for me to come to your city or even to Troy." He explained that his family in Syracuse was also "a very strong inducement to stay." In sum, he felt more secure in Syracuse because, he said, his friends "promise to stand by me let what may come. And I think that I can stand if they can for me."[11]

With similar thoughts in mind, when family and friends in Syracuse urged him to return home from Troy after the approval of the new law in 1850, he made haste to do so. He arrived back in Syracuse on October 2, 1850, one day before a citizens' convention was held in the city to consider the new legislation.[12]

The Cazenovia convention that Loguen attended in August 1850 had proved to be a mere prelude to northern organizing against the new Fugitive Slave Law, which triggered an explosion of resentment throughout the North. The reaction was especially strong in the Burned Over District of New York. The new legislation energized various factions of abolitionists and provoked debates about the appropriate way to resist the law and protect fugitives. It sparked fear in the hearts of northern Black Americans and led to an increase in Underground Railroad activity throughout the nation as men and women vulnerable to seizure made their way farther north toward Canada to avoid arrest and enslavement. Other Black northerners refused to flee and instead worked in vigilance committees to provide mutual aid in resisting arrests attempted by slave catchers. In some cities, white Americans joined in with them in their readiness to resist. The law also created such outrage that many white northerners who had previously been ambivalent toward the slavery issue (or had, in fact, supported the right of southerners to own slaves) came to resent the southern "Slave Power" and support efforts to limit its reach.

The town of Syracuse was at the forefront of protests against the new law. Although Loguen had found it wanting in its spirit of reform on his first arrival, during the 1840s and 1850s the city gained a reputation as an abolitionist stronghold. Between 1845 and 1850, Syracuse hosted no fewer than twelve major antislavery meetings as well as numerous smaller gatherings. By 1850, several prominent abolitionists resided in town. Samuel J. May, an outspoken Unitarian minister who was among the AASS leadership, moved there from Boston in 1845. He became the minister of Syracuse's Unitarian church and took the lead in organizing many antislavery meetings. An acquaintance of Loguen's from the colored conventions and the Liberty Party, Samuel Ringgold Ward, came from Cortland to Syracuse in 1848, where he published the *Impartial Citizen*, a Black newspaper with Liberty Party sympathies. And several of Loguen's AMA colleagues were members of the town's antislavery-oriented Congregational church. In addition, Liberty Party leader Gerrit Smith lived in nearby Peterboro, and in 1849, Loguen's friend John Thomas moved from Cortland to Syracuse, where he edited the *Liberty Party Paper* until 1851. America's most famous Black abolitionist, Frederick Douglass, made frequent visits from Rochester after he moved there in 1848. Douglass, who broke away from the Garrisonian wing of abolitionism soon after this move, would eventually team up with Thomas in the production of *Frederick Douglass' Paper* in 1851. All of these newspapers supported the Liberty Party, and apart from Samuel J. May, the abolitionist leadership of Syracuse generally supported the political wing of abolition. The Liberty Party reigned among the town's reformers.[13]

The Congregational church in Syracuse was a center for the town's abolitionist activity, but several other churches in Syracuse also supported the abolition movement. Loguen's AME Zion church and John Lyles's African Congregational church were among these. In addition, the town's Baptist church, led by Robert R. Raymond, and the Wesleyan Methodist church, led by Luther Lee, joined in the fight against slavery. They all formed a loose alliance, with church leaders and congregation members working together as they held meetings and organized aid for the town's fugitive population.[14]

The Fugitive Slave Law presented a challenge to northern abolitionists in that it required them to actively support federal slave law if necessary, but Syracuse had already proved itself a place where those who sympathized with the slave were willing to defy such laws. In 1839, a young woman named Harriet Powell arrived in Syracuse with a family of Mississippi planters, and a group of Black and white residents of the region conspired to liberate her and send her to live in freedom in Canada. Loguen told Harriet's story in his narrative, and it is undoubtedly one of the reasons he felt safe in Syracuse.[15]

And so there was precedent in Syracuse and its environs for the outright defiance of American slave law, and an active antislavery element was present in the city when the new Fugitive Slave Law was ratified. Although some residents still opposed abolitionism, by 1850, antislavery sentiment had permeated upstate New York. Abolitionists in Syracuse thus unsurprisingly moved quickly to organize against the new, more stringent law. Also unsurprisingly, it was Black townspeople who initiated the resistance.

On September 23, just five days after the Fugitive Slave Law was ratified, Black residents in Syracuse held a meeting at the African Congregational church to discuss the legislation. Loguen, who had not yet arrived home from Troy, was not present. At the meeting, they pledged to support and protect one another, and they organized a vigilance committee to oversee this process. They rejected suggestions that they flee for the safety of Canada in the wake of the law, as so many fellow Black northerners felt driven to do, pledging instead to stay put. "Liberty which is not worth defending here is not worth enjoying elsewhere," they proclaimed. Like those who had gathered at Cazenovia, they did not shy away from the notion of violent resistance to the law, proclaiming that if one of them were threatened with reenslavement, they would be "justifiable in resorting to any means, even if it be the taking of the *life* of him who seeks to deprive us of what is dearer than life."[16]

Following this meeting, one of the members of the newly appointed vigilance committee, Thomas G. White, produced a circular inviting all the residents of Syracuse to a candle-lighting ceremony in protest of the Fugitive Slave Law. He enlisted the aid of the town's abolitionists to publicize the event. Charles Wheaton helped to produce handbills and newspaper announcements, and the *Liberty Party Paper* also promoted it. Syracuse thus became one of the first places to call a formal townwide citizens' meeting to protest the new law. Loguen arrived back in town just in time to attend.

On October 4 at the Syracuse city hall, the Democratic mayor of Syracuse, A. H. Hovey, presided over the meeting that White arranged. The attendees of the meeting held a variety of opinions that anchored their inclination to protest. Black townspeople felt directly threatened by the legislation. Abolitionists were concerned that it bolstered the institution of slavery and ate away at the rights of northern Black residents. Some members of the white community, however, came primarily because they believed that the federal government was overstepping its authority in upholding slaveholder rights in northern states. There also were differences of opinion about how to protest the law. Some members of the meeting insisted on peaceful resistance, while others were more willing to advocate defensive violence.[17]

With more at stake in their protests of the law, Black abolitionists spoke against it in the most aggressive terms. Samuel Ringgold Ward criticized northerners for their role in allowing the passage of the new Fugitive Slave Law, calling it an act of "open warfare upon the rights and liberties of the black men of the North." He said that because it "strips us of all manner of protection, it throws us back upon the natural and inalienable right of self-defense—self-protection." Loguen agreed with Ward.[18]

When Ward concluded his speech, Loguen stood up to talk, giving his most famous address. In it, he summed up his position on the Fugitive Slave Law: "It outlaws me," he said, "and I outlaw it!" Loguen urged his fellow northern citizens to join in his resistance to the law: "The time has come to change the tones of submission into tones of defiance." He called out President Millard Fillmore and Secretary of State Daniel Webster, who had been promoting obedience to the law for the sake of the Union, daring them to "send on their bloodhounds." They would meet with no success in the face of resistance. "I feel no chains, and am in no prison," he said. "I received my freedom from Heaven, and with it came the command to defend my title to it." He pledged not to purchase his freedom or flee the United States for Canada, and he called on the white population of Syracuse to support the claims that all Black northerners, including himself, made to their liberty.[19]

This speech signaled no shift in Loguen's position, for he had always been willing to fight for his freedom. But now, with the ratification of the new law, he insisted that others do the same. In this speech Loguen made it clear to his fellow Syracuse residents that he expected them to provide sanctuary to all fugitives from slavery and to resist any attempt to reenslave a person taken by a slave hunter in Syracuse, physically if necessary.

The citizens' meeting of Syracuse was a success. Its attendees approved resolutions that portrayed the Fugitive Slave Law of 1850 as unconstitutional, arguing that due process, habeas corpus, and legal counsel were all denied to a fugitive who might be arrested under it. Because of this, it was their duty to declare the law "null and void" in Syracuse, and they agreed that they should resist any attempt to enforce it. A committee was formed to petition Congress urging the repeal of the unconstitutional law, and a new, biracial vigilance committee was created, replacing the one that had been organized at the African Congregational church.[20]

Loguen was pleased with the result of this meeting as he took his place on the new vigilance committee. Loguen was at the forefront of the committee's work and, personally invested in the cause, took the lead in speaking out against the Fugitive Slave Law in the coming months, encouraging the people of Syracuse and of upstate New York to maintain the region as a sanctuary for freedom seekers. For several months their efforts consisted of talk. They gave speeches and held meetings, seeking to influence public opinion. Soon, however, the resolve of Loguen, the vigilance committee, and their supporters would be tested.[21]

Amid this northern organizing against the Fugitive Slave Law, those who wished to see the Compromise of 1850 as a final settlement of the American sectional division over slavery also went to work, promoting obedience to the law in the North. The measure, they argued, was key to the preservation of the Union. In Syracuse and elsewhere, many within this faction were members of the Whig Party, which was declining in influence as anger about the law spread and more northerners became concerned that there was a "Slave Power Conspiracy" to dominate the nation's politics. The Whig Party had habitually avoided addressing the problem of slavery for the sake of party and national unity, and many former northern supporters became dissatisfied with this approach. Growing numbers bolted from the party to join up with the rising Free Soil movement to limit the expansion of slavery and thus slaveholder power. Whig leaders therefore believed that they were fighting not just for the nation but for the party's integrity. They sought to reinvigorate the organization with assertions that the compromises they proposed would preserve the Union and that failure to uphold them would lead to division and, perhaps, war. The highest members of the Whig administration, President Millard Fillmore and Secretary of State Daniel Webster, actively insisted on obedience to the law, and in 1851, the two men went on a speaking tour in upstate New York, promoting compliance with the Fugitive Slave Law wherever they went. The future of the nation, they asserted, depended on it.

Webster had presidential ambitions, and so he had a special mission during the tour to promote an image of himself as a man dedicated to the Union, an image that had always served his political career. He already had presented himself in this light in the Senate during the debates over the Compromise of 1850. Webster, in fact, had been instrumental in drumming up support for compromise legislation. After Henry Clay proposed the original compromise bill in March 1850, Webster addressed his fellow statesmen for four hours about the necessity of preserving the Union. Although Webster was from New England and had a reputation of being an antislavery man, he laid much of the blame for the sectional crisis over slavery on the agitation of northern abolitionists, who, he said, "for the last twenty years have produced nothing good or valuable" and who had succeeded only in dividing the nation by placing the South on the defensive. In his congressional speech, he asserted that approval of the proposed Fugitive Slave Law would represent an important concession to the South that would alleviate sectional tensions.[22]

At the invitation of a group of Whig businessmen and lawyers who called themselves Friends of the Union, Webster visited Syracuse in May 1851 to promote obedience to the law. There, on May 26, Webster gave perhaps his most provocative speech on the subject. Addressing a Syracuse audience gathered in Market Square, he told onlookers not only that agitation against the Fugitive Slave Law fed sectionalism but that refusal to obey the law was an act of treason. He called for patriotism and a spirit of union in the city, and he predicted that, despite the antislavery reputation of Syracuse, "even in the midst of an antislavery convention," citizens of the town would uphold the law.[23]

Webster's speech was inflammatory, and abolitionist leaders worried that the Friends of the Union might try to make an example of the city by pursuing the detention of a fugitive within its boundaries to make a point. They especially were concerned that Loguen might be targeted after this speech, for he was not only a fugitive but also one of the most outspoken agitators against the law. In June 1851, Rev. Joseph R. Johnson, a Syracuse associate of Loguen's in both the Liberty Party and the AMA, expressed his fears to the AMA leadership: "Daniel Webster shook his fists at the City Hall where our conventions are usually held and declared in the fullest emphasis that a fugitive slave should be taken from this city and that very likely from the midst of one of our most fanatical gatherings." He added, "Webster was so excited about this that he stamped his foot." Johnson wrote that he had special concern for Loguen's safety, for he had heard rumors that authorities had been delivered papers for detaining him, and he thus proposed that the AMA provide funds to purchase Loguen's freedom. Loguen, however, refused the suggestion and dutifully continued to fuel the growing sentiment against the Fugitive Slave Law, speaking out against slavery, racial prejudice, and the dangers that the new legislation brought to the northern Black population.[24]

During the summer of 1851, Loguen traveled through New York and into Pennsylvania, giving antislavery lectures. On August 11, he wrote to Frederick Douglass to report on his progress and congratulate him on the establishment of his new periodical, *Frederick Douglass' Paper*. Thus began an extended correspondence with

Douglass, who often printed Loguen's letters in his newspaper. It also initiated an important alliance for Loguen, for he and Douglass would become consistent colleagues in the decades to come.

In this early exchange, Loguen described his travels through nine counties of New York. He had presided over "some grand meetings," he told Douglass, and believed that many northerners had been converted to the antislavery cause by the Fugitive Slave Law. "I never saw the time during the last ten years, that I have been in the anti-slavery field when the public ear was so ready and willing to hear on American Slavery," he said. He hoped that those now "willing to hear on the subject" would be driven to action, "as action is what we need at present."

His letter to Douglass also expressed concern that there were not more lecturers in the field at this crucial time. He reported that he had had enough invitations to speak to keep five men busy. If more like himself were able to travel and speak on their experiences of slavery and freedom in the United States, they could help the antislavery movement to grow. Unfortunately, he noted, many had felt compelled to flee the United States after the passage of the Fugitive Slave Law. He suggested to Douglass that they organize conventions throughout the northern states to agitate against the law, and he asked his famous friend to speak out against it. He believed that if they could fuel more northern opposition to the new law, they could "make it a dead letter." He knew how dangerous the task would be for himself and other northern refugees from slavery who did not flee to Canada. "If a few of us are carried back," he said, "then I believe we will make it hot for them even in the prison-house of woe." For his part, despite all the dangers, he said that he was determined to "stand my ground and fight until the war shall end."[25]

Loguen's opportunity to fight would soon materialize, but despite the fears of his allies, it was not his own freedom at stake in the first battle against the law in his town. Instead, it was that of a recent arrival in Syracuse, a man named William Henry, who had escaped slavery in Missouri and now worked at the town cooperage. In Syracuse, he went by the name of Jerry. Fulfilling Webster's prediction that a fugitive could be arrested in the town during its next antislavery gathering, Jerry's ordeal began on October 1, 1851, on the same day that New York members of the Liberty Party met for a state convention at the Congregational church in Syracuse. As Jerry was at work, federal marshals grabbed him from behind, threw him to the ground, and handcuffed him, hauling him off to the office of US Commissioner Joseph Sabine for a hearing regarding his status. When news of the arrest spread, Syracuse residents remembered Webster's prophecy that a fugitive could be taken from their city, even amid an antislavery convention. Now the question was whether they would allow that prophecy to come true.[26]

Loguen's narrative recounts that the Liberty Party meeting of October 1 adjourned around noon when Charles Wheaton interrupted the proceedings with news of the arrest. The conventioneers, "probably to a man," assembled at Sabine's office to lend Jerry aid, gathering supporters as they walked through the streets of Syracuse. All the church bells in the city tolled, apart from those of the Whig-dominated Episcopal church, their harmony bringing together "an amazing mass of citizens, men and women, friends and enemies also."[27]

The town was crowded on the day of the arrest, for the Onondaga County Agricultural Fair was also meeting nearby, and the judges of the court were holding their term in Syracuse. Loguen recalled that he was worried by the presence of so many visitors, for he was unsure of their sympathies and believed they might support the federal marshals, thus providing "the best opportunity . . . to help the government suppress an attempt to rescue the slave." Loguen and his friends also were suspicious about the timing of the arrest, on the day of the Liberty Party convention and when so many outsiders were in town. Rumors flew that James Lear, the Missouri agent who represented the man claiming Jerry as a slave, had been in Syracuse for days and been urged by the marshals to wait for the meetings in town to take place in the hopes that it might ensure his success, thus supporting Webster's prediction about the execution of the Fugitive Slave Law. This was "an amazing error," Loguen mused, that led them "into a blaze of light in regard to the pride and courage, spirit and integrity of Syracuse."[28]

The courthouse was thronged with people when Loguen arrived. Before he made his way up the stairs to enter the courtroom, he paused to speak to a Black acquaintance about Jerry's predicament. Both agreed that it was "the time to try the spunk of white men" and test "whether they have the courage only to make speeches and resolutions when there is not danger." They agreed to assemble members of the Black community for a rescue, and "if white men won't fight, let fugitives and black men smite down Marshals and Commissioners." The two men then pushed up the stairs and into the courtroom, "presenting themselves boldly before the armed officers of the court."

As they did so, Loguen caught his first glimpse of Jerry, who sat in the courtroom "like a chained tiger." Liberty Party men Gerrit Smith and Leonard Gibbs, both attorneys, had taken seats beside the prisoner, offering impromptu services for the prisoner's legal defense. Their concern appeared to calm Jerry as the hearing commenced, but when Commissioner Sabine called a brief adjournment, Jerry seized what he believed to be an opportunity to make an escape. He threw himself on the crowd in the courtroom, the front of which was "composed mostly of colored persons," and, his hands still manacled, made his way out of the building and into the street.

His handcuffs slowed him. The people who were gathered around the courthouse attempted to shield Jerry from those who pursued as he fled, but he was soon overtaken and returned to custody. Jerry put up a fight, resisting his captors, who ripped his clothing and threw him into a cart, bloodied and bruised. After recovering their prisoner, officials decided not to return Jerry to the courthouse but to transport him to the police station on Clinton Square, where they could more easily secure him. There they put him in a back room, adding shackles to his feet and placing him under armed guard.[29]

That afternoon, the biracial vigilance committee gathered supporters and met at dusk in Dr. Hiram Hoyt's office, twenty to thirty people strong. All agreed that Jerry must not be taken back into slavery. They discussed the likely possibility that Commissioner Sabine, who was not sympathetic to the Fugitive Slave Law, might deny Lear's claim, but Gerrit Smith pointed out that "the moral effect of such acquittal will be as nothing, to a bold and forceable rescue." Those gathered agreed that they must seize the opportunity to demonstrate strong public sentiment against the law. They devised a plan to have a horse and buggy drive around the city in wait while they prompted the crowd to break through the doors and the windows of the police station to free Jerry. There was a debate about the use of physical force in the rescue, with most of the white abolitionists encouraging nonviolence while Loguen and other Black abolitionists "justified defensive violence" if needed. Ultimately, though, there was no getting around the fact that it would be a forcible rescue executed by a crowd: "If anyone is to be injured in this fray," Samuel J. May mused, "I hope it may be one of our own party."[30]

While the vigilance committee met, federal officials were making plans to resume Jerry's hearing. Federal Marshal Henry Allen, wishing for more security, instructed Sheriff William Gardner to call out the militia, and so Gardner called in the Syracuse Citizens Corps, the Fifty-First Regiment of the National Guard, and the Washington Artillery to stand at the ready and help control the crowd. The call was unsuccessful, however, because Charles Wheaton, on hearing of it, convinced the members of the National Guard regiment, led by an antislavery man, not to assemble. He also persuaded the sheriff that he had no obligation to call out the militia for the purpose of "slave-hunting," pointing out that the presence of so many armed men was bound to cause trouble. Sheriff Gardner agreed and retracted his call. The National Guard regiment and Syracuse Citizens Corps thus did not assemble, but the Washington Artillery heeded the original call and arrived to aid in crowd control. It would be ineffective in executing its charge. Jerry's hearing resumed at 5:30 p.m. in the police courtroom, and outside the crowd was roused, becoming loud and unruly, hurling stones at the building. Commissioner Sabine attempted to continue with the proceedings, but it became too difficult to speak over the noise outside. When a stone crashed through the window and narrowly missed Sabine's head, he adjourned until the next morning. Though the hearing was postponed, the crowd, which Loguen estimated to number around 2,500 to 3,000 people, remained. Charles Wheaton had placed clubs, axes, and iron rods outside the door of his hardware store, and many had come to the scene with these tools. One man brought a large wooden beam to be used as a battering ram, and they all prepared for the moment they would storm the building.[31]

Loguen and members of the vigilance committee arrived outside the police office around 8:00 p.m., dispersing among the crowd. At 8:30 p.m., someone gave a signal to move. In reenactments of the rescue in the years that would follow the event, Loguen's son Gerrit Smith Loguen played his father and was assigned this role, and so it is possible that Loguen himself gave the signal. Following this cue, several men used the wooden beam to break down the doors of the building as the crowd fell upon it. Inside, two members of the vigilance committee turned off the gas, extinguishing the building lights.[32]

The crowd poured into the building, slashing away at interior walls, eventually making an opening to the room where Jerry was held. By this time, most of the federal officials had fled, leaving Jerry under the charge of only a few men, including Federal Marshal Henry Fitch, who had come to Syracuse from Buffalo to aid in the arrest of Jerry. Several of the men who continued to guard Jerry claimed that Loguen was present in the crowd inside the police office when their prisoner was liberated, but other witnesses to the event swore during the police investigation that Loguen did not enter the building at the time of the rescue. For his part, Loguen claimed that he witnessed the rescue from the street outside.[33]

As the angry rescuers attempted to push into the room where Jerry was held, Fitch fired twice. Fortunately, his arm was struck away from the crowd as he did so, and he injured no one. Fitch then turned and jumped out of a second-story window to escape the onslaught. He suffered a broken arm in the fray, the only real injury incurred during the rescue, save those Jerry himself suffered.[34]

Although some disputed the claim later, it was reported that the other men who were guarding Jerry covered themselves with boxes and hid in a closet as the mass of people advanced. One of them pushed Jerry, still shackled hand and foot, out of the room into the crowd as he dove into his hiding place. However it took place, Jerry, unable to walk, was carried out of the building by members of the crowd to the carriage that waited for him. From there they spirited him away, taking a circuitous path to the eastern part of the city where most of Syracuse's Black residents lived. Once Jerry found refuge in a home in that part of the city, his shackles were removed and his wounds dressed. He was then taken to several different homes, where he hid until it was safe to leave Syracuse. When things calmed down, Jerry was transported to an Underground Railroad station in Mexico, New York, and then boarded a ship at Oswego Harbor that took him to Canada, where he could not be touched by the terms of the Fugitive Slave Law. There, Loguen said, "he lived, respected for his industry, morals and general character, until taken off by death."[35]

In his narrative, Loguen concludes his tale of the rescue by calling it "a model tragedy of sublime significance." He expressed pride in the Syracuse citizenry for standing against the Fugitive Slave Law. He wondered, however, whether his fellow citizens "would meet the recoil of their heroic conduct with persistent resolution and wisdom"; for now, more than ever, "pro-slavery partisans and officials hoped to clutch the ephemeral pluck of Syracuse and crush it." Loguen knew that "the test of character" was still to come as those who planned and executed the rescue, including himself, faced the consequences of their successful act of resistance.[36]

CHAPTER 5

Aid

SOON AFTER JERRY'S RESCUE, a group of Loguen's friends visited him at his home. They had come to encourage him to leave Syracuse immediately for Canada "until the skies cleared up" in town. They felt that he was in danger of arrest, not only because he was a member of the town vigilance committee that planned the act, but also because of his outspokenness about defying the Fugitive Slave Law in the year since it was passed. Loguen initially rejected the suggestion that he take refuge in Canada, for he felt that to run or to hide would be "a concession that his dignity and manhood would not consent to" after all the declarations he had made about standing his ground in Syracuse. He told the visitors that "he intended to go and come as before, in the face of day." But Loguen's friends, perhaps calculating that this would be his response, had approached him in front of his family. As his children looked on, his wife, Caroline, seven months pregnant, cried and begged him to take their advice and be cautious for their sake. Her pleas forced Loguen to reconsider his position.[1]

The government was indeed organizing to act against participants in what soon became known as the "Jerry Rescue." There was talk about indicting the leading rescuers for treason, but ultimately, the authorities chose to target the men who took an active role in the liberation of Jerry and prosecute them for violation of the Fugitive Slave Law. Abolitionist leaders in town urged that there be no resistance to the arrests. "If our Government shall punish them for giving to a man his 'unalienable rights,'" one man proclaimed, "the disgrace will attach to the government and not the sufferers."[2]

Among those who had participated in the rescue, however, were men like Loguen who themselves were fugitives from slavery. In fact, according to Loguen, fugitives who resided in Syracuse had "to a man" supported the rescue in some way. And like Loguen they feared a return to slavery should the government act against them. In the aftermath of their act of resistance, many of them fled to Canadian soil. Loguen was among them. Taking into consideration the entreaties of his wife and children, "he submitted to what he regarded a sad mortification—not for his sake but for theirs," and he agreed to leave Syracuse temporarily until, as his friends had suggested, "the skies cleared up."[3]

In the years after the dramatic rescue, Loguen would devote himself more and more to aiding those targeted by the unjust Fugitive Slave Law. By the end of the decade, he was known throughout the northern states as the King of the Underground Railroad. It was a reputation hard-earned, but he also owed much to his family and community, for—as we see in the aftermath of Jerry's rescue—he leaned heavily on them to protect his own freedom.

Within weeks of the rescue, Loguen was safely in exile in the community of St. Catharines, on the Canadian side of the Niagara River. Out of reach to slave catchers and federal marshals, he settled in to watch the situation in Syracuse and, while there, to aid fellow refugees from slavery. He stayed at the home of his friend and fellow Oneida Institute graduate Hiram Wilson, who was then working with Canadian fugitives on behalf of the AMA. While in

Canada, Loguen helped Wilson in his mission—teaching, preaching, and giving temperance and antislavery lectures. He also worked as a traveling agent for the Anti-Slavery Society of Canada, which had just organized in Toronto the previous winter to promote abolition and collect funds to aid Black refugees.[4]

The situation in Syracuse was this: in October and November, the federal government indicted a total of thirteen men, four Black and nine white, for violating the Fugitive Slave Law. Loguen was heartened that those arrested would not face treason charges, but there was bad news for him personally. In his absence from Syracuse, two men present at the rescue, Charles Woodruff and Alonzo Torrey, had accused Loguen of assault. Both men claimed that Loguen was inside the police office and at the forefront of the crowd that liberated Jerry. Woodruff, who was one of the marshals from whom Jerry was taken, asserted that Loguen had hurled objects at them while making statements of an intention to kill and that he was himself struck by one of Loguen's missiles. Torrey, a bystander who was in the police office building at the time of the rescue, testified that Loguen "jerked" him from the stoop of a stairwell during the melee after a heated verbal exchange. In response to these accusations, District Attorney James Lawrence drew up an arrest warrant for Loguen on the charge of "assault with intent to kill." News soon reached Loguen that Lawrence planned to seek his extradition from Canada to face these charges.[5]

Loguen immediately wrote a letter to Lawrence, denying the statements of Woodruff and Torrey. He said that he was not inside the police office during the rescue but just outside the building conversing with some men on Salina Street. He had witnesses who would vouch for him. Loguen also questioned the character of both Woodruff and Torrey, speculating that they might have been "paid for such wholesale shameless lying and perjury." He told Lawrence that he did not fear extradition. He had friends, he said, who would "disprove the falsities to be brought against me" and "make it plain to the British authority that the object of the requisition will be as much to put me into the hands of those who claim me as a slave, as to punish me for an alleged violation of that abominable Fugitive Slave Law."[6]

Loguen recognized the strategy being played. The Canadian government had a history of refusing to surrender accused fugitives from slavery to American slaveholders, and it certainly didn't wish to give teeth to the new Fugitive Slave Law. The Webster-Ashburton Treaty of 1842 had declared that Black refugees from slavery who entered Canada from the United States were safe from the demands of slaveowners for their return but that Canada would surrender fugitives from justice for other crimes committed in the United States, including "murder, or assault with intent to commit murder." It is unclear whether Woodruff and Torrey were indeed lying under oath as Loguen claimed or whether Loguen and witnesses who said they saw him outside the building during the rescue were lying in an attempt to protect his freedom. What is clear is that the district attorney was using the inflated charge of attempted murder as a pretext to bring Loguen back from Canada.

For his part, Loguen expressed confidence that Canadian authorities would not fall for the ruse. "Indeed, Mr. Lawrence," he wrote to the district attorney, "were I not assured that your ulterior object is to re-enslave me, most willing would I, upon American soil, meet the charges and refute the sworn—falsely sworn, allegations." Abolitionists in Syracuse also spoke publicly about the motives behind the charges levied at Loguen. In *Frederick Douglass' Paper*, John Thomas wrote that there was strong "reason to believe the perjured wretches who procured his indictment, did it, not to convict him of a crime, but to enable a diabolical kidnapper from Tennessee to steal him out of state."[7]

Although he felt certain he was safe if he remained in Canada, Loguen was frustrated, for he now knew that he would not be able to return to Syracuse without putting himself in danger of reenslavement, and he wanted to be on the front lines of the fight. He worried about the loss of income during his exile and his inability to provide for his family. Even more important, he wanted to return to Caroline, who was due to have their sixth child within a matter of weeks. Loguen thus set about writing letters to New York in an attempt to secure support for his family and as early a return home for himself as possible.[8]

On December 18, he wrote to his AMA colleague Rev. Joseph Johnson. "If ever I was in deep trouble and distress to know what to do," he said, "it is now." He told Johnson that if he were put on trial "for rescuing Jerry, and that alone," he would return immediately to "meet the charge like a man"; but he would not place himself in a position to be reenslaved. He told Johnson that he would wait patiently in Canada, continuing to work among the poor, preaching, teaching, and promoting temperance. For this work, however, he would not be paid and would not be able to support Caroline and his children. He therefore asked Johnson to "be a brother and friend to my poor family, while the husband and father is an exile."[9]

That same month, Loguen wrote to the governor of New York, Washington Hunt. He urged Hunt to consider his precarious position as a fugitive from slavery: "It was my misfortune, not my fault, that I was born in the South, contrary to the declaration of American Independence, which solemnly avers that 'all men are created equal.'" He continued: "I was born unconstitutionally. . . . I have never been able to produce any other certificate of freedom than the one which was indelibly written upon my constitutional nature, by the finger of the almighty." Loguen freely admitted that he was present at the rescue and pleased at its result, ending "as it did, in favor of freedom." He asserted, however, that the indictment's charges of assault with intent to kill were false and based on "mistaken or perjured testimony" intended to manipulate the legal system against the maintenance of his freedom. He would willingly answer those charges, but he feared that they were a pretext to lure him home so that he could be returned to slavery in Tennessee. Therefore, he requested that Hunt give assurance of protection from reenslavement should he return to face the charges against him.[10]

Hunt never responded to his request, and so Loguen's exile continued. On December 30, 1851, his second son, Jermain William Loguen, was born in Syracuse, his father absent.

As Loguen's refugee experience continued into the new year, he yearned to return home. He corresponded with his friend John Thomas to stay abreast of the situation in Syracuse. "I suppose the trials of those noble men who are charged with the rescue of Jerry are in progress at Albany," he wrote to his friend in January. "I trust it will not be long till the reign of pro-slavery terror will explode and I shall have the unspeakable happiness of returning to my family, to dwell with them securely, even if perils have to be encountered in the attempt." The rescuers' first trials, however, did not take place as scheduled. They were postponed several times throughout the year, and hearings would not commence until a full year later. The men indicted for their participation in the rescue remained in a state of limbo as they awaited their court dates, and so did Loguen as he waited for a safe time to return home.[11]

While the federal cases against the rescuers were delayed, the state of New York pursued its own legal action. In the immediate aftermath of the rescue, under pressure from the upstate antislavery men, the state government brought kidnapping charges against Jerry's claimant, James Lear, and Federal Deputy Marshal

Henry W. Allen, who had taken Jerry into custody. Lear returned to Missouri and died soon after, and so he was never brought to trial; but Henry Allen faced a New York jury in February 1852. Gerrit Smith appeared as special counsel for the prosecution in the case against Allen, and he used the trial as a vehicle for presenting a legal argument against the constitutionality of the Fugitive Slave Law, asserting that it violated the rights of the accused to a trial by jury and that the Founding Fathers never intended for the federal government to be "a gigantic slave-catcher." Indeed, he argued, the Fugitive Slave Law should be declared unconstitutional on the basis that it denied the natural rights of man. As a federal official, Allen had taken an oath to uphold not "an Act of Congress" but the Constitution. Because the law was unconstitutional, Smith concluded, "neither judge nor marshal can obey it with impunity."[12]

Smith was not successful in his prosecution. After the arguments were heard, Justice R. P. Marvin instructed the jury that they must find Allen "not guilty" because he was executing a federal law, and "the presumption is generally in favor of the Constitutionality of a law." Smith marked his effort as a victory, however, for he was able to use the trial to present a legal argument against the Fugitive Slave Law.[13]

During the Allen trial, sentiment against the Fugitive Slave Law continued to simmer in Syracuse. John Thomas, who edited *Frederick Douglass' Paper*, reported on events, and while doing so, he responded to Loguen's expressions of his desire to return home. "The people can hardly keep hands off from J. R. Lawrence now," he wrote in February 1852. Thomas predicted that should the district attorney "attempt to arrest Loguen as a slave, he would at last be compelled to pull up stakes and move to the south. The people would not endure such a wretch." Knowing the support he had always received from friends in Syracuse, Loguen took

Thomas's prediction to heart. Although he had received no official assurances of his safety, he soon decided to return home. He felt that his friends would keep him from the grasp of slavery.[14]

In late spring, Loguen left St. Catharines to return to Syracuse after a seven-month absence. As he departed, two of his Canadian colleagues—ministers to Black churches in that town—wrote an open letter to Loguen that was printed in *Frederick Douglass' Paper.* They praised Loguen's work with their community, thanking him for his dedication to his "colored brethren in this town and vicinity." They expressed gratitude for his work as a teacher at the juvenile and adult night schools aimed at increasing literacy as well as for his "candid and talented advocacy" of Black Canadians, which had "reduced the amount of prejudice heretofore existing, even in this free land, against the colored race."[15]

Placing his faith in friends and family in New York, Loguen made his way home from Canada in the late spring of 1852 in open defiance of the Fugitive Slave Law. He was happy to return to Syracuse, where friends had pledged to keep him safe, and to his home at 293 East Genesee Street, where his family had resided since 1848.

Following his return, the brown-shingled, two-story house became perhaps the most well-publicized Underground Railroad station in the north. The Loguen home was comfortable but unassuming, sitting on a quarter-acre lot with a large porch that faced Genesee Street and a second porch, surrounded by lilac bushes, facing Pine Street. It included front and back parlors, a dining room, a kitchen, a pantry, and a summer kitchen on the first floor. On the second floor were two front bedrooms, three back bedrooms, and a middle room with no window, which the family designated as the "Fugitive Chamber." There, freedom seekers could rest without attracting undue attention.[16]

The house was no secret refuge, however. Despite his vulnerability to reenslavement, Loguen placed notices in local newspapers between 1852 and 1861, advertising his address as a place where those who had seized their freedom would find a haven. He also made regular reports of his activity, openly flouting the provisions of the Fugitive Slave Law that mandated strict penalties for providing aid to those in flight. For one notable event, Loguen even published an invitation in a local paper for "friends of the Underground Railroad" to come to his home, where they could meet twenty fugitives who were currently taking shelter with the family, so that they "may see what kind of persons they are helping." Loguen's work for and with freedom seekers like himself became a full-time affair. Under his leadership, and through his direct and confrontational public style, Syracuse gained a reputation as a central depot for the Underground Railroad in New York.[17]

On his return home from Canada, Loguen's abolitionist colleagues held a donation party, inviting Syracuse citizens to an open house to drop off supplies and monetary support for the Loguen family, who had been deprived of Loguen's income during his exile. For his part, Loguen quickly returned to his ministry and activism, resuming his relationship with the AME Zion Church in Syracuse. Although there was an indictment for his arrest for his alleged actions during the Jerry Rescue, Loguen believed that his friends in Syracuse would protect him from any attempt to return him to enslavement in Tennessee as he resumed his work. It would not be long before this faith would be put to the test.[18]

The summer months of 1852 appear to have been quiet for Loguen. He was happy to be home with his family, but he also was eager to resume his travels throughout the state, giving antislavery lectures, raising opposition to the Fugitive Slave Law, and encouraging support for southern refugees from slavery. Loguen had gained moderate fame throughout the region after his initial protests of the Fugitive Slave Law and his participation in the Jerry

Rescue, and on his return from Canada, his determination to continue despite his vulnerability to arrest attracted attention. He received many invitations to speak, and he wanted to capitalize on the interest in his story to promote antislavery sentiment in New York.

He needed transportation to become more active in the field; and so, a full year after the Jerry Rescue had taken place, he traveled to nearby Skaneateles to pick up his horse and carriage, which he had left for safekeeping at his friend Lydia Fuller's house while he was in Canada. Little did he know that this short journey would provoke a wave of great excitement in Syracuse.[19]

On October 5, Loguen boarded the train that would take him west to the Skaneateles junction. Several passengers took note of Loguen's presence and became worried as they spotted Federal Marshal Allen, infamous for his role in arresting Jerry and for his subsequent trial for kidnapping in state courts, on the same train. They also spied two police officers from Syracuse.

The observers kept watch as Loguen exited his car at Skaneateles and were alarmed to see one of the officers and Marshal Allen exit, too. Anxious for Loguen's safety, they left the train at the next stop at Auburn and spread word of what they had seen, attracting a crowd of concerned citizens in that city. They also telegraphed news of what they believed was the kidnapping of Loguen to abolitionist friends in Syracuse. All hell broke loose.[20]

On receiving the alert from Auburn, William Crandall, an antislavery man and reporter for the *Syracuse Standard,* immediately set the bell ringing at the Congregational church, the signal that a fugitive had been taken. Word spread through town that Loguen was in trouble. A crowd gathered, and abolitionists hastily called a meeting at the church to make plans for a response. Years later, a writer to the *Syracuse Journal* would reminisce about the event: "We will remember how the news spread like wild-fire not long after the passage of the Fugitive Slave Bill of 1850 that Loguen was kidnapped by slave catchers at Skaneateles Junction. The signal bell was rung to call the people together. An extra train was chartered, [and] leading citizens, editors, capitalists, &c., armed themselves and rushed to the depot, to follow on and rescue him at whatever hazard—our humble self among the rest, pistol in pocket—all anxious to break the fugitive 'law' if not the necks of his captors." An unpublished biography of Loguen's daughter Sarah Marinda Loguen, written by her own daughter, Gregoria Fraser Goins, paints a vivid picture of the Loguen family's response to the rumors of Loguen's arrest, for the story had become part of family lore. As "citizens filled the streets, some with revolvers to attack the kidnappers, others handling their bank notes and offering money if it was needed," it reported, friends filled the Loguen home. Caroline was "taut with fear," and "the children sensing danger were weeping and clinging to their mother's skirts."[21]

Soon, however, everyone's worries were allayed. Marshal Allen returned to Syracuse on an afternoon train and, having been informed of the reason for the crowd gathered at the train station, proceeded to address those present. He explained that he had been aboard the train to travel to the circuit court at Auburn, where he had been subpoenaed to appear. It was a coincidence that Loguen was on the same train, but when he saw Loguen and a police officer depart the train car at the Skaneateles junction, he stepped out himself to assess the situation before continuing to Auburn. The two policemen's presence on the train was also a coincidence. They were chasing down a "nest of thieves," and one exited to pursue some men at Skaneateles while the other continued to follow others into Auburn.

Crandall stopped ringing the bells of alarm after Allen's explanation, but many members of the crowd distrusted the federal marshal and remained ready to act on Loguen's behalf. That evening, however, Loguen returned home with his horse and carriage, putting everyone's concerns to rest. Goins's account of her grandfather's return to town paints a triumphant picture: "As his carriage passed through the streets, he was hailed by many citizens who informed him of the commotion. Immediately he went to the Congregational Church where a meeting was in progress, and after assuring them of his safety, hurried as fast as he could, intent on getting home to comfort his wife and children." When he arrived, Caroline greeted him with her youngest child in her arms. She "rushed down the front steps to her husband as he stepped out of the carriage. Picking them both up and holding them close, he entered his home." There, "his children and friends surrounded him, weeping and laughing." He sat with his children and wife, holding them late into the night, and the next day he met with many friends who were eager to congratulate him on his safe return. He showed himself at meetings held throughout the city in the aftermath of the scare, thanking the citizens for their generous support.[22]

Loguen's friends in town were gratified by the vigorous response of so many Syracuse residents to their call for action. In a letter to the *Religious Recorder,* the town's Congregational weekly, Charles Wheaton expressed satisfaction that the "faithful servant of the church is permitted to run at large a little longer." John Thomas, in an editorial printed in *Frederick Douglass' Paper,* praised the city for honoring the "Free Democratic principle" in their popular demonstration of support when they heard the rumor of Loguen's arrest. He was happy that there was talk of "rescue, and vengeance, and even of blood" when they thought he had been detained. He felt confident that "if Marshal Allen had returned from the actual arrest of Loguen, his person would have been the subject of dreadful violence." Syracuse had proved itself to be "an asylum to the oppressed." Of Loguen's supporters in town, he noted that "it is all in vain to talk to people as we are about the sanctity of laws to enslave him."[23]

Others were less happy about the quick mobilization to rescue Loguen. Reports of the rumor and the crowd that formed in response reached newspapers throughout New York and beyond, and there was a fair share of criticism of the intention to organize against an arrest that would be sanctioned by American law. The *Syracuse Star*, which positioned itself as the supporter of "law and order" in Syracuse, called the episode "a ludicrous scene of excitement," and stated that the only good outcome of it was "that of showing the citizens how ridiculous our abolitionists are making themselves in their rabid zeal to overstep the laws." In a report of the event, the *Buffalo Morning Express* editorialized that if Loguen did "owe service and labor to some Southern gentleman" then "of course he must be caught and sent off to the sugar mill. Verily, the law must be executed, and all agitation be put down." Farther away, a Milwaukee, Wisconsin, paper lambasted Syracuse as a "hot-bed of Fanaticism of all shades and phases" and mocked the abolitionists of the city, who "were elated at the prospect of an opportunity to 'agitate'" only to find they were reacting to a rumor after wasting "a great expenditure of words and gestures." And so, the arrest scare enhanced Syracuse's reputation as an antislavery city and fed into larger debates about obedience to the Fugitive Slave Law, increasing Loguen's fame in the process.[24]

Through all of this, the threat of arrest hung over Loguen's head, for there was still a grand jury indictment against him for his purported role in the Jerry Rescue. Marshal Allen had delayed executing a warrant against Loguen for a time, but in December 1852, he began to arrest the Jerry rescuers who had fled to Canada to avoid prosecution and had since returned. Among his targets was Loguen, but instead of formally detaining him, he contacted some of Loguen's friends and told them that he wished to immediately take bail so that he could avoid a physical arrest. Loguen discouraged his friends from providing the funds, telling them that he preferred to "have no name but his own on his bond." His wishes were circumvented, however, when Allen preemptively accepted bail from those wishing to support their friend. Immediately after the arrest, Samuel J. May and Charles Wheaton began to collect donations to provide for Loguen's legal expenses.[25]

The government, however, never brought Loguen to trial, although it did move to prosecute several of those arrested earlier for their participation in the Jerry Rescue. Dates were set, canceled, and reset throughout 1852, with no trials taking place during that year, keeping everyone involved on edge. Finally, in January 1853, the first of the trials was held. At it, the jury found defendant Enoch Reed "not guilty" of violating the Fugitive Slave Law, reasoning that Lear never provided a valid written claim to Jerry's service to authorities before he was liberated. Although Reed was free of that charge, the jury did find him guilty of resisting a federal officer during the melee. He appealed this latter conviction but died before it could be considered. The government was also unsuccessful in enforcing the Fugitive Slave Law in the other prosecutions of the Syracuse rescuers that followed: William Salmon was acquitted, and the cases of R. A. Cobb and J. B. Brigham both were dismissed due to a hung jury. The government pursued no more of the Jerry Rescue cases after these failures to convict, and the end of 1853 marked the end of the trials. Even so, Loguen and the remaining defendants could not rest easy, for the government did not dismiss the charges brought against them until January 1861.[26]

Although Loguen was never brought to trial, many in Syracuse remained poised to aid him. One Syracuse editorial, reporting on Loguen's arrest and bond, speculated that "the holding of Mr. Loguen to bail is the beginning of war" and asserted that if the government attempted to prosecute Loguen, "we bet it may not be a bloodless war." The editorial announced: "Rather than a slave be taken from Syracuse we would see it sink in its ashes, and the embers then quenched in the blood of its citizens."[27]

Rumors of slave catchers seeking to take Loguen reemerged from time to time, the most notable episodes taking place in July and September 1855. Word spread during those months that members of the Logue family were planning to come to Syracuse to lay claim to Loguen and take him back to slavery. In July, William E. Abbott, a Syracuse merchant who was a supporter of the Underground Railroad, received a letter from a friend in Tennessee warning him of this danger, and he suggested that Loguen leave town. In response, Loguen decided to make a public declaration of his refusal to run. To address his situation, he held a public meeting at the new Plymouth Congregational Church, which had been established in Syracuse in 1853.

The meeting attracted a large crowd, with every seat full and many standing in aisles and doorways. Although the atmosphere was stuffy and uncomfortable, reports of the gathering indicate that Loguen had the "full and undivided attention of the audience" during a two-hour-long speech that recounted his experiences of enslavement and escape and addressed the warning he had received. He asked for "no undue excitement" from those gathered over the matter, telling the audience that "he understood the power with which he had to deal." He asserted that he believed "it was his right, derived from God, to live where he pleased; he believed it his duty to stay in Syracuse, and he should stay here till he believed it his duty to go elsewhere." He took this position not just for his own sake, for he believed he must "maintain his manhood and his rights" out of an obligation not only to the enslaved but to the free Black population both northern and southern. "The slaveholders want the North to degrade and oppress the free colored people as they do—they do not want us to be men," he said, for they wished to point to the derelict condition of members of the free Black community to justify slavery. "Is it not our duty then to maintain our rights, and endeavor to be true men?"[28]

Loguen thus resolved to stay put despite the threat to his freedom. Nothing, however, came of the rumor. No Logue showed up in Syracuse in July, but whispers about the possibility of an attempt to take him back to Tennessee resurfaced in September 1855. This time, the newspapers treated the rumor more skeptically, but the pledges to protect Loguen continued nonetheless. The *Syracuse Journal*, for example, warned "the said *master*(!) that Loguen is too much a man to allow himself to be taken back, and also, that he has too many friends around him to allow such an outrage to take place. It must be remembered," it declared, "that Loguen lives in *Syracuse*."[29]

Despite the dangers he faced, Loguen continued his work, traveling, giving lectures against slavery, and working with friends and family to aid fugitives who came through town on their journey to freedom. "I feel my heart cheered and my hands strengthened to preach the Gospel to the poor and assist in working the underground railroad," he wrote in 1854. "My friends may rest assured that I will be ready in season and out of season to watch the track for the forlorn, and help the fleeing fugitives over to British dominions, or to defend them on our own soil. I am myself called a slave, but will wear no fetters,—I will be free."[30]

Soon after imparting these thoughts, Loguen left his church ministry to dedicate himself to Underground Railroad work full-time. It became his sole focus between 1855 and 1859, and Loguen leaned heavily on his family, especially his wife, Caroline, as he took on this task. Aid for those who sought shelter in Syracuse was at the center of the family's daily routine throughout the decade before the Civil War. During that time, Jermain and Caroline became more than just partners in marriage; they were partners in managing one of the busiest hubs of the Underground Railroad in New York State. They opened their home to those in need: nursing the sick to health; providing food, clothes, and shelter for the homeless; and assisting refugees from slavery in the procurement of permanent living spaces, either in Canada or in New York State, where they could settle and support themselves. Loguen helped many find jobs, and he conducted marriage ceremonies for couples who wished to formalize their bonds with one another in freedom.

Caroline's role in the family's efforts to aid fugitives cannot be overstated. Jermain recognized how important his partnership with his wife was in his work. In his memoir of slavery and freedom, he praised her character, which held "qualities which fitted her to instruct her household, and even her husband—and to receive, comfort and bless the hundreds of fugitives from slavery who found an asylum at her house." She had a background that served her life with Jermain well. Her parents had operated an Underground Railroad station out of their home in Busti, New York, as had two of her father's brothers. And like Caroline, her sister Catherine had married a fugitive from slavery, Lewis Clark, who gained fame as an abolitionist lecturer and writer.[31]

Although it is difficult to find documentation of Caroline Loguen's day-to-day activities, there were public acknowledgments of her work. On one occasion, a letter, signed "A Woman for a Woman," accompanied a notice for a donation party. The writer singled out the work of Mrs. Loguen: "I am persuaded that if the friends of suffering humanity only knew the labors of that lady . . . they would come prepared on this day to gladden her faithful heart by their warm sympathies and free will offerings." The letter writer noted that Caroline was frequently "in the absence of her

Caroline Storum Loguen
(Courtesy of the Onondaga Historical Association)

husband" due to his travels and was "often aroused from her bed to attend to the pressing wants of those flying for liberty." She characterized Caroline's acts as a "practical Christianity" and called on the women of Syracuse to "cheer our sister on in her labors, and show her that her hopes are our hopes and that she has our warm and heartfelt sympathies in her labor of love." In addition to recognizing Caroline's work in general, this letter touches on an important aspect of her life—the long absences of her husband from her home. Jermain was often away from their well-advertised Underground Railroad station, traveling throughout New York, the surrounding states, and Canada. Caroline was tormented with worry during these long absences, concerned that her husband would be taken by slave catchers—but she also was busy making sure that her home continued to be a safe and nurturing place for fugitives.[32]

Samuel J. May recognized Caroline's crucial role in the running of the Syracuse Underground Railroad depot. After her death in 1867, he wrote this tribute:

> For many years she consented that her house should be the temporary home of the fugitives from slavery. They came at any time of day or night, and often in numbers which it was difficult for her to accommodate, or to provide for elsewhere. They came, too, not unfrequently, in such conditions of destitution and uncleanness, as subjected her to the most disagreeable inconvenience. But she rendered efficiently the services that were needed, and spared no pains to get the fugitives into places of safety and self-support. Could the history of American slavery, its subversion and overthrow, be fully written, and the labors of those who conducted the underground railroad be adequately described, the name of Mrs. Loguen would stand conspicuously among the friends of the oppressed.[33]

The Loguens' partnership is an example of how Black Underground Railroad work disrupts typical preconceptions about separate spheres during the antebellum era. Their work politicized the home, for the Loguens' aid to fugitives was an act of defiance of American slave law. It involved the whole family, with Caroline taking a leading role in providing aid within her household when her husband traveled around the state to agitate and collect funds to support their efforts. At home, the public and private spheres merged.[34]

bell hooks' concept of the Black "homeplace" has special resonance when considering Caroline's role in the Loguens' affairs, for hooks acknowledges that the homeplace was the "special domain" of Black women. Black homes were "places where all that truly mattered in life took place—the warmth and comfort of shelter, the feeding of our bodies, the nurturing of our souls." In the homeplace, women such as Caroline created not only a haven from racial oppression but also a crucial site of resistance to that oppression. "The task of making homeplace was not simply a matter of black women providing service," hooks points out, "it was about the construction of a safe place where black people could affirm one another and by so doing heal many of the wounds inflicted by racist domination." This was especially true for Caroline, who literally healed the wounds of the formerly enslaved whom she took into her home.[35]

And although her work was primarily domestic, Caroline—like many Black women activists of her time—also pressed against the boundaries of what was deemed acceptable for middle-class women in more public arenas. At First of August celebrations of the anniversary of West Indian emancipation, Caroline gave rousing speeches. She also was active in organizations that raised funds for Black newspapers, education, and events.

The crux of the Loguens' story, however, is not just about giving Caroline her due alongside her husband. It is about understanding how the couple formed an antislavery partnership within their marriage. The Loguens' collaboration created one of the most public stations of the Underground Railroad, and their efforts highlight how the domestic, private sphere overlapped with the political, public sphere in its operations. Despite the danger Loguen himself faced, they brought their family's activities out of the shadows, making their work both a service for fugitives and a profound political statement.[36]

Traditional sources give us a limited glimpse into the Loguen household. A more personal view, however, is available in Gregoria Fraser Goins's biography of Sarah Loguen Fraser. Based primarily on verbal and written exchanges between mother and daughter, it contains several chapters that focus on Sarah's childhood. In it, readers are presented with a unique view of how Jermain and Caroline's daughter remembered her experiences growing up in the most famous depot of the Underground Railroad in New York.

According to Goins, Jermain and Caroline's marriage was a happy one. They "enjoyed their home" shared with children and so many others. "The lives of the Loguens revolved around the antislavery activities of the day," she wrote, meditating on how their house on Genesee Street was always full of guests as "fugitive slaves, abolitionists, ministers of God, friends, and relatives, made a constant and moving human stream" through their doors. At least one fugitive, Henry Kelso, stayed with the Loguens long-term. He had come to their home at the age of fourteen with a group of freedom seekers from Maryland. Other members of the group were sent along to Frederick Douglass's place in Rochester or to the Patterson home in Niagara Falls after a short stay, but Henry had become so attached to "Mars and Missy Loguen" that "he adopted the family, and lived off and on with different members until his death in 1907." As a young man, he worked alongside the family in the Loguen home and became absorbed in its activities.[37]

Although there was much excitement associated with the Loguen family's Underground Railroad work, there was also a great amount of fear. "All of Caroline and Jermain's children grew up in an atmosphere pregnant with incidents fraught with service and danger," according to Goins. Sarah and two of her sisters were young—ages four, eight, and ten years old—when their mother described their situation to them and "began to train them in the use of prudence." She explained to her children that while she had always been free, their father had been born in slavery and run away like the fugitives they saw coming through their home. She told them that if they were ever questioned by strangers about their family, they could talk freely about Caroline, but they were warned "to be silent about their father—where he was, how he was, what he was doing. They were to notice how many strangers there were and what they looked like, and then they were to run home and tell her about them right away." The three children, who had sensed the fear of their parents when rumors about slave catchers circulated in Syracuse, understood the danger and the importance of being careful.[38]

Despite their need for caution, the Loguens continued their public Underground Railroad activities, and Goins provides details about how it was run. She references barrels of clothing that constantly arrived at the house in plentiful supply, providing for the travelers who came to the Loguens for aid. The family home was only two blocks from Railroad Street, and nearby was a railroad tunnel where the trains could slow down and let fugitives exit from the cars. Some of the train engineers were sympathetic to the abolitionists, and as they came through town, these engineers would blow their whistle with a prearranged signal when they arrived with human cargo. Jermain, Caroline, and Henry would hurry to meet the freedom seekers at the tunnel. The Loguen home was also just a few blocks from the Erie Canal, a popular route for fugitives traveling west from Albany or New York City. Other fugitives traveled north from Pennsylvania to the Finger Lakes region, from which they might continue northeastward to the Loguen home. Most of the arrivals originally escaped from slavery in Maryland or Virginia. From their home, the Loguens would either help the fugitives find a place to settle in upstate New York or send wayfarers farther north toward Lake Ontario, where they could ferry across the border. At times, they sent them to Rochester, where they could choose to cross the lake or continue west to Buffalo, where they could cross the Niagara River into Canada.[39]

All of the household members welcomed fugitives to the Loguen home, even in times of grief. On July 31, 1855, the Loguen family was dealt a blow as they experienced the loss of Elizabeth Letitia, Jermain and Caroline's eldest child, at the age of thirteen. She had fallen ill and was unable to recover. Loguen's colleague John Thomas wrote a letter to *Frederick Douglass' Paper* with the sad news of her death. Noting her "cheerful manners and affectionate sympathies" as well as her educational accomplishments and talent at music, Thomas said she had been "the delight of her home and the centre of attraction among her friends." He paid tribute to her work with her family in providing aid to fugitives, noting that she had formed a society of Syracuse youth, over which she had presided, to gather support for their relief. "It would be strange if the child of such a father and mother did not feel deeply the wrongs of the slave," he said. She had grown up in a house that was "the slave's castle," where her family provided for their defense, and she had heard stories of slavery from her father her entire life. "Hence, compassion for the slave was incarnated into her spiritual being, and was a part of her nature." He grieved "the loss of such a child to such parents, to society, and the poor."[40]

Still, the fugitives came, and the Loguens' work continued. In November 1857, family friend Frederick Douglass gave an account indicative of the hospitality that the Loguens offered, day or night, to those who arrived at their home. He recalled a time when he was returning home to Rochester from the east on a train that stopped in Syracuse along the way. On his journey, he encountered nine fugitives—two men, one woman, and six children—who were headed to the Loguen home. Noting that the time of the stop in Syracuse was around 11:00 p.m. and that the night "was exceedingly dark, and the rain was very heavy," Douglass decided to escort the company to their destination. "The children were sick, and shivering with cold, and the rain increasing in violence," he said. Not able to find a hack to drive them from the train stop, they had to walk a full mile and a half to the Loguen home, arriving close to midnight. Douglass said he wondered how they would be received by a family roused from sleep at such a "late hour of a stormy night." When they knocked on their door, however, Loguen "knew the meaning of the rap, and sung out 'hold on'" even as he opened the door at once. Loguen invited the travelers in, and Douglass noted that all the family came to welcome them. "Candles were lighted in different parts of the house, fires kindled, and the whole company made perfectly at home."[41]

Douglass was not the only famous collaborator with the Loguens' operation. Boston abolitionist Thomas Wentworth Higginson once commented on a visit he made to the Loguens' home in Syracuse, where he was struck by both the public nature of their work and the number of fugitives whom the family served in central New York: "Everybody knows where he lives, and every fugitive slave goes there who escapes on that line." Higginson mentioned a ledger of fugitive names he was able to read during the visit. He said he was confused, however, when he saw one woman's name appear multiple times, and he asked Loguen why. Loguen explained that the woman returned to the South on a regular basis to bring out relatives and friends. "Again and again she has done it," he said. "Among those slaves she is better known than the Bible." The woman to whom he referred was Loguen's fellow fugitive agitator Harriet Tubman.[42]

At times those the Loguens took in were sick or wounded. Fugitives often arrived with frostbitten feet, requiring them to stay and recuperate for weeks and even months. One man showed up at their door with "more than a hundred shots in his body." Loguen wrote to Douglass in 1859 that he and his family had many sleepless nights, as those they aided "often came sick, and must be cared forthwith." It "takes about all the time of myself and family to see after their wants," he said. Goins's account of the Loguen family's work includes Sarah's descriptions of watching her mother apply ointments and bandages to the wounds of those who came to them for aid. Sarah, who would become one of the first Black woman medical doctors in the United States, attributed her interest in this field to the time she spent helping her mother tend to fugitives. On one occasion, she recalled, Harriet Tubman brought a group of freedom seekers to the house, several of whom had gunshot wounds in their legs. Sarah helped her mother bathe the leg of one of the little girls in the group. "For days she felt she was the most important person in the whole house," Goins said. "The seed was sown."[43]

In addition to tending to the needs of freedom seekers, Caroline also served as record keeper. She created the ledger that Higginson had read when he visited, and among Sarah's childhood memories were recollections of how she helped her mother, at her father's request, compile the list of all the fugitives who came through the home. From time to time, to keep their activities in the public eye, Jermain would publish updates in the local press of the numbers of fugitives the family had helped. "In respect for the fears of some good friends," however, he did not publish revealing details on most of the "passengers" of the Underground Railroad he assisted. Nevertheless, there was a regular flow of information in Syracuse and antislavery newspapers about Loguen's work, with yearly estimates of between 135 and 200 fugitives aided during the 1850s. In 1860, Loguen stated that he had received approximately 1,500 fugitives in his home throughout the prior decade.[44]

Sometimes Loguen's newspaper updates were simple accounts of numbers served, but in others, he used the material to make a statement about the growing northern opposition to slavery. On April 6, 1855, he wrote to *Frederick Douglass' Paper,* "I would like to say to the Slaveholders and all others, just here, that the Underground Railroad was never doing better business than at present. We have had as many as sixteen passengers in one week in this city. I speak officially, as the agent and keeper of an Underground Railroad Depot. Let them come; we have some true hearts ready to receive them, and God will raise up more." He also published notes of thanks and included stories and descriptions about the flight and condition of those they aided in some of these announcements. He used these reports to publicize his cause, pressing the community to do more. "The genuine friend of the colored man," Loguen said in one piece, "is not satisfied with simply delivering him from whips and chains." He would also "joyfully open to him, whether bond or free, the passages to employment and self elevation." He thus called on Syracuse residents to "take into their shops and on their farms, our colored youth, and discipline and educate them to the industry and arts of life, as white children are educated."[45]

But the records Caroline kept served as more than a source of publicity. They helped to reunite families that had been separated as they fled from slavery. In 1858, the *Syracuse Standard* reported a story of a mother who had been forced to leave her two babies behind in the South as she ran for freedom. When agents of the Underground Railroad heard of her situation, they sent friends to find her children. One of the babies perished soon after it was located, but they were able to transport the other to Loguen's home in Syracuse. Loguen promptly left town with the child to find the mother, and he was able to reunite the two after nearly two years apart.[46]

Another poignant episode that garnered attention throughout the northern states concerned a couple, the Harrises, who had planned their escape together from their enslavement on the Maryland shore. Mrs. Harris had been arrested when the man who enslaved her found out about the planned escape, but she had been able to send a warning to her husband, who immediately fled their home to avoid jail. After she was released from her imprisonment, about three weeks later, the woman was able to make her own way north. She eventually arrived at the Loguen household, where Caroline read her the list of recent visitors. Mrs. Harris "exclaimed with enthusiasm" when she heard her husband's name, and after speaking with Jermain, they were able to determine that Mr. Harris was in Auburn, New York, working as a machinist. Loguen had sent him to his colleague L. D. Mansfield, a professor at the Auburn Theological Seminary who was part of the New York Underground Railroad network, to help him on his journey to Canada, but Harris had found work in Auburn and elected to stay there. Jermain immediately drove Mrs. Harris to find her husband in the cold December weather, putting her up in an Auburn hotel while he went to find Mansfield, who could direct him to her husband's whereabouts.[47]

In addition to revealing Loguen's dedication to helping those in need at a moment's notice, reports of this episode reveal the mischievous side of Loguen's personality. According to Mansfield, he accompanied Loguen to a meeting that was underway at the African church in Auburn at which Harris was in attendance. Once they arrived and Harris answered their call for him, Loguen reproved the man: "What are you doing here; didn't I tell you to be off to Canada?" Loguen then told Harris that he was being pursued by a man who claimed him as his property but that he and Mansfield would take care of him and take him to safety. "Follow me and you will be safe," he said, and then he asked him, "Can you fight?" Harris responded that it depended on whom he had to fight. "Will you fight slaveholders if they have come to take you?" Loguen asked. "Yes," Harris responded, "I would fight a regiment of them."

Mansfield and Loguen then led the frightened man to his wife, who was waiting for him at the hotel nearly a mile away, all the while letting him think he was running for his freedom. "He was so frightened," Mansfield reported, "that he did not know his wife at first, until she called him James, when they had a very joyful meeting." The account of the reunion in the *Syracuse Standard* reported that on recognizing his wife, Harris "was so overcome that he almost fell to the floor, exclaiming at the same time, 'it is my wife!'" They ran to each other, "and a happier bride and bridegroom could not be found in the world." Following their reunion, the couple boarded with Mansfield—Mrs. Harris doing domestic work and Mr. Harris continuing his work as a machinist—and Mansfield pledged to "do all we can for them, and teach them to read and write, and endeavor to place them in a condition to take care of themselves."[48]

In 1872, William Still, a Black activist who aided freedom seekers in Philadelphia and sent many on to Loguen's home in Syracuse, published *The Underground Railroad,* a memoir that gave an accounting of those aided by the network of activists in the northern states. Still acknowledged the biracial nature of the network but also made clear the dominant role that African Americans such as Loguen played. He highlights Loguen's role as the "superintendent" of the Syracuse Underground Railroad "station," and his work documents some of Loguen's specific contributions: reuniting families, passing along information, conducting marriage rites, collecting funds and supplies, helping fugitives establish themselves safely in the northern states or in Canada, and facilitating their ability to provide for themselves.[49]

In his aid to fugitives, Loguen joined the rest of his family in creating a space of refuge for those who came through Syracuse and helping them to freedom. The provision of this aid was a family affair, with each member contributing in their own way. In the Loguen household, private and public life merged. Their home was a place where its members, at great personal risk, publicly flouted a law they deemed unjust. Together the Loguen family, with the support of the town's larger antislavery community who pledged to protect their freedom and provide them with money and supplies, helped build Syracuse's reputation as an "open city" where the weary fugitive, including Loguen himself, could remain safe from the grasp of slavery.

CHAPTER 6

Alms

During the 1850s, the effort to aid fugitives became an increasingly organized project that cultivated greater efficiency, support, and transparency in Loguen's work. It suited his businesslike mind and allowed him to create the robust Underground Railroad operation for which Syracuse became known, but it came with new demands. One of the most challenging of his duties was fundraising, for Loguen's family needed material support to provide for the freedom seekers who came through their home and to maintain their own household. As the number of fugitives the family served increased, collecting alms to support the operation took up an ever larger amount of Loguen's time. The practice also presented new challenges to Loguen as it provoked debates about how best to solicit resources, who was justified in doing so, and the way donations were used.[1]

The network of aid to fugitives predated the railroad terminology that would later be widely applied to it. During the 1840s, however, this network's shape had become more coherent as the United States simultaneously witnessed the emergence of an extensive web of railway lines, knitting communities together and providing new avenues of transportation, commerce, and communication. The growth of the railroads helped to forge a national culture and economy, and those aiding fugitives responded by linking their cause to the optimism and progressive vision associated with them. They began to refer to their humanitarian operation as the Underground Railroad. Within this network of aid, the people who regularly opened their homes, churches, or businesses to fugitives became "stationmasters," the havens they provided becoming their "stations." Abolitionists who guided fugitives between stations were the "conductors," and those such as Loguen who oversaw the work within their larger communities earned the title of "superintendents." Collectively, they all served as "agents" of the Underground Railroad.[2]

By the time of the passage of the Fugitive Slave Law in 1850, the concept of the Underground Railroad was entrenched, and it began to inform the activities of its agents even more powerfully. The law heightened the risk both for fugitives and for those providing for their aid, necessitating greater efficiency and organization. Recognizing the need for streamlined operations, agents began treating their endeavors as a business, consciously incorporating management techniques from the emerging railroad corporations. Although the work to aid fugitives remained a decentralized, grassroots effort throughout the antebellum era, many who were dedicated to this work strove to bring order to it. They used new management strategies to tackle the challenges of coordinating the resources of people, money, and materials. Superintendents maintained ledgers, recording funds received and fugitives helped, and submitted regular reports to benefactors. They created an infrastructure of organizations tasked with raising and distributing resources for their work. And they took advantage of the new technologies of the day—such as telegraphs, railroads, and mass-produced newspapers—to run their operations more efficiently. When speaking of their work, Underground Railroad agents increasingly referred to the "dividends" of fugitives aided and the "stock" of those who invested in their aid, embracing, as Andrew Diemer has pointed out in his work on the business of the Underground Railroad, the "language of enterprise."[3]

In Syracuse, this new approach was reflected in the creation in February 1856 of a Fugitive Aid Society by local abolitionists to bring efficiency to the town's effort to help freedom seekers and circumvent for town citizens the "inconvenience of taking care of them" in their homes. Instead of dealing with fugitives on an ad hoc basis, the society elected to employ Loguen and his family as the primary caretakers of fugitives from slavery who came through Syracuse. The society's officers directed freedom seekers to the Loguen home and dispatched essential supplies to help with their care. To sustain their work the society enlarged its "sphere of operations" by collaborating with vigilance committees and aid organizations in other cities including Albany and Philadelphia. Leading abolitionists of the town served as its officers. Samuel J. May served as president, James Fuller as secretary, and William Abbott as treasurer. Loguen joined the organization's executive board. The Fugitive Aid Society did well in its first year, reporting that it had aided almost two hundred fugitives by the end of 1856.[4]

By September 1857, however, the officers of the society decided that fugitives would be better served if they turned the operation over to Loguen to act as the sole superintendent of the Underground Railroad in Syracuse. They printed a circular that ran in Syracuse and antislavery newspapers announcing that the Fugitive Aid Society was to be dissolved, for the organization was "no longer convenient, nor necessary." Loguen had been doing most of the work since he had become their general agent, they wrote, and "having been a slave and a fugitive himself," he knew "best how to provide for that class of sufferers, and to guard against imposition." Loguen, they announced, had agreed to "devote himself wholly" to the cause. To accomplish his goals, however, he would be forced to rely on economic support from the antislavery community. The circular thus called for generosity toward the operation and instructed that all future donations go directly to Loguen. Loguen, in turn, agreed to provide semiannual reports on what he received and on the number of fugitives aided in the *Syracuse Standard* and *Frederick Douglass' Paper* and to keep his records open for inspection to anyone interested.[5]

This new arrangement was a vote of confidence in Loguen. Under the oversight of the Fugitive Aid Society, funds had been managed by its secretary, William Abbott, and Loguen was treated essentially as an employee. When the society was formed in 1856, its officers had allowed others to collect for their organization until, realizing Loguen's effectiveness, they appointed him as its general agent in early 1857. Now he oversaw the entire enterprise. He would have more freedom to provide for fugitives as he saw fit, but this independence came with a price. He would also have to take on more of the burden of managing his work, including the raising of capital to support it.

Fundraising took up much of Loguen's time, both before and after the dissolution of the Fugitive Aid Society. He printed regular calls for donations in the newspapers and hosted donation parties both at his house and at Syracuse's Convention Hall, where supporters could bring cash, clothes, and other items for those in need. He went on long trips to speak at churches and antislavery gatherings on the plight of both the slave and the fugitive, following which he took up collections for fugitive aid. In some of the places he visited, Loguen facilitated the creation of new local fugitive aid societies to coordinate operations. When not on the road, Loguen communicated with women's groups, churches, and abolitionist organizations at home and abroad who supported his work. Funding an Underground Railroad operation was demanding. It also embroiled Loguen in several controversies surrounding the solicitation of funds for his operation.

One of the first of these disputes concerned his practice of taking up offerings for his cause at church gatherings, a rich source of support. Loguen contacted ministers at churches throughout New York and surrounding states asking permission to speak and fundraise. Many of these welcomed him, but some others wished to keep politically divisive questions, such as slavery and the legitimacy of the Fugitive Slave Law, out of their churches.

Loguen and his colleague Frederick Douglass both spoke out against those ministers who would not allow antislavery speech at their meetings. In an antislavery tour they did together in New York's Chautauqua County in the summer of 1854, for example, the issue came up when the two men visited a church in Jamestown. When Douglass spoke, he mentioned a minister in the town, a Reverend Mr. Gillett, who, he heard, had refused to advertise their lecture because "it was not proper to give Anti-Slavery notices in the pulpit." Douglass was critical of this stance, saying that it sadly was "an index of the clergy on the subject." Douglass was unaware that Gillett was present in the audience when he made his remarks, but Loguen knew he was at the gathering. Therefore, Douglass reported that when he sat down from his speech, "Brother Loguen, kindly, and characteristically, said, that as Mr. Gillett had been quite directly alluded to, opportunity should be given for him to reply." This Gillett did, saying that he had indeed given notice of their talk at his church "and had done so with pleasure." Douglass retracted his criticism, and he would have left Jamestown feeling bad for having maligned Gillett except that the reverend then rose and defended the notion that antislavery speech should not be part of official church services. "I therefore retracted my retraction," Douglass said, "leaving the Rev. Gentleman to dispose of the matter among the people to whom his proslavery character is known." Following this event, Loguen wrote to Frederick Douglass with complaints about others who claimed they had sympathy for the enslaved but allowed lectures from Black antislavery speakers only if the meetings supported their coffers. He remained frustrated, as well, with ministers who did not allow him to speak at all in their churches.[6]

Appeals to the churches were an important source of funding, and on November 29, 1856, Syracuse's Fugitive Aid Society officially reached out to antislavery ministers to collect on its behalf. It printed a circular in the *National Anti-Slavery Standard*, reminding readers of the many fugitives who came to Syracuse due to its position as a central Underground Railroad depot in New York. More came to them in need than they could service without looking outside the city for aid. They therefore wrote to ask that church leaders appeal to their congregations for funds to support the work of the Fugitive Aid Society, take up offerings, and send them to the organization's secretary, William Abbott.[7]

As an agent of the Fugitive Aid Society and later as the sole superintendent of the Syracuse Underground Railroad, Loguen engaged even more directly in appealing for aid in churches, scheduling talks around New York and beyond and letting the ministers of the churches he visited know that he intended to take up a collection to support the Syracuse Underground Railroad operation. Most of the time, these prior arrangements prevented conflict, but in one well-publicized case, Loguen engaged in a public verbal battle with a minister who challenged his efforts.[8]

The man in question was Hiram Mattison, minister of the Methodist Episcopal church in the small town of Adams, New York, about fifty-two miles due north of Syracuse. Mattison's affiliation was with the more conservative wing of the northern Methodist

Church. During the previous decade, American Methodists had been riven by the slavery issue, with the Wesleyan Methodists splitting from the Methodist Episcopal Church in 1843 when the latter introduced strictures against discussing slavery from the pulpit. A year later, the church broke into northern and southern branches when southern churches refused to bar slaveholders from church leadership positions. Mattison, though a Methodist Episcopal minister, was known for his antislavery views, so Loguen requested through an intermediary the opportunity to lecture in his church. He received a positive response, and when he arrived in Adams, Mattison agreed to find time for Loguen to speak to his congregation outside his regular services.

When Loguen arrived at the church at the appointed time in July 1856, Mattison was thirty minutes late for the proceedings, and he took a seat in the pews while Loguen gave his talk. At the end of Loguen's lecture, which recounted the horrors his mother and siblings met under slavery and encouraged support for the plight of fugitives, Mattison rose quickly to give his benediction, dismissed the service before the choir gave its final hymn, and refused to let Loguen take up an offering. Those who wished to support Loguen as individuals could do so outside of the church meeting, he said, but not as a part of his congregation.

Loguen was disappointed in Mattison's reception and was not shy about speaking of the lack of support he felt from the minister. During a lecture at his next stop, in the town of Pierrepont Manor, he told his audience of Mattison's late arrival to his lecture, his decision not to join Loguen in the pulpit, his instructions that no offering be taken during the service for Loguen's cause, and his hasty dismissal of the service.

On July 29, 1856, Mattison published a public letter in the *Jefferson County News*, defending his decision to bar Loguen from taking up a collection at his church, saying that Loguen had made false assumptions about what was appropriate at his church due to Mattison's antislavery reputation. Speech against slavery was one thing, he argued, and collecting money to support the Underground Railroad from his congregation was another, for it promoted breaking federal law. As a minister, he felt it unwise to sanction such contributions within the church walls.[9]

The *Syracuse Journal*, a paper with antislavery sympathies, printed a summary of Mattison's piece in early August, and it came to Loguen's notice. Seizing the opportunity to challenge Mattison's position, Loguen penned a public response. When Mattison instructed church members that they could contribute to the Underground Railroad individually but "not as Christian Methodists under his charge," Loguen argued, it was a directive that "separates Christianity from the man, and of course annihilates it." He urged Mattison to consider the practical impact: without aid, fugitives would suffer hunger, cold, and deprivation. He asked Mattison, "Does your religion forbid you to do unto others as you would have them do unto you?" To the argument that members of the church should not be encouraged, as Christians, to defy government measures even when they were unjust, Loguen said of such laws: "If you say they obligate you and me, then you say God approves them." He concluded that if Mattison believed such things, he didn't "understand the Scriptures."[10]

Loguen had made his point, and he was prepared to argue it further as he awaited Mattison's response. But after this initial exchange, the minister's public correspondence quickly devolved into defensiveness and personal invective. Instead of responding to Loguen's argument about church support for the Underground Railroad, Mattison addressed the insult he felt at Loguen's representations of his visit to Adams. As he did so, he became increasingly emotional and abusive.

The minister first addressed rumors he had heard from the

town of Pierrepont Manor. Friends from the town informed him that Loguen had held Mattison up to ridicule in one of the town's churches, telling the crowd that Mattison showed up late to his talk and "sneaked away to a corner" when he did arrive, only to dismiss the crowd before the offering when Loguen finished. Mattison felt he needed to set the record straight. He said there was a mix-up about the time of the meeting, and he complained to Loguen that he acted in an unchristian manner when he seized on the accident to "weave it into your narrative of wrongs as an intentional discourtesy." He did not "sneak" into a corner, he said, but chose not to enter the pulpit as Loguen spoke out of respect. He complained that he did not prevent the people in his congregation from giving to Loguen but only said that there was "an obstacle in the way of a public collection" in the church. He told Loguen that he also did not abruptly dismiss the service as Loguen accused, "but having deliberately stated my wishes, and a few of my reasons for them, and seeing by your impertinent remarks in my pulpit that you was disposed to get up an altercation in the house of God, on the holy Sabbath, after saying what I wished to say about the collection, I dismissed the congregation." Mattison added that he had not been appropriately forewarned of Loguen's intentions in his visit, which he said he had learned about only when Loguen arrived in Adams. "I did not write and invite you," Mattison said, "and still you thrust yourself upon me!"

After defending his treatment of Loguen, Mattison then went on the offensive. He attacked Loguen's reference to himself as "a Methodist." He argued that identifying himself as such was misleading since Loguen was not a member of the Methodist Episcopal Church. Such a self-designation was therefore "well-calculated to deceive." He questioned why Loguen never went to the church conference for official approval to collect for his operation and speculated that he did not because, he told Loguen, "they would at once brand your schemes as inexpedient or as private speculation. . . . Your pathetic description of 'clanking your chains,' and all that sort of thing would be too thin in such a body to conceal the real character of your mission." Mattison said his only error during Loguen's visit was being "too credulous" of him because of his "sable complexion." He ought to have refused him access to his pulpit altogether, for he believed that Loguen's behavior had proved him untrustworthy. Mattison then insinuated that Loguen's stories of enslavement were fabrications: "I doubt if it is best to shed many tears over the case of Rev. Mr. Loguen and his mother and sisters at present. It may turn out, after all, like the story about a certain minister . . . who went into a church and 'sneaked away in the corner.'"

After relaying his assessment of Loguen's character, Mattison declared that not every Black man who appealed to northern sympathy should be "taken up, petted, and caressed by antislavery men." He criticized the prevalence of itinerant beggars in the North, using their color to gain sympathy and collect money for their personal benefit, and he counted Loguen among these swindlers. His solicitations were an act, he said, of "clerical vagrancy." Mattison concluded that he was "no more in favor of making white ministers at the North the slaves of wandering colored lecturers than we are of having the colored man at the South slave to the white planter." He believed "that while we are doing all we can to abolish slavery in the Republic, it is hardly safe to resign up our personal liberty and become the slaves of the colored race."[11]

In October, Loguen responded with a mix of surprise and disappointment. He noted that Mattison had ignored the substance of his previous letter, instead resorting to racial demarcations within the Methodist Episcopal Church. Loguen dismissed Mattison's personal attacks, focusing instead on the minister's harmful stance toward fugitive slaves. He criticized Mattison's adherence to the Fugitive Slave Law, suggesting that it showed his unfitness as a religious leader. Loguen received no further response from Mattison, but he continued to address the substance of their quarrel in a second public letter in November, which emphasized the church's duty to put God's laws over human ones and the importance of Christian charity.[12]

The content of Mattison's correspondence with Loguen highlights not only the racial paternalism that existed among some members of the northern antislavery community who gave only qualified support to the needs of Black Americans but how the Fugitive Slave Law complicated northerners' sentiment toward slavery by making protection of the institution the law of the land. It also reveals Loguen's astuteness as an agitator. Loguen responded to Mattison's vitriol in a pointed yet measured and rational way, bringing the conversation back to the main idea—which was that Christians and their churches should support attempts to provide aid to fugitives from slavery and should not be beholden to immoral American laws that supported the institution. Throughout the exchange, Loguen displayed his awareness that the letters were a source of publicity for the antislavery movement and the Underground Railroad, and he conducted himself accordingly in his responses to Mattison, taking care to make his point and avoiding words that would cast doubt on his own character and motives. Indeed, after the conclusion of this exchange of public letters in the *Syracuse Journal,* antislavery men in Syracuse arranged for them to be published in full in pamphlet form, extending the conversation about the church's position on aiding fugitives and abiding by the Fugitive Slave Law.[13]

Mattison was not the only person to question Loguen's motives. Syracuse's "law and order" crowd who had spoken out against the Jerry Rescue also targeted Loguen's provision of aid to fugitives.

The *Syracuse Daily Courier and Union* emerged by the middle of the decade as the main mouthpiece of this group, regularly running articles critical of "Brudder Loguen" and Syracuse citizens who either supported his Underground Railroad station or looked the other way as he ran a very public illegal enterprise that, the paper insinuated, was undertaken primarily to line Loguen's pockets rather than help others. Such aid that was provided, it said, was "an incidental matter."[14]

In April 1857, after Loguen became the general agent of the Fugitive Aid Society, the *Courier* printed a letter from a correspondent criticizing the town's abolitionists for allowing Loguen "to draw upon the public as an independent, self-appointed, self-auditing and self-distributing lecturer, ostensibly to aid the fugitives, but really to aid himself." It insinuated that the goal was to allow Loguen to build "an estate" of enough worth to give him the power to vote in New York. The correspondent also complained that town leaders had for several years allowed Loguen to use the city's Convention Hall to collect funds to provide aid for the influx of Black fugitives in New York and claimed that white men were denied the opportunity to use the hall for fundraising purposes. For at least some of the supporters of the *Courier,* Loguen's work was not just an illegal operation that might threaten the Union; it was a threat to the racial order of New York State.[15]

The article's complaint about the use of Convention Hall, however, had already been addressed in January 1857 by the Syracuse city council. For several years Loguen had used the hall to host an annual fundraising event to support his work. Because of this history, Loguen anticipated no obstacles for the coming year, and he began to advertise the annual "donation party" for fugitive aid at the turn of the year, announcing that Frederick Douglass would speak at the event. In an unprecedented move—for the hall had always been open to anyone who wished to reserve it—the city council took up the question of Loguen's use of the hall when one of the aldermen proposed that Loguen be required to pay five dollars in advance to reserve the space. That discussion in turn led to the larger issue of the "questionable" activity for which Loguen wanted to use it. In the end, the council voted six to one to deny the use of Convention Hall to Loguen altogether, forcing him to find a new location for the annual fundraiser in 1857.[16]

Official opposition to the use of the hall for such work, however, dissipated, for in 1858 and 1859, it was again opened to donation parties held by antislavery women in Syracuse on the Loguen family's behalf. Whether it would have been reopened to Loguen himself had he wished to reserve it is not clear, but the "questionable" act of raising funds for the Underground Railroad was apparently no longer a problem for city officials. With this turn of events, the *Courier* renewed its invective against Loguen and his supporters. "It is about time that the city Hall of Syracuse," it printed in 1858, "should cease to be prostituted to the orgies and 'donation visits' of the Rev. Mr. Loguen and his confederates, and that the swindling and treason of these operators, 'conductors,' and local agents should be shown up for the benefit of their dupes and for the benefit of society."[17]

Although the funds Loguen raised went both to provide supplies for fugitives and to support his own household, charges from such sources as Mattison and the *Courier* that Loguen was using the humanitarian cause of the Underground Railroad to line his own pockets were untrue. The goal of his fundraising was to provide for fugitive needs and to allow Loguen and his family to dedicate themselves full-time to their work. Loguen nevertheless frequently faced criticism from opponents who charged that, because the funds he collected in part supported his household, he was an opportunist. In a portion of one of his letters to Mattison, Loguen explained the need for these collections and how those funds were used:

> There is not a week passes, rarely a day, that I have not fugitive slaves at my house. I have had twelve and fifteen at my table at the same time. Some of them stay with me for days, and some for weeks. Some of them are ragged, and are provided with clothing. Some are sick, and are provided with nurses and medicine. Some of them want to work, and I provide places for them to work. . . . My house is a mile from the Depot, and I am obliged to keep a horse and carriage . . . to take the fugitives to and from the cars, which, alone, is an expense of no small amount. The time and labor of my wife and family are entirely occupied in the care of my suffering countrymen. . . . I have spoken above, only of those who receive temporary lodging and board, and assistance at my house; besides these, there are numerous others whom I receive at the Railroad, and furnish with tickets and funds, and provisions, to help them out of the country.

All these obligations, Loguen explained, required that he frequently call for donations: "Of course, my expenditures are very great, and I am obliged often to call on the wealthy men of the city to contribute liberally to meet instant necessities. Syracuse is overburdened with these charges, and therefore, I go into the country occasionally, and appeal to people at a distance." In the face of challenges to his integrity Loguen remained prepared to open his books to anyone who questioned his work and his expenditures.[18]

There were others, however, who did use the humanitarian impulse to aid fugitives to advance their own personal interests, and such charlatans were harmful to Loguen. Not only did they force him to prove the legitimacy of his own operation to the public but they also siphoned away possible donations by fleecing would-be benefactors.

Such charlatans could be either Black or white. In March 1857, the *Syracuse Standard* warned its readers against Black men calling on Syracuse residents to beg for money, pretending to be fugitives in need. The paper reminded readers that callers asking for alms should be sent directly to Loguen's house, where they would receive aid. Those who would not go to Loguen were deemed impostors. The same article also warned that "some unprincipled white persons" were "partners in the impositions," and told readers to be on guard. Loguen himself wrote to Gerrit Smith about the problem in 1859, commenting on a man named William Smith who came to him as a fugitive requesting aid. "I do not regard him as true," he said. He told his friend that he regretted there were many such frauds throughout the country. "How to get at them I know not," he said. "Some of them are white men and some are black men—but all of them are bad men."[19]

One of the white men who caused particular problems for Loguen and his allies was William Brown, who began circulating around New York and New England in 1857, soliciting funds on behalf of fugitives for his self-created African Aid Society. Brown started out as an agent for the Fugitive Aid Society in Syracuse, and he acted with a certificate of approval from Samuel J. May to collect for their organization. Although he raised funds in Syracuse and surrounding towns, no money was remitted to the organization for fugitive aid—only a few boxes of clothing. The officers of the society became aware that Brown, who styled himself varyingly as "Professor," "Doctor," or "Reverend," had a reputation as a dishonest man. In early 1857, the executive board revoked May's approval of Brown as their agent around the same time that they appointed Loguen as the organization's general agent, prompting Brown to form the competing African Aid Society so that he could continue his solicitations. To give it an air of legitimacy, he convinced several Syracuse residents to serve as officers for this organization with promises of salaries that never materialized. Funds collected for fugitive aid were never deposited in the coffers of the society, although Brown bragged about collecting hundreds of dollars in Syracuse and surrounding towns.[20]

When reports of Brown's new organization came to the members of the Fugitive Aid Society, its officers issued a circular warning the public about Brown, who represented himself as an agent collecting for fugitives and insinuated that his African Aid Society was the only one to serve such a purpose in Syracuse. Brown provided no accounting of how the funds were used, they warned, and in fact, they could find no evidence that the African Aid Society provided aid to any fugitives in need. The circular was printed in Syracuse's Methodist newspaper, the *Wesleyan,* which was known as a mouthpiece for the town's Underground Railroad operation, as well as in other newspapers with an antislavery bent. It criticized the "gross imposition" that Brown made on the public by collecting for an organization "which has no real existence in Syracuse, but is a mere sham." His work was supported neither by the city's Black population nor by their allies, and the public was urged to be wary of the "impostor."[21]

When Brown became aware of the warnings issued, he defended himself to Samuel J. May, explaining that his objects were to aid fugitives in Canada rather than New York. May seemed to initially accept this explanation. But Brown soon revealed that in addition to the obvious desire to raise money for his own benefit, he was waging a vendetta against Loguen both as a Black man and as the general agent for the Fugitive Aid Society.

On August 14, 1858, Brown wrote a letter to Loguen, bragging to him that he had collected over three hundred dollars in Utica and over one hundred in Rochester. "I do draw hard on some of your old customers and shall be at it again," he said, for "I oppose you as a man of color and I am determined to oppose you in every possible way of my ability until death." He told him that this antagonism had fueled him for the past two years and would continue as long as he lived, for he believed that Loguen was a "spoiled negro, in every sense of the word." If he had "common sense as much as vanity and pride," Brown said, Loguen would realize that "the popular Republicanism of this day has little sympathy with Radical Abolitionists and social equality with the most ungenial and dangerous specimens of humanity." He told him that the negro race belonged in the tropics and not the United States and that he expected the Black population to soon die out among the "far superior and boldly aspiring people" of the United States.[22]

Throughout the controversy, the *Syracuse Daily Courier and Union*, amid its own critiques of Loguen's Underground Railroad operation, printed several articles in support of Brown's purported work. On September 8, 1858, the *Courier* printed its take on Brown's position in "War among the Conservative and Radical Underground Railroaders." This article reported that the original arrangement between Brown and the Fugitive Aid Society was that Brown would focus on aid in Canada while Loguen would focus on aid in Syracuse, and it claimed that Loguen had arranged for Brown to be ousted from the Fugitive Aid Society when Brown refused to turn over his funds to Loguen. Brown "worked harder, talked louder, and by the way, succeeded better, generally" than Loguen had, it claimed. "This made trouble in the camp," and so Loguen "set to work in order to excommunicate the Professor—all because he wouldn't pay to him the money received!" The paper reported that Brown was now doing "a thriving business all over the country . . . and not molesting *Brudder* Loguen at all," when suddenly Loguen and his friends launched a campaign against Brown in "all the radical papers from the lake shores to the Atlantic Ocean." The article concluded that Brown was persecuted because he worked independently of the Radical Abolitionists, "does not go in for 'social' equality with the darkies," supported colonization as well as institutions to serve the Black population, and refused to "divide the spoils" of his efforts with Loguen.[23]

The paper continued its discussion of the matter in March 1859, referencing a pamphlet Brown had compiled that described the "trials and tribulations" he faced as he worked to support the "poor downtrodden slave" and expose the hypocrisy of Loguen and the former members of the Fugitive Aid Society. The goals of the African Aid Society, Brown explained, were conservative ones, aimed at relocating Black people across the border in Canada. Brown stated that it was Loguen, and not himself, who was "mixing up" the public's mind regarding the two societies, so that no one could tell "which from which." Because of the "tirade of abuse" that had been heaped on him from the "Lougenites," Brown had decided to seek redress in court "and make the sable engineer of the 'Fugitive Aid Society' and his minions 'smell woolen!'" Brown repeated earlier claims that Loguen enriched himself through his work, and he insinuated that the Fugitive Aid Society had disbanded in 1857 due to some sort of vague misdeed committed by Loguen. He proclaimed that since its dissolution there was no Underground Railroad in Syracuse, but only "a mere party of the deluded disciples" of Loguen and his radical friends who were "revolutionists and not reformers—church and state destroyers, who would feign mingle the blood of Ammon and Ashdod with the fair daughters of Judah; and put a sword into the hand of every slave, that he might gloat."[24]

Brown issued this pamphlet on the heels of initiating two libel suits in response to the circular that the Syracuse abolitionists had distributed throughout the press, warning against his work. One was filed against Cyrus Prindle, editor of the *Wesleyan*. The other suit was against the four Fugitive Aid Society officers who signed the circular: Samuel J. May, James Fuller, Abner Bates, and William Abbott.

In January 1860, a hearing commenced to deal with Brown's complaint against Prindle. At it, Prindle testified that Loguen had come to the *Wesleyan* offices on November 1, 1858, requesting that he publish the handbill on Brown. Prindle agreed to do so, he said, to support the public good. He was himself aware of the rumors about Brown's character. Further testimony from both the officers of the Fugitive Aid Society and those of the African Aid Society established that neither organization had received remittance of funds from Brown when he acted as general agent, and thus the claims that he was an impostor were not libelous but true. One witness claimed that Brown used the money to pay off his mortgage. Brown's character was also questioned at the hearing, and several bullying letters that Brown had sent to members of the Fugitive Aid Society officers were read into the record.

Brown did not come out of the proceedings looking good, but the outcome of the suit would not be decided on its merits. After all the testimony, the judge dismissed the case rather than sending it to the jury. He explained that he considered the matter a "nonsuit" because collecting aid for fugitives was an illegal act, and he believed that any complaint of libel associated with it was therefore invalid. Following this ruling, the attorney for the Fugitive Aid Society officers requested that, despite the judge's ruling in the Prindle case, theirs be scheduled on the next docket for a jury trial rather than dismissed. The society's officers did not want their fate to rest under claims of the legality of the Fugitive Slave Law. They preferred to pursue an acquittal based on their defense against the libel charges, which they felt was strong. The hearing never took place, however, because Brown dropped the suit. In the end, both defendants and plaintiff agreed to let the matter go, paying their own legal fees.[25]

In February, the *Weekly Anglo-African* printed a statement from Loguen on the William Brown affair. "You will agree with me that it is bad enough to bear the unavoidable hardship of our work, without having the charity intended for us intercepted by knavery," he said. The testimony given at the hearing revealed that Brown had "sponged several thousand dollars off of the people in his operations," and Loguen expressed frustration that "such an errant and shameless humbug should have possessed himself of our means." He held out hope for the future, however, that donations for fugitives would all reach those in need. Along with Loguen's musings, the paper reprinted the Fugitive Aid Society's caution against Brown that was the subject of the suit, and it also printed a letter dated September 10, 1858, from one of the officers of the African Aid Society in Syracuse claiming that it had been dissolved a year earlier. Brown had been collecting under the name of an organization with no real existence for months.[26]

On December 1, 1860, after the drama of the libel suits had passed, Loguen wrote a letter to the *Syracuse Standard,* thanking the city for its support of his work as superintendent of the Syracuse Underground Railroad. He reminded readers that he had all the provisions needed to aid fugitives in his home and explained that the designation of his address as the city's central depot helped to prevent benefactors from "imposition by imposters" by concentrating the work all in one place. He also noted that the annual fundraising event to support the station was held so that donors supporting the needs of fugitives weren't confronted with constant requests for funds. Last, he let them know that his family and friends were "ready to care for all at any time, if they will call," and "when we cannot we will let the friends know it." It was signed "J. W. Loguen, Superintendent of the UGRR."[27]

Ensuring the financial wherewithal to support his Underground Railroad enterprise remained a constant worry for Loguen throughout its existence. Although donations poured in from women's groups both at home and abroad, wealthy New York philanthropists, antislavery church congregations, and members of the free Black community, his resources were often stretched thin. Samuel J. May wrote as much in his memoir, remembering how the Loguen family had taken on the operation in Syracuse while relying on donations from antislavery supporters: "The charge thus committed to them, Mr. Loguen and his excellent wife faithfully and kindly cared for to the last, and I more than suspect that the fugitives they harbored, and helped on their way, often cost them much more than they called on us to pay."[28]

Because of the difficulties he faced, Loguen sought new sources of income to fund his work, and by the end of the 1850s, he had found one. He would publish an autobiography recounting his time in slavery, his flight to freedom, and his participation in the Jerry Rescue. He began to work with his old friend John Thomas, who had editorial expertise; and in March 1859, he reached out to Gerrit Smith, telling him he was "trying to get out a book." He hoped that Smith would "feel friendly to the idea" for "we need something to help us take care of the many poor that are calling on us for help, and we have a large family to care for at the same time."[29]

Beginning in March 1859, abolitionist friends began advertising Loguen's forthcoming book in newspapers, announcing that it would cost fifteen hundred dollars to publish, but when one thousand dollars was raised in subscriptions, the first copies would be issued and Loguen would assume further costs of production. The ad touted that "there are few men whose history is so marked with stirring incidents, instructive lessons, and encouraging examples as Mr. Loguen's." Loguen hoped not only that the book would raise money to support his Underground Railroad enterprise but that its stirring narrative would also open minds to the plight of both the slave and those who fled from slavery.[30]

The Rev. J. W. Loguen, as a Slave and as a Freeman: A Narrative of Real Life was published before the year's end, with five hundred copies offered for sale at one dollar apiece in September 1859. A second edition of five hundred was released a month later, and a third edition of one thousand copies came out in January 1860. Loguen's autobiography was well received, with positive reviews in the antislavery press and excerpts running in numerous newspapers. Reviewers compared it positively to Harriet Beecher Stowe's novel *Uncle Tom's Cabin,* of 1852, and to Frederick Douglass's narrative *My Bondage and My Freedom,* of 1855—both of which had clearly inspired the style and presentation of Loguen's narrative.[31]

The book's publication had the desired effect of allowing Loguen to have some self-reliant income for his operation, freeing him from wholesale dependence on charitable contributions. According to a letter published in January 1860 in the *Weekly Anglo-African,* Loguen had insisted on taking charge of the book's publication himself, vowing to employ only Black agents to promote its sale. Although several publishers had reached out to him with offers to publish his narrative, Loguen worried that this would eat into the profits of a book meant to aid "his own brethren." He thus insisted on "having everything in his own hands." Although this was initially expensive, "by thus doing he himself reaps the benefit—not some great publisher."[32]

If the book gave Loguen some self-sufficiency, however, it also opened himself to danger of retribution from Tennessee, for its publication caught the eye of his former "mistress," Sarah Logue. The year following the release of Loguen's book, she wrote her infamous letter to him, complaining that he misrepresented his treatment at the Logue plantation, that he had placed the Logue household in financial straits when he ran away, and that she would relinquish claim to his service only if he paid her for his freedom. Loguen responded by sending the woman a vehement rejection of her offer, publishing her letter in the antislavery press, and including it, along with his reply, in the appendix of the fourth edition of his book when it was issued in November 1860. One newspaper joked that in his reply to Sarah Logue, Loguen offered to sell her three thousand copies of his book for two thousand dollars, and she could apply the profits of the sale however she wished: "This, he says, is the best he can do for her."[33]

Although Loguen made bold proclamations that he did not fear his former enslaver's threats, her letter was nevertheless a reminder of his continued vulnerability under the Fugitive Slave Law. Even as he ran one of the busiest, most efficient, and most visible enterprises to aid and protect fugitives from slavery who came into the northern states, his own exposed status as a fugitive loomed over him, adding danger and difficulty to his work conducting a sophisticated enterprise that defied American law.

CHAPTER 7

Uplift

THROUGHOUT THE 1850S, in addition to providing for and shepherding many fugitives across the international border, Loguen regularly traveled to Canada to provide aid for and assess the condition of Black settlers who had made new homes in freedom at the "terminus" of the Underground Railroad. As he did so, he became embroiled in debates within the antislavery community, especially among his fellow Black activists, about the best way to assist Black refugees. These concerns were part of a wider conversation about how to elevate the condition of the free Black population at large, at home as well as abroad, and they were a priority for Loguen. Although during the 1850s he turned much of his attention to the needs of fugitives, he remained active, as he had the previous decade, in Black political and religious organizations in New York State that worked to promote aid, uplift, and equality for the state's larger free Black community. This work, both at home and in Canada, forced Loguen to confront important questions about how best to improve the free Black condition.

Although Loguen was both active in relocating fugitives to Canada and concerned with their fate as they settled there, he preferred that those he aided remain in the United States, where they could better participate in the fight against slavery and for equality in their homeland. The question of whether to promote emigration to Canada loomed over all Loguen's work with fugitives during the 1850s. Loguen, though he was willing to help those who wished to settle across the border, always refused to do so permanently himself, and he encouraged other freedom seekers to remain in the United States as well.

In August 1851, referencing the exodus to Canada precipitated by the passage of the Fugitive Slave Law of 1850, Loguen wrote to Frederick Douglass, who held views similar to his own on emigration. He expressed frustration at the number of possible agitators who had fled the United States: "Were to the Lord that they were all on the ground with their sword and battle axes in hand, to do battle against the foul monster of hell! They might do much for their country." Ironically, soon after writing these words to Douglass, Loguen left for Canada himself, seeking safety from arrest after the Jerry Rescue. He was determined, however, that his time there would be short.[1]

During his Canadian exile, Loguen attended the founding meeting of the Canadian Anti-Slavery Society in Toronto, where he gave a rousing speech against slavery and the Fugitive Slave Law. The speech was well received, but when fellow fugitive Henry Bibb, an antislavery ally who held different views from Loguen on emigration, reported it in his Canadian newspaper, the *Voice of the Fugitive,* he hinted at what he saw as Loguen's hypocrisy. Noting his friend's earlier statements implying that flight to Canada was "cowardly" and his pledge that he "was determined to stand his ground and defy the slaveholders and their posse," Bibb expressed surprise that Loguen had taken refuge on "the Queen's free soil." He addressed Loguen smugly: "That's right, brother Loguen, we told you that Canada was the best place for fugitive slaves, although you and Mr. Douglass opposed us. . . . You must now be convinced that we were right:—we welcome you here, and here you had better stay." Bibb felt that only outside the United States could fugitives truly have the opportunity to elevate their condition.[2]

Loguen did not stay, however. He soon returned home, and once there, he continued to discourage emigration to Canada. In March 1853, in fact, he chaired a Black anticolonization meeting in the city, and one of the resolutions passed opposed "emigration in large bodies to any country—whether it be to Liberia, Canada, the West Indies, or elsewhere," for those gathered believed their "right to remain in this country to be as indisputable as that of our white fellow citizens; and that our own well-being as well as that of our enslaved brethren at the south requires us to look forward to this land as the place of our burial as it has been that of our birth."[3]

This meeting was held in response to a resurgence of the American Colonization Society (ACS) in the northern states in the early 1850s, which came with the increase of sectional conflict in the wake of the Compromise of 1850 and the passage of the Fugitive Slave Law. Colonizationists proposed that a policy of removal would eliminate the cause of the tensions between North and South. In March 1853, Loguen editorialized in several newspapers about a gathering at the First Presbyterian Church in Syracuse to form a new auxiliary of the ACS in Onondaga County. The chief speaker at the Syracuse meeting was ex-governor of Liberia and corresponding secretary of the New York Colonization Society John Pinney, who, Loguen said, "affected great benevolence of feeling for the poor colored people . . . and pictured in glowing color, how happy they would be in Africa." Pinney, however, revealed the prejudicial underpinnings of his society when he contrasted this to what he believed to be their condition in the United States, where they would remain "nothing but 'the filth, the scum and offscourings of the earth.'" Although those present at the organizing meeting said they wished to create a benevolent society promoting uplift for Black Americans, Loguen informed the public that “the colored people . . . regard both the Fugitive Slave Bill and the Colonization scheme as coming (to a great extent) from the same class of men” and that it was indeed “hard to say which they are the most actively engaged in—the sending us back to the hell of slavery, or to Africa. Either of these destinations, it seems, will suit them.” They did not wish to see the Black man “stand and contend like a man for his God-given rights,” he asserted; instead, “they prefer to see us running and disgracing our manhood.”[4]

Loguen argued that the northern Black population must lead the fight against American racism. “We can never be respected by others,” he said, “till we demonstrate our self-respect to the world.” Black northerners had done so during the Jerry Rescue of 1851, and their efforts in that event “had given life and vigor to some of our white friends.” He believed that the colonization society feared the influence of Black activists and had formed, in part, “to get such colored men out of the country.” Loguen pledged that he would remain on American soil and “not quit the field so long as my people are held as slaves—preferring to suffer on here if need be until we all be slaves, or all be freemen together.”[5]

On March 17, 1853, when Loguen chaired the anticolonization meeting of Black citizens in Syracuse, he spoke against all expatriation efforts. Those present at the meeting resolved not to support any mass colonization scheme, no matter the destination, but they took special aim at the revival of northern colonization societies affiliated with the ACS, declaring that any Black person who supported its work “with the slightest degree of approval” was “a foe to his own best interest and those of his race.”[6]

As Loguen’s rhetoric during the early 1850s indicates, for many members of the northern Black community, the colonization issue had become intertwined with the question of voluntary Black emigration after the passage of the Fugitive Slave Law, but the emigration question was one on which Black reformers were divided. Fellow fugitives Henry Bibb and Samuel Ringgold Ward, who had both relocated to Canada following the passage of the hated law, contributed to Canadian newspapers that encouraged emigration, the *Provincial Freeman* and the *Voice of the Fugitive*, respectively. Ward worked with Mary Ann Shadd, the first Black woman publisher in North America, who founded and edited the *Freeman* and had strong proemigration views herself. And in addition to his newspaper, Bibb organized several Canadian conventions to promote relocation to the "Queen's free soil." In 1854, Black reformer Martin Delany, who had originally opposed emigration, began to argue that it was a viable option for his compatriots, and he organized several proemigration meetings in the United States to support the voluntary establishment of Black colonies elsewhere.[7]

In January 1854, Black leaders in New York took up the question of expatriation in general at the inaugural meeting of the New York State Council of Colored People in Albany. The council was a new organization meant to provide leadership and coordinate the activities of the state's Colored Conventions Movement, and Loguen served as vice president as well as on its ways and means committee. Among many other issues discussed at the founding meeting, the council issued a resolution declaring that it "opposed every system of Colonization of the people of color from these United States, whether by the 'American Colonization Society,' or the more dangerous and equally detestable scheme, the Emigration Convention intended to convene at Cleveland." This convention, which would take place the next August, would be the first of the proemigration gatherings planned by Delany. Larger meetings of the Colored Conventions Movement at both the state and national levels also issued resolutions opposing expatriation.[8]

Loguen stood firmly with his colleagues who opposed a mass

Black exodus from the United States, but it is important to note that he wasn't as unbending on an individual fugitive's decision to seek sanctuary on the free soil of Canada. Despite his alignment with those who opposed colonization and Black-led emigration schemes, Loguen was willing in his role as an Underground Railroad agent to help the weary fugitives who arrived at his home in Syracuse make their way to Canada if they wished. He understood their desire for the security that crossing the border would bring, for he had felt that pull himself. Even so, he encouraged those he aided to settle in New York State instead, preferring to help them secure lodging, education, and jobs in nearby communities. According to Loguen, he rarely sent fugitives on to Canada, except for those who were of a more "timid class, who dare not run the risk of remaining in the states."[9]

Although he urged Black Americans to remain in the United States, Loguen was as eager to provide aid to those who had made their way across the international border as he was to help those who settled in New York, and he took frequent trips between 1851 and 1856 to visit communities of Black Canadian settlers, distribute goods, and report on their condition for interested parties at home. Advertisements ran in Syracuse newspapers that donations of clothes and other supplies could be dropped off at Loguen's house in Syracuse for him to take to Canada, and he held additional meetings on his route to the Niagara suspension bridge, where he crossed the international border, collecting goods along the way. In 1856, Loguen worked with fellow fugitive and minister Rev. Simeon Hutchinson, who established a home for refugees on the Canadian side of the bridge near the steamboat landing and railway station. It would serve as a temporary place of shelter, rest, and nourishment until fugitive wayfarers could find permanent homes and provide for themselves. Loguen's Canadian colleague in

St. Catharines, Hiram Wilson, was also a proponent of collecting supplies to aid refugees in their transition to freedom. Loguen cooperated with these efforts to provide aid, distributing clothing he brought with him to Canada "to the best advantage he could among the destitute" and taking note that those "just arriving are the most needy." This work, however, was not without controversy.[10]

Some fellow reformers took exception to abolitionist and missionary "begging" for relief on behalf of fugitives in Canada. They argued that it was unnecessary, for Black settlers had a reasonable path to self-improvement without such aid. They also objected to the depictions of Canadian settlers as destitute, unable to care for themselves, and desperate for assistance. They felt that such depictions, often employed by those collecting on the settlers' behalf, reinforced slaveholder claims of inherent Black dependence. Others argued that the practice of distributing goods to fugitives encouraged corruption, believing that some supposed benefactors pocketed what they collected, mishandled money, or disbursed the goods in a self-serving manner.[11]

Loguen's allies Hutchinson and Wilson were both on the receiving end of such criticism. A letter to the editor in the *Syracuse Journal* in August 1856, for example, questioned the location and cost of Hutchinson's house of refuge, suggesting that he wasted money and that the operation was not run efficiently. Wilson was targeted in editorials in the *Provincial Freeman,* which accused him of using his supply of donated clothing to court Black support among established settlers rather than distributing it to new arrivals most in need, complaining that a large percentage of funds he secured on behalf of the Black church was used for his own living expenses.[12]

Loguen, however, believed that his colleagues acted in good faith and supported their work. Although he sympathized with concerns about the assumptions of Black dependence, he felt that the goods he brought to Canada "helped real suffering." Loguen remembered his own struggles as a refugee in the Canadian town of Hamilton in 1835, and he was gratified, he said, that in the 1850s more support was available to refugees from slavery. But when Loguen reported on the condition of Black Canadian settlers, he had to walk a fine line between impressing on his readers the needs of the community and acknowledging the strides they made in freedom.[13]

With time, Loguen learned that he needed to be careful with his words, for he came into conflict with colleagues more than once over his descriptions of Canadian Black communities. In a letter to his friend in Syracuse J. R. Johnson, he lamented the poverty of the fugitives in the town where he had taken refuge. He said their destitution was beyond description, and he blamed their condition on the "cruel working of slavery." The letter was intended to be private, but Johnson sent it to *Frederick Douglass' Paper,* where it was printed, and Loguen quickly received criticism for his comments. Samuel Ringgold Ward objected to the "deplorable case" Loguen made about Canadian fugitives, saying he had doubts about Loguen's representations of the settlers as "a pack of paupers." Although they arrived destitute, Ward explained that Canadian refugees living in a free nation all had the opportunity to elevate their condition. Realizing how his first report was received, Loguen quickly sent a follow-up letter for publication in *Frederick Douglass' Paper,* acknowledging that many of the fugitives he had met were industrious, happy, and comfortable—"respected *good men* just as any other class of *men.*" Some were temporarily dependent on charity, but he, too, believed in the possibilities of uplift they would achieve from industry, economy, and hospitality.[14]

Loguen believed in self-help, and he emphasized the importance of education, land, and labor as the ultimate vehicles for the elevation of the Black condition. In a letter sent to the *Voice of the*

Fugitive in March 1852, Loguen reported that he was working successfully with the Black settlers of St. Catharines, where he urged the refugees to acquire land and pursue farming as a path to independence. Agrarianism wasn't the only means of mobility, however. In 1854, he noted how many talented mechanics there were among the fugitive settlers in Canada, highlighting that he met one blacksmith who had become quite wealthy. Loguen made clear that he saw the provision of donated goods and supplies to Canadian refugees as a temporary, transitional measure. "I will say," he wrote in his report of 1854 from Canada, "though they may suffer *some* in Canada for the first year, yet their sufferings will not compare *at all* with what they endure for the same time in slavery, and after the first year they will take care of themselves." He remarked on the refugees' accumulation of property and independence. He said that although poverty existed, it was usually due to sickness or misfortune and not caused by bad character, although he qualified this statement by noting that some suffered from "bad economy," which Loguen saw as a legacy of slavery, for fugitives from slavery had never had the opportunity to learn how to handle finances while enslaved. During an extended tour of Black Canadian settlements in 1856, Loguen continued to trumpet the advancements he saw among the settlers. In Chatham, he reported, Black settlers competed with the white population in all fields and their meetings were as orderly and aligned with Christianity as any others. He made special mention of the work of Mary Ann Shadd, editor of the *Provincial Freeman*, who resided in the town and was strongly committed both to emigration and to Black self-help.[15]

To his surprise, Loguen's reporting in 1856 attracted Shadd's ire. In one of his letters to the press, Loguen emphasized that the fugitives from slavery he visited were morally upright and that the Black Canadians he encountered on this trip who were living more dissolute lives were not men who were fleeing slavery but freeborn Black men—criminals who lived in Canadian border towns to escape not slavery but the American justice system. He was frustrated that such men might prejudice Canadians against fugitives from slavery with their behavior, but he expressed gratitude that organizations such as the Canadian Anti-Slavery Society in Toronto were dedicated to the fugitive's cause. Loguen's differentiation between the formerly enslaved and freeborn Black criminals was meant to soften worries among white Canadians about the character of the refugees from slavery who poured across the border, but Shadd took issue with Loguen for applying different standards to the freeborn and the formerly enslaved. She accused him of falling into a proslavery trap with his insinuation "that slavery makes a better man of the colored man, than freedom can possibly do." One group of people should not be shielded at the expense of another class of people: there were good and bad of both sorts. Shadd also took exception to Loguen's praise of the Toronto antislavery society as the prime organ of Black uplift in her home country. She viewed the society as a white-led organization that did not truly understand the needs of the Canadian Black population and whose members considered most Black Canadians "too low in their estimation to approach." She informed Loguen that he was mistaken when he assumed that it provided "*all* the philanthropy" and held "antislavery under their lock and key" in Canada.[16]

Loguen had unknowingly placed himself in the middle of a larger conflict that existed among Black Canadian and American reformers. Shadd's complaints reveal the underlying tensions that existed. Although the two groups both wished to point to the Canadian refugee population as successful examples of Black independence, they approached the issue from different angles, each with their eyes on problems at home. Loguen and many of his

American colleagues were concerned with the acceptance of fugitives they shepherded into Canada, and they concentrated on what the Black settlers' condition there meant for the larger fight against slavery at home. Black activists in Canada, in contrast, focused on nurturing the Black Canadian community, supporting emigration to Canada from the United States, and promoting the acceptance of refugees on an equal footing with the rest of the Canadian population. Loguen once commented on the differences between the antislavery meetings he attended in Canada and those at home: "It is worth going from Syracuse to Canada to attend an anti-slavery meeting of fugitive slaves. . . . They did not meet to instruct the ignorant of the nature of Slavery, but to recount their trials, their hardships, their outrages, their conflicts, and to show the scars the best made upon them" in the United States. Black Canadian leaders wished to highlight that refugees in Canada had opportunities there that they didn't have in the land of their birth.

There was also an element of a turf war between the two groups as they competed for resources. Some American abolitionists discouraged collecting aid in the United States for Canadian refugee relief, arguing that there was more need for support for fugitive aid on the American side of the border. For their part, many Canadian reformers, including Shadd, expressed resentment of American intrusion into Canadian antislavery affairs, believing that it drained resources from their own reform efforts. Shadd, as her comments on Loguen's visit to Canada indicated, was also skeptical of white-dominated organizations such as the Canadian Anti-Slavery Society, which she saw as overly connected to abolitionists abroad and less concerned with the needs of the Canadian Black population at home.[17]

Another issue that faced Loguen as he visited Canada was the question of integration. Some abolitionists, Black and white, supported the establishment of separate Black settlements in Canada where refugees could develop their own institutions and avoid white prejudice, while others felt that this type of separatism only bred further inequality and discrimination. Loguen was in the latter camp. He addressed this topic in several ways during the tour of Black Canadian settlements he made in 1856. After a stop in St. Catharines, Loguen wrote home condemning missionaries for the practice of establishing separate Black schools. "It is plain that some of our Missionaries have done the fugitives great harm, with the best intents, no doubt," he wrote. "They have succumbed to caste, and opened schools separate from the whites." He complained that the teachers in these schools, as a general rule, did not promote equal rights. "I am told," he said, "that where they had no separate school there has been no trouble on this score."[18]

In his next report from this tour, Loguen wrote of his stop at the site of the Wilberforce Settlement, a colony that had been organized for Black Canadian refugees in 1829 with aid from a group of Ohio Quakers. He wrote with some satisfaction that the colony had dissolved, and the Black settlers had integrated among white Canadians in the surrounding area. He saw this as a good thing. "God made the human family a unit," he wrote. He felt that the exclusively Black settlement had been established "by a wrong principle, and they had been scattered among the whites by a right one." This dispersion, he said, benefited both Black and white settlers who could support one another as well as refugees from slavery. Loguen argued that it was time that white men, who owed a great debt to the Black community for past harms, "pay it by giving us our rights and ceasing to burden themselves with futile attempts to enslave us, or cage us in colonies, in this or any other country." Instead, he said, "they must allow us to roam at pleasure in search of happiness among the blessings and privileges which our sweat and blood have earned. It is the only payment we demand."[19]

The debates about emigration, self-help, and separatism that Loguen faced in his work in the Canadian borderlands during the 1850s were not new to the North American Black community, nor were they concerns that ended in Canada. They were issues that had emerged after the free Black communities of the northern states took shape following the emancipations of the postrevolutionary era, and debates surrounding these questions would linger as more Black Americans achieved freedom. The flight of fugitives into Canada in the 1850s, however, provided a flashpoint for these concerns in the decade before the Civil War and foreshadowed questions surrounding how to nurture Black independence and uplift that emerged after emancipation. They were questions Loguen would continue to consider for the remainder of his life.

Loguen was a busy man, and he stayed in constant motion in the decade before the Civil War. Although he maintained an interest in Canadian refugee communities, his central concern was for the elevation of the Black condition within the United States. He believed that it would primarily be through the efforts of free Black community members that equality and upward mobility would be achieved, and the theme of self-help was thus a constant one in his activism as he traveled around New York and the surrounding states.

Loguen's outreach took him away from home for long periods, and his trips were physically arduous. Reports of his lecture circuits show that in addition to traveling by train and by horse and buggy (or sleigh), he often had to walk many miles. Inclement weather made travel harder in the winter months, and his time on the road was filled with unceasing work during all seasons. "I have spoken two or three times every Sunday, and with a few exceptions, every evening throughout the week, for the last three weeks," he wrote to Frederick Douglass from one of his tours, lamenting, as he often did, that there were not more lecturers in the field. Loguen's reception varied in the different communities he visited. Sometimes he was taken in and fed by town residents, but during other visits he was not provided with food or accommodation, and he had to speak several times in one day and then travel to a new location on an empty stomach with no rest.[20]

Loguen also had to negotiate the prejudice of much of the northern white population. In 1850, for example, when Loguen attempted to join the "Sons of Temperance" in Syracuse, he was denied membership on the basis of his skin color. Other expressions of hostility came from those who resented the abolitionists in general. In December 1855, Loguen and Frederick Douglass were prevented from holding a planned meeting when pipes were purposely obstructed and the stoves inside the meeting place were lit, filling the room with smoke before the gathering could take place.[21]

Sometimes northern prejudice could lead to attempts to intimidate. In 1850, while traveling between Herkimer and Jacksonburgh, New York, Loguen was rudely harassed. A group of "rowdies" rode up behind Loguen as he was driving his horse and sleigh, hurling insults. They passed him and then waited "in a narrow place" of the road where they continued to taunt him as he passed, relentlessly repeating the process for about two miles. Loguen felt safe only when the perpetrators turned off the main road.[22]

Although these situations certainly angered Loguen, he was well known for maintaining his wit and poise in the face of hostility. A story told in the Syracuse *Wesleyan* of a confrontation on a train car in Albany provides an illustration of the way he handled himself. As he boarded a full car, Loguen spotted a white man taking up a whole seat, and he asked if the place beside him was taken. The man curtly told him that he was holding it for someone who had stepped away. Loguen said that he would take the seat until the passenger returned, upon which the man informed him, "You will have to give it up pretty quick." Loguen agreed to those terms, but the man bristled as Loguen sat and then became angry when Loguen, whose "dimensions," the *Wesleyan* stated, "are quite expansive," bumped his leg. The man yelled at Loguen for touching him, and Loguen apologized and adjusted his legs to provide more space. As he did so, however, the man demanded that Loguen move aside so that he could switch seats. With what the *Wesleyan* described as "a bland air," Loguen told the man, "I'm afraid if you go away, I shan't know the man whose seat I've got when he comes."[23]

In general, these encounters with hostile white northerners were common enough that Loguen refused to let them get under his skin. Instead, he used them to fuel and further his cause. They served as concrete examples of the need to elevate the condition of his fellow Black community members, fugitive or freeborn, and to counter white assumptions of Black inferiority. In October 1860, Loguen gave a speech that revealed his perspective on northern white prejudice, saying he felt that the problem grew "not so much from any hardness of the heart in the generality of northern Christians." Instead, it grew from their tendency toward "yielding unduly to prejudice, and in listening to those whose interest it was to detract as much as possible from the colored man's claims to their regard and sympathy."[24]

Loguen knew that one avenue to the elevation of the condition of Black Americans was the encouragement of political awareness, and he felt that Black newspapers were an especially important vehicle for this undertaking. He thus served as an agent for a number of them, beginning in 1840 with the *Colored American.* In addition to his role encouraging subscriptions for the paper, he wrote letters for its columns, reporting on the needs of the Black communities he visited. Throughout his career, he took on both tasks with other Black and antislavery publications. During the 1840s, he worked with the *Northern Star and Freeman's Advocate,* an Albany paper "devoted to the cause of temperance, reform, education and equal rights," and, later, the *Impartial Citizen,* a vehicle for the Liberty Party published by Samuel Ringgold Ward. In the 1850s, he served as an agent and correspondent for Henry Bibb's Canadian *Voice of the Fugitive* and *Frederick Douglass' Paper,* based out of Rochester, to which he was a frequent correspondent. His agency expanded beyond newspapers in 1855 when he began promoting the sale of Frederick Douglass's book, *My Bondage and My Freedom.* The *Syracuse Standard* urged readers to "buy a copy from Mr. Loguen," pointing out that "one persecuted fugitive acting as an agent for another one" was fitting. Loguen's work as a newspaper agent continued into the 1860s, when he promoted the *Weekly Anglo-African,* a paper that frequently served as a mouthpiece for the AME Zion Church.[25]

Loguen felt that encouraging the readership of Black newspapers was important, and in addition to promoting the papers on his lecture circuits, he gently cajoled friends and family to keep up-to-date with their subscriptions. One can see his approach in a letter to his sister-in-law, Mary Ann Storum. "You say that you have not seen *Frederick Douglass' Paper* recently," he wrote to her in 1853, informing her that the paper "makes a friendly visit" to his own house every week. "I am afraid, dear Mary, that you do not treat it well. It is a great lover of company. It likes to talk with all about the house; and it will be found to have talked matter enough to interest all." He called on her to promote the paper in her town of Busti. If she could send him fifty new subscribers, he told her, "you will have a grand and glorious party visiting your neighborhood daily."[26]

Loguen's concern about subscriptions grew out of his desire to promote antislavery and Black uplift, but he also worried about keeping those papers afloat, for they came and went quickly due to financial difficulties. Their audience, a relatively small and marginalized population, made it difficult to generate sufficient revenue through subscriptions, and those producing the papers generally had limited capital. Maintaining a newspaper required financial resources for printing equipment and skilled personnel. Loguen, who served on the finance and business committees of numerous organizations and spent much of his time fundraising, was well aware of how hard it was to fund such operations; but he felt that with good management and good marketing the problem could be addressed. Indeed, he could be very critical of those who encountered financial setbacks.

Unfortunately, this attitude damaged one of his close friendships in the Black reform community. Loguen and Samuel Ringgold Ward had worked together and participated in the Jerry Rescue but became embroiled in conflict when Loguen wrote a letter to Henry Bibb in June 1852 describing the difficulties he faced in collecting subscriptions for the *Voice of the Fugitive.* Loguen sent one dollar with the name of one subscriber to Bibb, and he expressed regret for not being able to send more. He attributed his difficulties to the abrupt discontinuation of Ward's *Impartial Citizen.* Loguen had worked with Ward on the paper as an agent, and his wife, Caroline, helped raise funds for it, but the paper had nevertheless failed to stay afloat. Ward declared bankruptcy in 1850, and Loguen claimed that many of the *Impartial Citizen*'s subscribers were never told why they failed to receive the papers for which they had paid in advance. Loguen said that it was "a very hard matter for me that is not an editor to get along with such things" and alleged that Ward, who held this role, could provide a better explanation for the paper's demise than he could.[27]

Loguen's letter was meant to be private, but as often happened, it made its way into the press. Bibb printed it in the columns of the *Voice of the Fugitive,* and on reading it, Ward took exception to the insinuation that he had mismanaged the newspaper. Ward wrote a response for the *Voice of the Fugitive,* claiming that Loguen was well aware of the difficulties that caused the newspaper's failure. Many subscribers were in arrears, and that was why he could not keep it going. He felt the coy way Loguen addressed the issue was disingenuous, and he was angry. Ward thus turned to Loguen's own work, launching accusations that Loguen inappropriately took payments from Black settlers on Gerrit Smith's Adirondack lands, charging them a fee for obtaining deeds for them. On the defensive, Loguen responded to Ward's accusation with indignation, explaining that he never charged settlers for his work in procuring deeds, although he did accept gifts that some offered him in appreciation of his efforts. The accusations caused a lasting rift between the two men that went beyond professional disagreement, for each felt that the other had attacked their character. Loguen was frustrated by the public dispute, telling Bibb, "I think every man will allow that I have enough to do, warring with slavery and slaveholders without stopping often or long with those who misrepresent and traduce me." He had "neither time nor taste for personal altercations especially with those who ought to be united with me in contending against a common enemy."[28]

Loguen indeed remained busy throughout the 1850s. In addition to encouraging free Black northerners to stay informed about issues affecting their community and condition, Loguen focused on spiritual elevation. Despite his decision to step away from official church duties for a time for his Underground Railroad enterprise, Loguen was at heart a minister. Many of his activist speeches and lectures were thus delivered from the pulpit, both when he was employed by AME Zion and while he operated independently as an Underground Railroad agent. For Loguen, moral improvement went hand in hand with the material and intellectual elevation of the Black community. Through the antebellum years, Loguen attended AME Zion conferences and supported the church's uplift efforts. Like Loguen, the church emphasized Black self-help. At a Zion conference in Rochester in 1852, Loguen served on the business committee, which presented to the meeting a resolution pronouncing that "the elevation of the colored people is the work of their own hands." It asserted that the best way to promote such elevation was through "*practical business pursuits*" of every sort. "If these are the means by which white men are elevated," the resolution reasoned, "colored men can also be elevated by the same means, and therefore, should pursue them."[29]

After Loguen's return to the ministry in 1859, he became a leading voice within the church, and Black self-help remained an important part of his agenda. Loguen helped to organize a church literary society, the purpose of which was "to take ignorance by the throat and choke it to death," and he helped to create an essay-writing contest for its members, awarding prizes for the best pieces on various topics. He served on a temperance committee to dissuade church members from using alcohol, which, the church proclaimed, promoted "a sweeping tide of moral death." He also served on an education committee that encouraged a "thoroughly educated and pious ministry."[30]

Loguen also remained involved in the Colored Conventions Movement, addressing the question of Black uplift at its meetings. In 1853, he was excited to attend a national convention at Rochester as a delegate from Syracuse. In a letter to his sister-in-law Mary Ann, Loguen described how he departed from a temperance and antislavery tour in Maine, where he had been for several weeks, traveled some seven hundred miles, and stopped in Syracuse for only a few hours to see Caroline and the children before leaving on the lightning train for Rochester. After visiting with several of his antislavery colleagues in town, he went to the meeting place at Corinthian Hall, and the scene he encountered pleased him, for those assembled "looked like men of war, earnest, and prepared to do their duty." The stated purpose of the three-day convention was to determine the needs of the Black community. They were indeed at war, but they exclaimed, "Our warfare is not one where force can be employed; we battle against false and hurtful customs, and against the great errors of opinion which support such customs."[31]

The delegates organized to confront these errors of opinion, and they did so directly with an address of the Colored National Convention to the People of the United States. "We address you as American citizens asserting their rights on their native soil," they boldly stated. They pledged to "speak, write and publish, organize and combine" for equal treatment. "We are many and strong," they said, and they professed no need "to assume a tone of excessive humility" as they claimed their just rights.[32]

To help coordinate their efforts, they created a National Council of Colored People and instructed delegates to form state councils at home to address various aspects of Black elevation, including the encouragement of landholding and agricultural pursuits, the establishment of manual schools to develop technological expertise, and the promotion of equal social and political relations. One aspect of uplift that was deemed especially important was the education of Black children, not only in the schoolhouse, but also at the "fire side." Encouraging an investment among free Black parents in "culture, training, and the future prospects of the child" would be an answer to many of the problems in the community and would combat "false ideas of natural inferiority, wicked prejudices, foul hatred, and all kindred bars to our progress." The delegates felt that free Black Americans had a duty to improve their position in the United States and, by doing so, change the minds of white Americans about Black inferiority.[33]

Loguen applauded the convention's work, for it aligned closely with his own ideals. "I regard that Convention as an era in the history of the free colored people of this country," he wrote Frederick Douglass. He explained that he did not take a leading role because some of the delegates felt it "unwise" for those without legal freedom to play a "conspicuous" part. Despite this, he said, he felt "as a man among men" at the gathering, and he pledged "to carry into effect, the doings of that Convention" with all his power. In the years following the meeting, even as Loguen continued his work with fugitives, he thus took on an increasingly visible part in the New York Convention Movement.[34]

In January 1854, Loguen chaired the first meeting of the New York State Council of Colored People in Albany and was elected the organization's vice president. At the meeting, delegates pledged to keep up with statistics that would reveal the condition and needs of Black New Yorkers, including total population, the numbers of those who farmed, the level of landownership, and the number of mechanics in the state, as well as the amount of capital invested in the Black community. The council promoted the establishment of an industrial school based on the manual labor principle in the state of New York, which they believed would provide opportunities for greater independence. They furthered the tasks entrusted to the national council, but they also recognized a special concern in New York State—the lack of equal access to the franchise. The efforts of Black agitators and their allies in the 1840s had failed to produce change in New York's constitutional property requirement for Black voters, and their access to the franchise as a community remained limited. The New York Council delegates thus formed a standing committee to petition the state legislature for equal suffrage and to publish material advocating for their voting rights.[35]

Loguen supported these objectives, but he wanted more. Two months before the council meeting, he served as one of the vice presidents of a women's rights convention held in Rochester to advocate "for the removal of the legal disabilities of women." The cause struck a chord with Loguen, who held a broad dedication to justice, equality, and the rights of all individuals as well as great respect for the strong women in his family and community. He therefore opened the state council meeting with a speech advocating for women's rights. His thoughts, however, were "earnestly objected to, as being irrelevant to the business of the council." Others supported Loguen's position, asserting that "human rights were not to be defined by either sex or complexion," but even so, the business of the council remained exclusively dedicated to issues related to the elevation of the race.[36]

In March 1855, Loguen chaired a meeting in Syracuse to form an auxiliary to the New York Council and to make plans to host its next meeting. The state delegates arrived in Syracuse in August, and the issue of suffrage predominated. It was presented in terms of what it could do for Black uplift, for, as Loguen's colleague George Vashon pointed out, the right to vote was "a lever of elevation." Loguen agreed. There were members of the meeting, however, who referenced how many New Yorkers had voted against equal suffrage in 1846, and they felt that putting resources into renewing the agitation for equal access to the vote was a waste of time. After a lengthy debate, the council nevertheless adopted a resolution in favor of petitioning the New York legislature to amend the state constitution to allow for unrestricted suffrage for Black men, and they encouraged Black voters to give their votes only to those who supported such change. Council delegates appointed Loguen, along with its president, William H. Topp, to travel around the state to promote the cause.[37]

The council movement was a grand attempt to coordinate work supporting the goals put forth in colored conventions, but it did not last. In March 1855, an appeal went out to northern Black reformers urging a renewal of the council's work. Acknowledging that they had been stymied in the previous year due to the "commercial gloom" of the period, they hoped for a resurgence of effort. Further council meetings, however, are absent from the antebellum historical record.[38]

The Colored Conventions Movement nevertheless remained strong, and the issues that the state and national councils had considered remained alive within it. In September 1855, there was a Colored Men's State Convention in Troy, New York, at which delegates set out to reorganize their push for access to equal suffrage in the state. Loguen served as one of the convention's vice presidents. The meeting issued resolutions justifying the demand for equal suffrage as consistent with the nation's founding principles and documents, declaring that they regarded the vote "as a grand safeguard against oppression" and asserting the right to exercise the vote as "essential to the respectability and well-being of every citizen." They appointed lecturers to stump throughout the state and lobbyists to attend the state legislative sessions in Albany. Loguen again was appointed as a traveling lecturer, and he was assigned fourteen New York counties as his circuit.

The most profound piece of business at the Troy meeting, however, was the creation of the New York State Suffrage Association to promote the equal right of suffrage for Black New Yorkers. Its president was Frederick Douglass, and Loguen served as one of the organization's vice presidents. The Suffrage Association would last longer than the councils that preceded it, continuing its work throughout the antebellum years. Its members toured New York, promoting the election of antislavery candidates at both the national and state levels and agitating for equal suffrage resolutions in the state legislature. It encouraged the registration of Black voters in New York and published a newspaper, the *Voice of the People*. Its members' efforts to promote constitutional change, however, proved fruitless before the Civil War. The question of suffrage in New York State was again voted on in 1860, and the measure failed in a vote of 345,791 to 197,889. Even so, the Suffrage Association succeeded in providing a Black political voice in areas where it was strong, primarily in upstate New York, and in creating a platform on which later political organization could grow.[39]

As usual, even in the face of failure, Loguen continued to press for change. In a speech at the New England Colored Convention held in Boston a year before the failed vote, he had told the delegates "that there was more necessity for action than for talking. The time for action had come." The failure to achieve suffrage in 1860 emphasized the stakes involved. So, too, did the escalation of sectional politics throughout the 1850s, which reached a climax at the end of the decade. As the sectional crisis loomed, Black debates about uplift and equality in the North increasingly became intertwined with parallel debates in American politics about slavery and the larger place of Black people in the nation. For his part, Loguen looked forward to a great reckoning over these issues, which he hoped ultimately would lead to an elevation of the position of all members of his race.

CHAPTER 8

Reckoning

"THE COLDNESS WITH WHICH the politics and religion of this country turn away from the slave, is sad but irresistible proof that slavery must go down in blood." This prescient last line of Loguen's narrative of enslavement and freedom was published on the cusp of civil war. Throughout the 1850s, as debates raged over the expansion of slavery into the western territories and the property rights of enslavers in free states, tensions grew between proslavery southerners and an increasingly antislavery North. The political crisis that resulted kindled abolitionist debates about how to respond, and front and center were concerns about antislavery political action and violent resistance to slaveholder claims, two issues on which Loguen had strong opinions. Throughout the crisis, he held steadfastly to his belief in the power of political engagement and never wavered in his conviction that forcefully resisting slavery was justifiable. As the decade drew to a close and the next began, the American sectional crisis reached a crescendo with John Brown's raid on Harpers Ferry, Abraham Lincoln's election, the secession of the southern states from the American Union, and finally, the Civil War. Loguen expressed little surprise at the progression of events; in fact, he welcomed them as instruments of divine intervention in the affairs of a sinful nation.[1]

In October 1852, on the one-year anniversary of the rescue of Jerry, Loguen and his fellow Syracuse abolitionists hosted a celebration of the town's act of defiance, setting aside the first of the month as "a Festival Day in the Calendar of Freedom." It became an annual meeting, and each year throughout the rest of the decade, Loguen took time from his travels to be in Syracuse for the occasion. The Jerry Rescue commemorations did more than honor what Loguen and his antislavery associates saw as a sacred event in Syracuse's history; they became a venue for registering continued opposition to the Slave Power's influence in American politics.[2]

The annual Jerry Rescue festivities, like the rescue itself, united supporters of the antislavery movement writ large. At the celebrations, one could find political as well as Garrisonian abolitionists, members of the free Black community as well as white Free Soilers, local Syracuse reformers as well as leading abolitionist lights from other cities, and women as well as men. While the anniversary festivities initially promoted a spirit of unity, celebrants increasingly used the meetings to wrangle with divisive issues that arose within the antislavery movement alongside the escalation of sectional tensions. Rescue attempts of other fugitives and the violent conflict over the status of slavery in federal territories fueled these debates. Over time, the meetings became more conflict-ridden, for some of the participants issued more aggressive calls for violent resistance to the Slave Power as the events of the 1850s tilted more and more toward its interests. Some condemned those who advocated confronting slavery with violence, while others, like Loguen, had come to believe that violent conflict was inevitable.

The celebrants' disagreements were local versions of the larger schism within the abolition movement. On one side were the Garrisonian abolitionists, who endorsed moral suasion, denounced violent resistance, and distanced themselves from the corruption of American politics. On the other side were the pragmatic political abolitionists, who supported political and legal measures against slavery and who increasingly acknowledged the need for defensive violence against slaveholders and their supporters. At the Jerry Rescue celebrations, the conflict between the two manifested as a geographical contest between abolitionists from the Garrisonian bastion of Massachusetts and those from upstate New York, where political abolitionists dominated.

Although Loguen was firmly aligned with his region's political abolitionists, he wished fervently for unity of action among the reformers. In 1854, he wrote a letter to William Lloyd Garrison, praising the sentiments present in his antislavery newspaper, the *Liberator*: "I want you to set me down as a Liberator man. Whether you will call me so or not, I am with you in heart. I may not be in hands and head—for my hands will fight a slaveholder, which I suppose the Liberator or some of its good friends would not do. But I do not say they are doing more good in their way than I am in mine. I am a fugitive slave, and you know that we have strange notions about many things." Garrison responded with gratitude for Loguen's words and said he was not surprised at his rejection of the Garrisonian doctrine of nonresistance while his freedom remained under threat. Still, he wished Loguen could see that "it is solely because of war and violence that slavery exists."[3]

Loguen did not participate in the divisive debates between the Garrisonians and political abolitionists at the Jerry Rescue anniversary meetings. He nevertheless figured into them, for his involvement in the celebrations was considerable—giving speeches, making prayers, arranging the finances, and extending calls for meetings. Even more, Loguen's fugitive status and his tenuous freedom were objects of discussion at the gatherings and had many abolitionists elevating him into a symbol: he was a freedom seeker who had found sanctuary in Syracuse and who was willing to risk his life to defy slave law and protect himself and others.

At the celebration in 1854, Loguen served as vice president of the meeting, and the clash between the Massachusetts and New York antislavery factions was particularly heated, for the meeting took place against the backdrop of the failed rescue of fugitive Anthony Burns from custody in Boston. Burns had been detained by federal authorities in May, and when a crowd attempted to storm the courthouse where he was held, in much the same fashion as the Jerry Rescuers had done in Syracuse, they were met with the force of several thousand federal troops who prevented the action. The failed attempt to liberate Burns proved to be more violent than the successful rescue of Jerry, for one of Burns's guards was fatally wounded.[4]

In addition to the continued enforcement of the Fugitive Slave Law, the sectional conflict over the expansion of slavery in the West cast a shadow over the celebration. In January 1854, Senator Stephen Douglas introduced the Kansas-Nebraska Bill to Congress. The bill proposed that the status of slavery in a territory that was considered free soil under the terms of the Missouri Compromise of 1820 be decided instead by "popular sovereignty." Territorial residents would make the decision. Douglas's measure became law the following May, and northern concern about the influence of the Slave Power over federal policy multiplied as the new approach to the territories shook the nation.[5]

The combined issues of the Burns rescue attempt and the status of slavery in the territories pushed many northerners into expressing more radical views on how to fight the ever-influential Slave Power. For his part, Loguen celebrated the intensification of northern hostility toward the South. He wrote Frederick Douglass to express his delight at the impact of Stephen Douglas's proposal: "Nothing in the world is so good for the slave as this Nebraska bill.

It is such an outrageous assault upon all laws, all compacts, and rights of honor, that a political slaveholder will be no more respected hereafter, than a political Satan. I want the North strongly committed against it; and then pass the bill, and we need not look for the day when Northern freedom will begin to grapple his iron sinews about the enemy, and crush him to death wherever he can find him, be he North or South." Loguen reiterated this perspective after the bill became law in a speech to a Syracuse audience in which he "rejoiced that slavery was beginning to show its true character." He noted that those who understood the evils of slavery "had long known that it respected not the rights of the white man any more than the black man," but most northerners had "been blind" to this fact. He was happy, he said, that "Fugitive Slave Laws and Kansas Nebraska Bills are beginning to open their eyes."[6]

Loguen was quiet at the Jerry Rescue celebration in 1854, but in response to the growing sectional tension, Frederick Douglass and other New York colleagues gave aggressive speeches insisting on the need to oppose the Slave Power. Douglass, now fully aligned with the political abolitionists of New York, locked horns with William Lloyd Garrison over the meaning of the rescue after Douglass gave a speech praising the act of resistance in Syracuse. He passionately advocated for continued defiance of the Fugitive Slave Law, holding up Jerry's broken handcuffs as a symbol. He mocked the idea of moral suasion as ineffectual and proclaimed that the Fugitive Slave Law must be resisted at all costs, "even to the shedding of blood." Garrison, the leading advocate of nonresistance, predictably took exception to Douglass's words, and he criticized the glorification of Syracuse as a sanctuary for fugitives. Syracuse was "still slave-hunting soil," he said, noting that Jerry was not safe in the town but had to be sent to Canada to find true security. In response, Douglass pointed out, "Loguen is still here."[7]

In 1855, Garrison declined an invitation to attend the Jerry

Rescue celebration, saying that the event had turned into a venue to promote the agenda of New York's political abolitionists. He could not countenance their proclivity toward violent resistance. Indeed, the aggressive rhetoric of the festivities escalated as the passage of the Kansas-Nebraska Act led to violence on the ground in Kansas. The announcement for the Jerry Rescue celebration of 1855 called for attendees to come and protest southern dominance over the nation's affairs: "How clearly in the light of the Fugitive Act, the Nebraska Act, and still more astounding the attempt to compel slavery in Kansas, does the Slave Power declare that the only issue it will accept is the legality of slavery anywhere and everywhere." At the meeting, Abraham Pryne, an associate of Frederick Douglass, gave a speech justifying making war against slavery, and Syracuse abolitionist Samuel J. May, who represented the Garrisonian nonresistants, initiated yet another debate on the use of violent means to eradicate slaveholding.[8]

Loguen stayed out of these conflicts between the abolitionist factions at the celebrations, but he accepted his symbolic role as a defiant fugitive. He served as a living example of a man who stood his ground, continued to speak out against slavery, and provided aid to others despite his own vulnerability to reenslavement. As he did so, he sought to keep the meetings focused on altruistic purposes. In 1855, he addressed the gathering, acknowledging that it "is regarded by some as a dangerous step, to celebrate the rescue of a black man," but he saw in the event an opportunity to do something for those still bound to slaveholders. The object of the meeting, he said, was not so much to honor those who rescued Jerry as to do something about those still enslaved. "They are yet clanking in their chains," he said. "Jerry had gone to his long home; but these are yet in bonds."[9]

The sectional division over slavery did not let up. By 1856, the skirmishes between proslavery and antislavery forces over the legality of slavery in Kansas had become a protracted affair known as Bleeding Kansas. In May, violence entered the halls of the US Capitol when South Carolina representative Preston Brooks attacked Senator Charles Sumner with a cane. The beating was a response to Sumner's speech "The Crime Against Kansas," in which he had hurled insults at slaveholders and, specifically, at Senator Andrew Butler, Brooks's cousin. That year the Jerry Rescue Committee, of which Loguen was a member, issued an invitation to the annual October 1 celebration that reflected the fraught nature of sectional discord. It invited "all who will strike for freedom when freedom demands it . . . who will meet force with force to that end, either the enemy be armed with the forms of law, or, as in Kansas, marches without a mask upon our constitutions, laws and liberties." The need to remember the Jerry Rescue was more important than ever, as "the bold blow that rescued Jerry anticipated the impudent aggressions of each year, until freemen have no alternative, but to use the bayonet and other weapons as slavery uses them to kill the enemy or be killed by them."[10]

At the celebration in 1856, Gerrit Smith, who presided over each annual meeting, lamented the discord among the abolitionists who had spoken from the platform in previous years, hoping to "let Garrison and May be as much encouraged as Douglass and Loguen to occupy it." He admitted that he believed that "American Slavery must end in blood," for he had long "despaired of its peaceful termination" and, in the last few years, had "come totally to despair of it." Even so, he wished to clarify that although he expected a violent confrontation over slavery, he never desired it. His preference was to "put away slavery by political action." But the political abolitionists had failed to attract enough support, "and now it is too late to hope for it."[11]

Smith's speech effectively communicated the despair many political abolitionists felt at the progression of abolitionist third-party politics during these years. The titular head of the Liberty Party in New York, Smith had witnessed its rapid decline in the early 1850s. By this point, its influence had been largely confined to upstate New York, for in 1848 most of its membership had left the abolitionist party to join the new Free Soil Party, which focused on attacking the expansion of slavery in the western territories. In doing so, it cast a wider net for supporters than the purely abolitionist Liberty Party. The Liberty Party survived under Smith's leadership, but even many Black voters believed that the Free Soilers offered a more pragmatic option in countering the Slave Power, due to their ability to wield more political might.[12]

Loguen sided with Smith and stayed active in the Liberty Party, which remained dedicated to universal abolition through political means. As the party's numbers dwindled, Smith and Loguen attempted to keep the party alive in New York. In 1853, Loguen presided over a Liberty Party convention in Canastota, and in 1854, he went to a sparsely attended meeting in Syracuse. He did all he could to revive the party, but the numbers continued to shrink as members fled to the flag of Free Soil. One of the reasons Loguen celebrated the discord of the Kansas-Nebraska Act was that he hoped it might spark enough anger to attract northerners to a purer form of antislavery politics. In June 1855, hoping to revive the cause of political abolition, Loguen and his colleagues met in Syracuse to reorganize under a new banner. There, they formed the Radical Abolitionist Party.[13]

Loguen's colleague James McCune Smith, a Black physician and writer with whom he had worked on the National Council of Colored People a few years before, headed up the new party along with Gerrit Smith and Frederick Douglass. Loguen assumed his usual position on the finance committee. The party platform was straightforward; it advocated a constitutional attack on slavery everywhere, in the states as well as the territories. In May 1856, the Radical Abolitionists held a convention in Syracuse, and Loguen served on a committee tasked with nominating candidates for the election of 1856. Gerrit Smith would be the party's presidential candidate.[14]

The Radical Abolitionists hoped to wield political influence by nominating candidates for the upcoming election, but just as the Free Soil Party had done in previous years, a new party based on the same principle of slavery's nonextension eclipsed their efforts. The Republican Party, a coalition of former Free Soilers, antislavery Whigs and Democrats, and frustrated abolitionists, nominated John C. Frémont as its presidential candidate, and even Loguen and Douglass recognized that success for the Republicans would benefit the antislavery cause. Both men retained their affiliation with the Radical Abolitionists, but they also encouraged New Yorkers to vote for the new party's candidates. Loguen, in fact, gave a lecture at a Frémont rally in Syracuse, urging all there to "do something for the Slave; if you can do nothing more, elect Fremont."[15]

Loguen recognized that the Republican Party did not rise to an abolitionist standard. It did not promote universal abolition and had no commitment whatsoever to racial equality. Even so, he hoped for its success because he saw growing support for the party as an expression of rising antislavery sentiment in the North and a blow to the Slave Power. Loguen had taken this pragmatic view of the party from its beginnings. In 1854, as the Republican Party was gaining traction, Loguen wrote to Douglass expressing his satisfaction that many were starting to "flock to the Republican standard." They had begun to recognize that slaveholders would "cheat white men as black ones, if they got a chance." He knew that these voters joined the Republicans to protect their own liberty "whether they care for the black man's rights or not," but he said that although support for free soil was not a pure form of abolitionism, "I am glad to see it. If we cannot bring them up to the true ground of Anti-Slavery gospel, let them come up as far as they will." If the Republicans had electoral success, perhaps it would "strengthen up their back bones a little. So that they will 'come up' nearer the broad, true ground of Radical Abolitionists." Conversely, he believed, "they will backslide, unless the thing works well."[16]

For his part, Smith rejected support for the Republican Party altogether. It was the rise of the party that had produced such despair in his speech at the Jerry Rescue celebration in 1856. The following year, at the rescue anniversary meeting Smith noted that the new party, which claimed to be a "Friend of Freedom," was diluting the effectiveness of political abolitionism by drawing people out of the Radical Abolitionist Party, thus hindering the effort to bring an unconditional end to slavery through political means. Far from being a friend of freedom, Smith said, the Republican Party was "its most deadly enemy." Eventually, his disdain for growing Republican support among those attending the Jerry Rescue celebrations caused Smith to withdraw from them. In 1859, Smith rejected his usual invitation to preside over the annual event, for he felt that the celebration, attended by so many who had migrated to the Republican Party, was now a "grand annual hypocrisy." The rising power of the new party crowded out the possibility of ending slavery peacefully, for it would leave it intact in the southern states and Washington, DC, uphold enslavers' rights to hunt fugitives in the northern states, and allow the interstate slave trade to continue. He pointed out that the rise of the Republicans had not prevented the Slave Power from asserting more dominance over the federal government. A case in point was the

Dred Scott decision of March 6, 1857, which denied the constitutionality of Black citizenship and declared that an enslaver's property rights were protected in the US territories. "Slavery has never strengthened itself so rapidly as during the existence of the new and misnamed Republican Party," he declared. Because American voters abandoned Black men and women, Smith said, there was no longer any alternative but to fight, and he warned, "for insurrections, then, we may look any year, any month, any day."[17]

Six weeks after Smith's prediction, John Brown led his infamous raid on a federal arsenal in Harpers Ferry, Virginia. In mid-October 1859, after years of planning for what he termed "railroad business on a somewhat extended scale," Brown set out with a party of twenty-two armed Black and white men to seize the arsenal with the intention of using its stored weapons and ammunition to foster a slave uprising in the South. Smith was aware of Brown's plans, for he had met with the abolitionist at his Peterboro estate in February 1858, where Brown informed him of his desire to wage a southern campaign of liberation.[18]

Brown had been circulating among the abolitionists in New York for a decade by the time of the raid. He purchased lands from Smith in North Elba in 1849 and settled there among the Black colonists that Smith brought into the surrounding Adirondack lands. In 1855, after the passage of the Kansas-Nebraska Act, he moved with several family members to Lawrence, Kansas, to promote antislavery settlement in the region. While there, he emerged as a central figure in the protracted violence that erupted in the contested territory. Smith was a confidant of Brown and provided funds to support his work throughout the 1850s. Although Smith preferred to combat slavery through political action, by the end of the decade, he had come to think that Brown's more aggressive approach was more effective.[19]

Brown also became close with Loguen, Douglass, and other leading Black abolitionists in the North. He actively sought out these men, for he felt they would be dedicated allies in his effort to bring war against slavery. In 1853, Brown wrote to *Frederick Douglass' Paper* about Loguen. He had read correspondence from the Syracuse abolitionist appearing in the paper that, he said, "has a certain music in it that so fills my ear that I cannot well suppress the pleasure it affords." In the correspondence, Loguen had commented on his arrest for his participation in the Jerry Rescue and his expectation that he would soon be tried in court. Loguen had said he would be glad to stand trial for the action. Brown addressed Loguen's position in his own letter to the paper: "Go then, noble spirit—go to your trial, and to suffering, too (if need be). The blood of martyrs will be the seed of the church. I go for agitating and agitating again in the true Loguen style." Brown also referenced Loguen's statements that death was preferable to slavery. He wrote that he could not "too often repeat" such sentiments. "I have been waiting and watching with longing eyes for many years to see some full sized colored men leaping their full length above the surface of the water," he declared, "and I hope someday to see Loguen and to give him such a shake of the hand as will make his snap."[20]

It is not clear exactly when Loguen first met Brown, but he was certainly aware of Brown's work by June 1855. That month, Brown attended a Radical Abolitionist Party convention in Syracuse. Shortly after Loguen offered a prayer to open the first day's afternoon session, Brown gave a speech appealing for support for his work in Kansas, which "deeply stirred the hearts of the audience." Douglass was present at the same convention, giving a speech in the evening that promoted a constitutional attack on slavery.[21]

Despite earlier brushes with Brown, Douglass would later claim that it was Loguen and his fellow Black colleague Henry Highland

Garnet who first made him aware of Brown's work. He noted that their voices "dropped to a whisper" when they spoke of Brown, making Douglass "very eager to see and know him." By January 1858, Douglass had developed enough of a friendship with Brown that the man came to stay at his home in Rochester for several weeks. While he was there, the two worked on developing a provisional constitution for a biracial republic that would integrate men and women liberated from slavery. That meeting occurred one month before Brown traveled to Peterboro to discuss his plans for a southern invasion with Smith. Following his visit to Peterboro, Brown then departed to see Loguen. There is no record of what the two men discussed when they met, but the previous May, Brown had written to Loguen: "I will just whisper in your private ear that I have no doubt you will soon have a call from God to minister at a different location." He said he trusted that Loguen would obey that call, for his planned community of freedpeople would need "a strong religious influence among the early settlers."[22]

Loguen helped Brown recruit others to his cause. In April 1858, Loguen traveled to Ontario with Brown, and the two men met up with Harriet Tubman at her home in St. Catharines, where they discussed a plan to enlist fugitives from slavery to support Brown's mission. Loguen was rumored to have later traveled throughout Canada with John Brown's son, John Brown Jr., to organize Black men into "Leagues of Liberty" to support the plan. Following this initial organizing, Brown held a convention in the Canadian town of Chatham on May 10 to adopt the provisional constitution on which he had worked with Douglass. Loguen's name was put forth at this meeting as a nominee for president, but it was withdrawn because Loguen was not present and had indicated beforehand that he "would not serve if elected."[23]

Loguen continued to encourage Brown's organizing with his words, although his own efforts to help began to flag. He wrote in

May to congratulate Brown on the convention at Chatham. He also expressed regret that he could not provide him with more recruits. "I have seen our man Gray," he said, "and find it as I feared—that he was not ready yet. I do not think he will go to War soon." He told Brown that others he spoke to "have not the money to get there with, and I have concluded to let them rest for the present." He inquired about Brown's communication with other allies, including Harriet Tubman. "Let me hear from you soon," he concluded. "As I cannot get to Chatham, I should like much to see you and your men before you go to the mountains." Although Loguen would not accompany Brown, he told him, "My wife and all unite in wishing you success in your glorious undertaking."[24]

Loguen was not the only prominent ally who would not be by Brown's side at Harpers Ferry. Frederick Douglass was willing to provide funds but warned Brown that the invasion was risky and a likely death sentence. He would not accompany him south either. For her part, Harriet Tubman agreed to support Brown, but she did not participate in the raid, due to either illness or doubts about his odds of success. In the end, only five Black men accompanied Brown on the raid, with most of the key Black leaders holding back, believing the attack was a suicide mission. They knew Brown lacked the resources and a clear plan to carry the raid off successfully.[25]

Their fears were manifested on October 18, 1859, when Brown and his fellow raiders were defeated by a company of US marines at Harpers Ferry. Ten of the raiders were killed in the skirmish; seven, including Brown, were tried and executed; and five managed to escape. Brown's raid had failed to liberate any of the enslaved, but it had produced martyrs to the antislavery cause.

Loguen's daughter Sarah had vivid memories of the reactions to Brown's actions in Syracuse. She recalled the day in October when the Loguens heard the news of the southern invasion. For "that night, and for a week after," Caroline and her three oldest children "searched for, and burned, every letter, paper and report found in books, book cases, and desk drawers, that had John Brown's name on them." Many of Brown's other acquaintances did the same. Loguen once again took temporary refuge in Canada, expecting that he might be vulnerable to arrest owing to his connection with Brown, as did many of his colleagues. On December 2, the date that John Brown was executed, church bells tolled in Syracuse and black drapes hung on the town's buildings. The flags all stood at half-mast as the city mourned. Caroline and her children attended memorial services for the antislavery martyr, and Sarah "never forgot the pictures she saw of John Brown draped in crepe, nor the tension and fright of the days of searching, and her father's hurried departure."[26]

Loguen gloried in Brown's martyrdom. After Brown's execution, Loguen wrote to Douglass, proclaiming that "the 2d day of December 1859, will hereafter be looked upon as a sacred day to the holy cause of human freedom; made so by the noble sacrifice of John Brown and his brave compeers." Their act signified the willingness of white men to fight for Black freedom. Loguen declared that "the signs of the times are ominous of a glorious future." In typical fashion, he called on the free Black population to take the lead in ushering in that glory. They needed to be "wide awake to the development of God's providence in relation to slavery. They have a very important part to act in the work of emancipation. Let them learn bravely to do and dare for the cause of Freedom by the heroic example of John Brown."[27]

As Loguen hoped and predicted, John Brown's raid further polarized the divided nation, inching the United States closer to a reckoning over slavery. Taking place a little over a year before the presidential election of 1860, the raid intensified the contest's political stakes as many southerners blamed Brown's invasion on the Republican Party and insinuated that its presidential candidate, Abraham Lincoln, supported Brown's desire to promote a slave uprising. Although Lincoln and other Republican leaders officially distanced themselves from Brown's actions, other antislavery northerners portrayed Brown as a hero and a martyr, increasing southern anxieties about northern intentions toward slavery. More and more, southerners argued that should Lincoln win, they would have no future within the American Union.

Loguen continued to support the Radical Abolitionist Party during the campaign for the election of 1860. Again, the party nominated Gerrit Smith for president, but Smith had no chance of success. Antislavery northerners saw Lincoln as their best chance at combating the Slave Power and rallied around the Republican Party. Lincoln, the first presidential candidate to make a pledge to curb the influence of slavery in the United States, was elected its sixteenth president in November 1860. The next month, South Carolina was the first of the southern states to secede from the Union.[28]

Lincoln's election not only widened the breach between the northern and southern states but led to discord in the North between the abolitionists and those who were anxious for the survival of the American Union. This division intensified after South Carolina seceded and Congress sought to prevent the dissolution of the nation through various compromise proposals. Most controversial was a measure put forth by Senator John J. Crittenden of Kentucky that proposed constitutional amendments to reinstate the Missouri Compromise line dividing free and slave territory and guarantee that there would be no future attempt to attack slavery where it existed. The anxieties that grew in the North as its citizens contemplated compromise or disunion eventually led to an eruption in Syracuse.

In January 1861, Samuel J. May hosted an abolition convention in the city at which Susan B. Anthony and Beriah Green were special guests. In reaction to the Republican win at the polls and the discussions in Congress of compromise proposals, their purpose was to reiterate that the nation should brook no compromise with slavery. Loguen did not take an active role in the meeting, but as was true in the Jerry Rescue anniversary meetings, his name was lifted up as a symbol of the city's defiance of slave law. This time, however, it was the antiabolitionist faction in Syracuse who did so.

The abolition meeting was scheduled to begin at 2:00 p.m. on January 30 in Syracuse's Convention Hall. Forty-five minutes before that time, the antiabolitionist faction in town entered the meeting room, filling it to capacity. They began their own meeting, speaking out against "the fact that Syracuse had been trampled upon for years by Abolitionists" and issuing statements promoting compromise with the South for the sake of the Union. As they proceeded with speeches, Samuel J. May, Susan B. Anthony, and several other abolitionists arrived and informed those gathered that the hall had been reserved for their abolition meeting. May then attempted to speak, but protests from the crowd drowned him out. His colleagues had no more success, and when Black members of the community attempted to enter the hall, they were shouted out with racial slurs. The antiabolitionists then proceeded to present their own resolutions denouncing the long-held abolitionist influence in the town and declaring that they supported giving to southerners "all their constitutional rights, both in the States and Territories." They blamed the dissolving Union on abolitionist agitation and took special aim at the "Jerry Rescue traitors, headed by Fred. Douglass, and the depot of the Underground Railroad, marshaled by negro Loguen." They declared that Douglass and Loguen had disgraced the city, their work giving "rise to the bloody raid at Harper's Ferry." Finally, they resolved to commit themselves to the Union and to promote the Crittenden Compromise measures to guarantee its survival.[29]

The abolitionists were effectively driven out of Convention Hall. That evening the antiabolitionists struck again as a mob of around twenty people gathered with a band and marched through the city with effigies of Samuel J. May and Susan B. Anthony and signs that read: "The Jerry Rescue Played Out!" "The Rights of the South Must Be Protected!" "Freedom of Speech, but Not of Treason!" and "Abolitionism No Longer in Syracuse!" They stopped in Hanover Square and made inflammatory speeches while they burned the effigies on a bonfire. The participants in the mob were subsequently arrested. Unionist forces in Syracuse praised their actions while Republicans and abolitionists denounced them.[30]

Driven out of their original meeting, the abolitionists reassembled the next day at a private home where they were able to issue their own resolutions declaring that American slavery was sinful and would "be a perpetual trouble" to Americans as long as it existed. There could be no peace until it was abolished. They insisted that northern citizens were complicit in the sin of slavery as long as it existed and that emancipation therefore should be "the great concern of the American people." Without it, "there can be no union, no peace, no political virtue, no real, lasting prosperity in all these once United States."[31]

Neither the radical abolitionists nor the unionist crowd would get their way following their confrontation. Lincoln and Republican politicians remained committed to limiting the extension of slavery in the territories and so rejected the Crittenden Compromise proposal. Neither would they advocate for federal abolition of slavery in the southern states, which they deemed unconstitutional. In just two months, the nation would be at war.

On April 12, 1861, Confederate forces launched an attack on Fort Sumter, a federal fort in Charleston Harbor, marking the first military action of the Civil War. When the fort fell to the South the following day, Lincoln began preparations to fight for the preservation of the American Union. Immediately following these events, Loguen helmed a meeting of the Black residents of the Eighth Ward of Syracuse, where they pledged their loyalty to the "stars and stripes" until death. Thirty to forty Black men at the meeting organized a company and volunteered their services in support of the war.[32]

At the outset of hostilities, however, Loguen emphasized that he did not share the Republican government's narrow perspective on the war, which framed it solely as a battle to uphold the Union. He firmly believed that the Union could not and should not survive if slavery continued to exist, and he insisted that the war was therefore one to eradicate the evil institution. In May 1861, he gave a speech in Syracuse arguing that the war wasn't about secession or the shots fired at Fort Sumter; it was about slavery, the cause rooted in the colonial settlement of North America and festering in the nation since its beginnings. Although he wished for peace, he was glad for a war on slavery, he told his audience, for it had been a long time coming. "So thoroughly was he a peace man that he would *fight* for peace," for slavery was an inherently violent institution that must cease. Having framed the war in this way, he insisted that Black men should be at the forefront of battle: "I feel it a glorious thing to fight for liberty, and I want my colored brethren to have that privilege. I want them to share in so great a cause." He maintained that his people wished to prove to their fellow Americans that "we are not mean enough to shirk out of responsibility, and see our white brethren's life flowing for our sakes. Rather let us share in the hardships, dangers, and finally the glory of war."[33]

After Sumter, Loguen therefore spent much of his time trying to enlist Black men to fight for the United States. He hosted recruitment meetings in Syracuse and other New York cities and traveled to Canada to raise units among the refugees of St. Catharines and Montreal. Loguen threw himself into recruiting in the months after the war's outbreak, but he paused in his efforts when it became clear that Lincoln had no intention during the first year of war to call Black troops to service.[34]

In September 1861, he wrote to the editor of the *Syracuse Standard* expressing his frustration. He stated that his people were "ready to do their duty, when the government would permit, and we are ready now." The government, however, would not accept them and "seems afraid to touch the cause of the present rebellion," which was "slavery, we all know." Referencing Crispus Attucks's contributions to the American Revolution and the willingness of Black men to fight in the War of 1812, Loguen noted that Black men had fought for liberty in the past, and he found it strange that they were barred from fighting when so much was on the line for the nation in the present. Not only did Black men want to contribute to the war effort alongside white soldiers, but they would also be a superior force in battle because of their investment in emancipation: "One colored regiment of brave men . . . would do the cause of liberty more service than half a dozen regiments that are merely fighting for the Constitution and Union." Slavery must end for the war to have meaning, for the Union with slavery, Loguen said, "is worse to us than nothing."[35]

Beyond his efforts to encourage the participation of Black troops, Loguen spent most of his time during the war years in his ministry, for he had resumed his duties with the AME Zion Church in 1859. As a whole the members of its Genesee Conference, to which Loguen belonged, also expressed a frustration with the limited vision of the Republican Party. In September 1861, the conference met, and Loguen served on its first-ever committee on slavery, helping it to carve out its position statement on the war effort. Because the leaders of the US government refused to attack slavery, the committee pledged that they would "stand still, and see the Lord use up slavery in his own way." In April 1862, Loguen reiterated this position more emphatically in a letter written to the *Weekly Anglo-African*. "The slave must be delivered, come what may to this nation," he said. "It is God's will and it must come." He cared nothing for the American Union, he said, for "souls must live—nations will decay, and be no more." He prayed that God would help "Pharaoh Lincoln" to "take another step, and another, until Liberty is proclaimed for every slave in this land."[36]

In 1863, it appeared that this trust in God's will was well founded. Loguen and other members of the northern Black community rejoiced when Lincoln shifted the war's aims and means with the Emancipation Proclamation, issued on January 1. It would affect only those areas still in rebellion, and thus Loguen remained vulnerable to slavery, for conquered Tennessee was excluded from the proclamation. Nevertheless, the measure transformed the purpose of the war and opened the door for the participation of Black soldiers. After it was made clear that Black men could fight, and fight no less as part of an army of liberation, Loguen resumed his efforts to recruit soldiers. In his pastoral duties, Loguen spent the years of war splitting his time between his Syracuse congregation and a church in Binghamton, New York, and he used his pulpit in both cities to promote enlistments. In Binghamton, a militia unit known as Loguen's Guards was formed, and Frederick Douglass visited Loguen's church in Syracuse several times, recruiting men for the Massachusetts Fifty-Fourth Infantry.[37]

In the aftermath of the Emancipation Proclamation, Black community leaders in New York, including Loguen, expressed delight that the Civil War was no longer just a "fratricidal conflict" but had evolved to become "one of the most justifiable wars that was ever inaugurated." They met at a colored convention on July 16, 1863, to issue a "Manifesto of the Colored Citizens of New York," which expressed their desire to fight in what had become a contest between "civilization and slavery." All hope was now tied to the Union, and the convention therefore tasked "trusty and able men of color to canvas the entire state for recruits" and to encourage Black women "to form themselves into colored soldiers aid societies all over the state." A central committee was appointed to coordinate such efforts, and Loguen served as its vice president.[38]

At the AME Zion Genesee Conference in September 1863 in Binghamton, Loguen headed up an antislavery committee, and he drafted its report on the war, declaring it to be a "holy war" and "a righteous visitation of the provoked wrath" of God on a sinful nation. The report expressed pleasure in the number of their Black brethren who had been set free from slavery as a result of the Emancipation Proclamation and also in the heroic actions of Black troops who were "refuting the charge of those who have said . . . that colored men were unfit to be soldiers or freemen." It praised Republican leaders for "bringing about justice" to their people but gave ultimate credit to God for "bringing them to see the expediency of such an equitable movement." At the next annual Genesee Conference, held in September 1864, another committee on which Loguen served reiterated its support for Republican leaders: "In this struggle between the North and South, the place for every colored man is by the side of the Federal Government."[39]

CHAPTER 9

Reconstruction

EVEN AS LOGUEN and his colleagues celebrated the turn toward emancipation and expressed confidence that God's will would help the United States to triumph in its "holy war" against slavery, they recognized that their work would not be done once freedom came. At the Genesee Conference meeting of the AME Zion Church in 1863, Loguen looked ahead to the need to provide aid for the freedpeople. In the last resolution of the antislavery report that Loguen penned for the conference, he set forth a task for himself and his fellow Zion ministers, calling on them to "hold ourselves in readiness to go to any of the many freed portions of the South at the first call to preach the Gospel to the poor, and to educate our war-freed brethren to respectable citizenship, and a manhood perfect in the beauty of holiness." Loguen believed this to be a precondition of creating a "permanent peace," for the future of the nation rested not only on the eradication of slavery but also on the "complete enfranchisement of the whole slave population." Any other result, he wrote, "will make us a nation of murderers," as they will have allowed "our brothers and sons to perish in vain."[1]

At the time of this declaration, Loguen had already committed himself to freedmen's aid, for just a month after Lincoln delivered his Emancipation Proclamation, he became a member of the Freedmen's Friend Society, an organization presided over by his Brooklyn colleague James Gloucester. Formed on February 4, the Black-led society's purpose was to assist the government in providing education and relief for those who had liberated themselves from slavery. Loguen served as a vice president of the organization along with other leading lights of the abolition movement, including Frederick Douglass and Gerrit Smith. The society faced many challenges when it came together; not the least was the anti-Black violence of the New York Draft Riots that erupted in the city in the summer of 1863. The savagery of the riots physically threatened many members of the organization, and the Brooklyn office in which it met was almost destroyed. By 1864, however, its members were able to proceed with their work.[2]

One of the society's first areas of focus was on education in Norfolk and Portsmouth, Virginia. These cities were among the earliest gathering places for freedpeople during the war, making them strategic locations for its efforts. As the Freedmen's Friend Society became involved in Virginia, it built on the earlier work of the AMA, one of the first and largest of the organizations dedicated to aiding the formerly enslaved. In 1861, the AMA had established Sabbath schools in federally occupied areas of Virginia, and as the number of refugees from slavery grew with the progress of war, other organizations such as the Freedmen's Friend Society became involved. Their work often overlapped and intertwined, and under the oversight of dozens of such organizations, schools and missions were eventually created throughout the South to promote literacy, self-discipline, political awareness, and spiritual growth.[3]

In July 1864, Loguen embarked on a "tour of observation" in Norfolk and Portsmouth to assess the work being done in the freedmen's schools and report on ways to assist them back home.

While in Virginia, he also spoke to several large congregations across different churches. His speeches emphasized the urgent needs of the newly emancipated and the importance of collective action on their behalf. Loguen was impressed with the exertions on behalf of the freedpeople that he witnessed, which he described in the Syracuse *Wesleyan* and the *American Missionary*, both journalistic mouthpieces for the AMA. He was happy to see that children in Norfolk attended "nice schoolhouses" that were "well fitted out with maps and blackboards," and he commented on the discipline of the students, who were drilled "with military precision" by some instructors. He commended the teaching at the Ferry Point Orphanage, noting how well managed the institution was. While there, he christened a six-month-old baby and said he was gratified that the infant and his siblings had found refuge at the institution, where administrators achieved "bloodless, social victories" with their work. After visiting Norfolk, Loguen went to Portsmouth, touring freedmen's colonies in Fortress Monroe and the "finely-conducted schools at Hampton" on the way. Loguen praised the commitment to Black uplift evident in the operations he witnessed.[4]

Despite the valiant efforts of those who aided the freedpeople in Virginia, Loguen nevertheless expressed some misgivings. He was struck by the "sickness and inevitable wretchedness" of many of the "dear souls who have suffered so many years beneath a Southern sun." Although the authorities in Virginia "act well their part," he felt that there was much more to be done and that Black northerners had a special role in effecting change. Commenting on his time in Norfolk, he said that while he was gratified that Black and white teachers toiled together "without distinction of color" to educate the freedpeople, he wished there were more Black teachers among them. He was happy that "white friends" wanted to "remove the blot" of Black dependency in the nation, he said, "but I am convinced that the work is ours. They may be pioneers while we are gathering influence. But we must come forward, make sacrifices, and take our own position for the elevation of our people." He called on northern friends to "direct their charities to these localities and help those who are helping themselves."[5]

Loguen's further contributions to the freedpeople were grounded in his ministry. The AME Zion Church grew quickly after emancipation in 1863 as it sought to bring the newly freed into its orbit. Many of the enslaved had attended the churches of their enslavers and had nominally been associate members of the mainstream white churches in the South. With freedom, the Black congregations in the North—including AME Zion—sent out missionaries and built new churches to provide spiritual guidance to the freedpeople who wished to worship without white oversight. Because of his stature as an antislavery lecturer, Loguen had risen to a prominent position in the church, and in May 1864, he was elected to the office of bishop. Fearing this would mean relocating to the South, however, Loguen turned the position down, for slavery remained legal in Tennessee at that time, leaving him subject to the Logues' claims over him as a slave. For the time being, even as he worked to aid the newly emancipated, he remained himself a fugitive from slavery.[6]

And so Loguen took on a different role within the church. In the fall of 1864, he agreed to serve as the central agent for the Genesee AME Zion Conference Missionary Society. In that position, he maintained Syracuse as his home base. From there, he traveled around upstate New York, enlisting Black missionaries and schoolteachers to work among the southern freedpeople and soliciting funds to support their work. As the leader of the church missionary society, Loguen could further his vision of Black self-help, for it was similarly committed to that object. "This society feels that the colored people of the Free States have not only the right but the imperative duty to share in the labors and honors of this work," read a society statement in 1866. Referencing a letter from agents in the South requesting more Black educators to join them, the statement noted that "both the white and colored citizens of this state are in favor of colored teachers," who were more easily able to connect with the freedpeople and gain their trust.[7]

For his part, Loguen argued that it was God's plan for former fugitives to teach the freedpeople. "Forty thousand were colonized in Canada," he said, as part of a divine plan to provide teachers in the South after emancipation came. These early refugees from slavery would better understand the needs of the newly emancipated than white teachers and missionary agents would. In addition, Loguen pointed out, Black teachers could do good in the South at lower cost than white teachers, for they could eat and sleep among those they ventured to help.[8]

Beyond his trip to Virginia in 1864, Loguen initially eschewed travel in the former slave states, feeling that it was safer to sow seeds of interest in freedmen's aid in New York. In January 1865, however, the Thirteenth Amendment to the Constitution, abolishing slavery in the nation for good, was approved in both houses of Congress and sent out to the states for ratification. The next month, the Tennessee Constitution was amended to recognize the emancipation of all held as slaves within the state. With that development, Loguen shed his status as a "defiant fugitive" from slavery. He was a free man.

Loguen was therefore receptive when he received a letter in March 1865 from fellow AME Zion clergymen in Tennessee, inviting him to visit and confer with them. Noting the nation's new commitment to universal emancipation, they said, "The way is open for you to come to your native state."[9]

Loguen was eager to accept the invitation, but his abolitionist allies were still concerned for his security, for although slavery had been abolished in Tennessee and Union victory seemed imminent, the war had not yet come to an end. On March 31, Loguen's friend Samuel J. May penned a letter to Secretary of War Edwin M. Stanton requesting a letter of endorsement and protection from the government for Loguen's journey. Cosigners with May included prominent AMA representatives Charles Sedgwick, Sherman Canfield, George Whipple, and Lewis Tappan. Shortly after May made this request, on April 9, Robert E. Lee surrendered to Ulysses Grant, signaling the end of war, but a letter of protection was still desired as the nation came to terms with the end of hostilities. On April 14, Abraham Lincoln was assassinated, shattering any notion of peacetime stability, and so Loguen was grateful when he received the government endorsement his friends sought. On April 20, five days after taking office, President Andrew Johnson forwarded a letter to Syracuse recommending Loguen "to the favorable consideration of the Civil and Military authorities of the State of Tennessee whither he goes."[10]

Thrilled at the prospect of universal emancipation that came with the end of the holy war against slavery, Loguen prepared to visit Tennessee that summer. He had several items on his agenda. He went to evaluate the condition of the freedmen and women in the aftermath of war and emancipation, speak to southern audiences on the need for Black empowerment, organize schools and churches on behalf of the AME Zion Church, and—on a more personal level—reunite with the family he had left behind when he had run from his life in slavery on Manasseh and Sarah Logue's Tennessee plantation. He would finally be able to reunite with his mother.

The letter from the president would prove to be helpful. He left Syracuse on June 1 and proceeded to Louisville, Kentucky, where he preached and lectured before taking a train to Nashville.

When he tried to board a car, he was stopped by an officer who demanded to know who his master was. Loguen told him that he was his own master, and the officer tried to deny him entry. After he presented President Johnson's letter, the man backed down. Loguen then proceeded to Nashville, where he "found the slavery atmosphere very different from Kentucky," for it had been under a more sustained attack than in the border state to its north.[11]

Loguen remained in Nashville for five days, preaching on Sunday and visiting schools and freedmen's colonies the rest of the time. From there, he proceeded south to the town of Columbia, where a committee of Black people welcomed him. "They seemed to be very glad to see me," he said, "and the rebels didn't know what to make of it." Loguen had not expected such a reception, and he was touched by their demonstration when he arrived: "The people had not forgotten me in this country, although I had been absent over thirty years. But my escape from the state with 'Old Rock' [the horse he had commandeered from the Logue farm] has never been forgotten by the slaves nor the slaveholders. They all say it was the greatest 'strike' ever made by a slave in this state."[12]

On July 15, Loguen hired a horse and buggy and set out with a companion to visit his "old slave home" and find his mother. When he arrived, he barely recognized the place. Loguen asked after Jane and was told she was in the log cabin behind the house that served as a kitchen.

When he found her, he said, "our meeting can be better imagined than described." She was "quite unwell, all bent up, walking on her cane," and stood among twenty other members of the household, both white and Black. Loguen said they "were looking as if some unexpected person had come; which I suppose was a fact." Jane knew him immediately. Loguen recognized her as well, although he admitted that he "had to look at her some time before I could get her all right." He was joyful at their reunion but also saddened that his brothers and sisters were all gone, "all dead, for all they knew," when he asked where they might be.[13]

A few days after he visited with his mother, Loguen gave a speech in Columbia, around ten miles from the old Logue farm. After he spoke, he looked out into the audience. He saw Jane in the crowd, and she approached him and took him by the hand. Her presence at the lecture was a moving testament to the opportunities that freedom brought. In the past, Loguen had used their story of separation to generate sympathy for the enslaved; now, he used their reunion to speak to the possibilities of freedom. When he returned home, he continued to do so, relaying to audiences the emotional tale of his reunion with his mother in Tennessee.[14]

Loguen also told of his reunion with his former enslaver, Sarah Logue. When he saw her during his visit to the old farm, he noted that she "at first was inclined to exercise a little of her old authority over him." She scolded him for stealing Old Rock when he was a young man and complained that he had "used his old master so shamefully." Still, she invited Loguen to stay and to preach, for she was interested in his story. Loguen declined her request, however, "feeling that the audience that would assemble might not be inclined to listen attentively to his abolition gospel."[15]

In a public letter describing his travels, Loguen told northern audiences of the hostile climate of postwar Tennessee. He said that the defeated Confederates "hate the northern white man because he has succeeded, and hate the black man because he assisted the north," and they "pour out their vials of wrath upon the heads of the freedmen whenever they think themselves beyond the reach of United States soldiers." And it was not just ex-Confederates who posed a threat, for "many of the copperheads from the North, who are in military power, are meaner than the Southerners." Loguen asserted that the safest places for Black people in the South were areas where Black soldiers were stationed: "I never spoke to a more noble set of men in my life than the colored soldiers at Chattanooga." They endured hostility from white troops nearby yet performed their duties "with dignity and manliness." Equal rights and the ballot for Black men were more important than ever, he argued, for only such action would protect Black southerners. Describing their tenuous situation, he predicted that it would be "a dark day for the friends of freedom" if Union troops withdrew from the South before Black people gained full equality with whites. He urged Black men and women at home "who can leave for a time their Northern laboring fields, to go and spend all the time they can in the South." Those who could not travel should also "get acquainted with the freemen," for they had much to teach them about the needs of their race.[16]

Although there was indeed great need among the formerly enslaved, Loguen also noted some of the positive changes that emancipation had wrought in Tennessee. When he visited Columbia, Loguen celebrated the removal of the old whipping post and auction block in the town. He was also happy that the slave pens had "changed their inmates" and been replaced with prisoners, some of whom had been slaveholders. "Their sins have found them out," he said. He preached several times near the old slave pen where, Loguen reported, "colored and white came to hear me," many, he acknowledged, out of curiosity because they knew of his escape from the region. "It is almost impossible for a person to realize the changes brought about by this war without visiting the South," he said. "In the place of slave pens, you will see churches and school rooms filled with happy souls. In the place of auctioneers there are missionaries who preach a full, free Gospel to the eager listening ones." Of the freedpeople, he said, "they are anxious to learn to read and write, and the privilege to do so makes them appear happier than any other people in that part of the country." He thus, again, pressed the need to encourage this status with the provision of schoolteachers and missionaries from the northern states. Hundreds were needed in Tennessee, and the same was true of the other former Confederate states.[17]

All in all, Loguen's trip to Tennessee was successful. One highlight was a Fourth of July speech he gave in Nashville, the only one in the city that summer. Loguen reported that three to four thousand people, mostly Black, attended the speech in which he called for equal rights and the ballot. When he returned home, he followed up his travels with fundraising and calls to action as he spoke and wrote to audiences throughout New York. A year later, Loguen received a letter from Bishop J. J. Clinton of the Tennessee AME Zion Church informing him that the "seed sown" during his first trip to the region had "produced abundant fruit." Enough Zion ministers and churches had appeared in the state to organize a conference, and schools for the freedpeople had been established throughout Tennessee. He requested that Loguen continue his work and emphasized that teachers were still in great demand. Loguen responded to this call for aid and continued his work at home in New York.[18]

His efforts were limited at first, however, for shortly after returning home from Tennessee, Loguen fell ill. It may be that he contracted tuberculosis, the disease that would eventually take his life, during his journey south. A contagious illness that affects the lungs and other organs, tuberculosis was known to many during Loguen's time as "consumption" because it appeared to consume the body over time. It was often deadly in this era before antibiotics. Tuberculosis could be persistent even for those who appeared to recover, for the disease at times became latent, reappearing later in life due to stress or age. Loguen did not feel well when he returned home, but his symptoms disappeared, and he was happy to return to work on behalf of the freedpeople. Shortly after Loguen's recovery, however, his wife, Caroline, became ill, eventually succumbing to tuberculosis on August 17, 1867. Tragically, just as Loguen had been able to reunite with the first important woman in his life, he lost the second—his wife, partner, and soulmate. He continued his work, but his grief was evident to those close to him.[19]

Gregoria Goins's biography of Loguen's daughter Sarah describes the scene following Caroline's death. "Dressed in her best black silk gown and Cashmere shawl," it said, her body lay in repose on a couch in the Loguen home for two days, "black fringe draped in the back parlor, tall lighted tapers in a silver holder at her head and feet." She was placed in her coffin and laid to rest on the third day. Loguen "shut himself in her room and would see no one" in the days after her death, and when he did emerge, he wanted only to be with his children. Goins described the funeral services as "very impressive," for Caroline had done so much for others that "there seemed no end to the expressions of appreciation." She was buried in Syracuse's Oakwood Cemetery. Following Caroline's death, Loguen insisted that there be no mourning attire for friends and family, though he wore a black crepe armband under his coat for the rest of his life. He "never recovered from the shock of his wife's passing," Goins noted. His bearing changed. "He not only stooped," she said, "the spring had gone out of his step."[20]

Loguen, of course, was not the only one with personal struggles in the war's aftermath. In 1866, the town witnessed the return of many who had served in the military, some healthy, but others maimed or traumatized. The Loguen family did what it could to ease their situation. For her part, Sarah visited their homes and played piano for the men who returned from the South. "Strange as it was," her daughter commented, "they wanted to hear war songs." Many also did not return home from battle. During the war, Sarah's older sister Amelia kept up a correspondence with

Lewis Douglass, Frederick Douglass's eldest son, whom she would eventually marry. Lewis served along with his brother in the famed Fifty-Fourth Massachusetts Infantry Regiment, the first official Black unit in the US Army, and he wrote to Amelia about the action he saw in battle and the injuries and losses of men they both knew from the region around Syracuse.[21]

In 1864, Lewis was himself injured with a wound that would leave him unable to have children. He was discharged and went to work in Washington, DC, but in the years before their wedding, he often visited Amelia in Syracuse. Sarah had memories of Lewis, "a tall, very thin youth with prominent eyes," spending time at her home, and she noted that he used to "tease and frighten" her and the younger Loguen siblings. She remembered that her sister, who "affected the wearing of bloomers and a Woman's Rights attitude," was always with Lewis when he was in town and that she wrote letters to Lewis when he was away. Despite their affection for one another, their courtship was an extended one, in part because Amelia was committed to her work as a teacher and reluctant to give it up to become Lewis's wife. Eventually, however, on October 7, 1869, the son of Frederick Douglass and the daughter of Jermain Loguen wed in a "strikingly solemn and beautifully effective" ceremony in front of a large gathering in the Loguen home.[22]

The Reconstruction years were bittersweet for Loguen. Although his children flourished, even in the midst of hardship, and although he witnessed the end of slavery and other changes in the Black condition for which he fought during his life, he and his old antislavery friends were aging. Loguen had also entered a period of loss. In addition to Caroline's passing, several of his close colleagues died in the years after the war. John Thomas, the man who had brought Loguen into the circle of New York's political abolitionists and who had edited his narrative of slavery and freedom, died in April 1866. And in July 1871, his good friend Samuel J. May died. May's obituary noted Loguen's prominence at his funeral, as the "noble looking man of gigantic stature . . . spoke very tenderly of this friend of himself and his people." It was the end of an era.[23]

Throughout these years of loss and change, Loguen never stopped working to elevate the condition of Black Americans. During the early years of Reconstruction, Loguen maintained his busy lecture circuit throughout upstate New York, speaking on the condition of those formerly enslaved in the South, describing the work done among them, and soliciting support for its continuation. Education of the freedpeople was high on Loguen's agenda. In the years following the Civil War, he tapped into his past pursuits in erecting Black schools in New York as he shifted his focus to the needs of the newly emancipated in the South. He put his experience in fundraising, teaching, and school administration to work.

As with his previous Underground Railroad work, his family became involved. Before her death, Caroline and her daughter Amelia had helped to organize the Colored Ladies' Freedmen's Aid Society of Syracuse, which hosted concerts to raise funds for schools. Loguen's son Gerrit served as the music conductor. The ladies of the society also organized fairs and festivals to benefit the freedpeople. They forwarded all funds they raised to Loguen for distribution, and Loguen referred to the ladies of the society as "angels of mercy." Transparency remained important to Loguen. As he had done for his Underground Railroad operations, he issued semiannual reports with the AME Zion missionary society, listing funds received and remitted for the freedmen's benefit.[24]

Loguen's lecture circuit extended his influence beyond Syracuse. Freedmen's aid societies, run primarily by women, were created in other New York towns in the wake of Loguen's visits. Loguen also succeeded in encouraging Black northerners to take an interest in working with the freedpeople in the South. He insisted that fugitives had a special duty to aid those who had been left behind in slavery. It was God's plan for them, for God had allowed them to make their way north to the refuge of free soil not just to elevate their own position but to prepare themselves to help less fortunate members of their race.[25]

In his emphasis on education, Loguen joined other leaders of the northern Black community in the aftermath of emancipation. In 1865, following Lincoln's assassination, Loguen participated in an organization to establish a Colored People's Educational Monument to the Memory of Abraham Lincoln. Loguen became a "life director" of the organization, which was established in Washington, DC, and presided over by Henry Highland Garnet. The group appealed to the public to memorialize Lincoln, but instead of advocating for a traditional structure, its members encouraged the establishment of an institution dedicated to Black education. "Marble may crumble, brass may tarnish, but the light of learning is as enduring as time," they proclaimed. On July 4, 1865, as Loguen gave his Independence Day speech in Nashville, other members of the organization participated in a celebration of Lincoln's memory in Washington. The festivities featured speeches from Black leaders and leading politicians and promoted a biracial vision of the nation's future. Unfortunately, this celebration was the zenith of the organization's work. The grand monument to Black education that its founders envisioned never came to fruition. The exertions of the organization's members, however, demonstrate the centrality of education to the Black community's vision of freedom.[26]

As Loguen participated in these Reconstruction Era efforts to encourage Black education, his views on how it should be carried out had shifted somewhat from his early years. Loguen's first ventures in this arena had been to set up schools under the wing of

Black churches, since so many of his people were excluded from public facilities. In the 1850s, however, access to public schools became less restrictive in many New York communities, and Loguen moved away from building Black schools to encouraging integrated education in the state. Loguen eventually saw success in Syracuse when the doors of its public schools were opened to Black students in 1855. Loguen rejoiced at this development until he realized its limitations for his people. It soon became clear that although these schools would welcome both Black and white students, they would not employ Black teachers. In addition, the problems of racism and discrimination hung over the educational experiences of Black children. In time Loguen, and many other Black reformers who saw schooling not just as an avenue for personal elevation but as a tool for racial justice, became concerned about the lack of Black role models in the schools. Thus, by the time Loguen became involved with Black education among freedpeople in the South, his experiences in New York had convinced him that Black students needed Black teachers and that separate schools were, initially, the better way to foster racial justice. "Colored people with colored people and white people with white people," he wrote about his approach to education for the newly emancipated. "Each party (as society is at present) are better satisfied among their own particular people."[27]

Loguen's work with the missionary society flourished as he concentrated on aid for the education of the freedpeople, and in 1868, Loguen was again elected to the position of bishop in the AME Zion Church. This time, he accepted. His role entailed a continuation of his missionary work, for he was given a two-year charge of leading the Fifth District of Kentucky, Allegheny, and Western Missions. After Loguen became bishop, he was in greater demand on the lecture circuit, and he spent much time traveling and giving sermons at churches in his diocese. He also worked to establish new churches, a job that, again, tapped into his fundraising and management skills.[28]

In addition to his recruiting and fundraising, both before and after he was made bishop Loguen visited the former slave states to organize schools and churches on the ground. In this effort, Loguen joined many of his Black colleagues who "streamed south" following the Civil War to work with the freedpeople. In 1867, Henry Highland Garnet, John Mercer Langston, and Howard Day were among the prominent Black leaders who joined Loguen in this enterprise, each going to different southern states. They all recognized that the task of elevating the condition of free Black men and women could "no longer be called sectional." Now that slavery had ended, it was a national cause. One sympathetic newspaper article reporting on these southern visitors expressed gratitude that "the work of political, moral and social reform at the South will not be left to intriguing politicians" but was also in the hands of these Black reformers. A letter printed in the *Syracuse Journal* made its own assessment: "We are now doing what should have been done long since—nationalizing our agitation." Along with his Black colleagues, Loguen transformed his local efforts on behalf of the African American community in his home state to a national one, aimed at elevating Black people throughout the nation.[29]

Loguen continued to emphasize the need for Black teachers. Because Kentucky and Missouri were within his diocese, Loguen made several trips there following his appointment as bishop. In 1869 and 1870, he traveled through those states, preaching and encouraging the establishment of schools and churches. In his report on one of his visits, Loguen proclaimed that his work had "confirmed me more than ever in the belief that educated colored teachers are better adapted to this work than white." They were less expensive and could "live with the people and become part of the people." Wherever he went, his brethren in Kentucky and Missouri begged for more "colored teachers and preachers from the North" until they could train some of their own.[30]

After two years in the Fifth District, Loguen was moved to the Second District of the AME Zion Church, serving as bishop for the Genesee, Philadelphia, and Baltimore Conferences. Although the new diocese was closer to home, Loguen continued to take an interest in growing the church's presence farther south. In 1871, he went on his most extensive southern tour, traveling for several months as far south as Georgia and Alabama. A letter from Wilmington, North Carolina, to the editor of the *Syracuse Journal* described Loguen's impact as he traveled and spoke through the former Confederate states. The writer noted Loguen had been in the South for a month, and he estimated that up to fifteen hundred people came to hear him speak in his city alone. Loguen "interested the people very much," the letter said. "He is a sight to see with his immense form and head and bushy hair. He preached repeatedly and gave lectures and addresses," telling his story of slavery and freedom. "With his irresistible humor and pathos, his attacks on the vices of his people, with wit and sarcasm and mimicry as well as argument, and his manly advice to them to respect themselves and rely on themselves and educate their children and make attractive and happy homes for them," he said, Loguen's speeches "were a great attraction."[31]

One of the reasons that Loguen spent so much time encouraging education was that he appreciated its importance in promoting economic uplift for individuals in his community. Loguen understood that meeting the freedpeople's immediate needs was not enough; reformers must also help those who were struggling to achieve economic independence. And so, during the Reconstruction Era, Loguen also participated in formal efforts to organize Black workers.

Black labor reformers during the postwar years envisioned a biracial working-class movement, but because they were excluded from mainstream labor unions, they met in their own colored labor conventions. In 1869, Loguen served as a delegate to the National Colored Labor Convention in Washington, DC, a gathering of those "who think that colored men should have the right to work, and should be protected in the same on an equality with white men." On the fourth day of the convention, Loguen opened the meeting with a prayer, and later that evening, he gave a speech. "Leaning upon his gold-headed cane," Loguen, who was introduced as the King of the Underground Railroad, spoke for an hour on his escape from enslavement and his aid to others who struggled not only for freedom but also for economic self-sufficiency. He deemed the work of the labor convention important, for access to skilled labor positions was crucial for financial independence, and as with his other work, Loguen felt that Black leadership and organizing was needed to secure the economic elevation of his people. Members of the convention realized this as well and not only demanded better job opportunities and higher pay for Black laborers but also issued a call "to organize colored labor throughout the land, to effect a union with laborers without regard to color." While the delegates hoped eventually to participate in a biracial working-class movement, their strategy began with the organization of Black workers. This was in many ways similar to the approach Loguen and other Black reformers took with education—Black teachers for Black schools due to the challenging circumstances of Reconstruction, but with hopes for eventual integration on an equal basis. Black solidarity was a necessity to make inroads for a truly equal future with white Americans.[32]

Along with employment with fair wages and equitable working conditions, the convention delegates knew that land ownership was an important element of economic independence. They complained of the lack of attention that the Republican Party gave to the material needs of the freedpeople, especially regarding land. "We should be secured in the soil, which we have enriched with our toil and blood, to which we have a double entitlement," they stated. This issue of Black land ownership was especially important for freedpeople in the Reconstruction Era, emancipated but often with no wealth to speak of, but it wasn't a new concern. Loguen and other New York Black activists had recognized the importance of land to their community decades before the Civil War when they became involved in the land scheme hatched by Gerrit Smith. Again, Loguen's postwar concerns for the nation were a continuation of the local problems he had addressed as a younger man.[33]

In addition to organizing for material well-being, Loguen was happy that the convention also highlighted the importance of education and moral elevation within the Black community. He reported on the convention at a "meeting of the laboring people" at his church in Syracuse a few weeks after the proceedings. His son Gerrit, who became ever more involved in the same causes as his father, served as secretary. Loguen told his audience of the measures passed in Washington and was especially "eloquent while commenting on the resolutions passed by the convention on education and temperance." Loguen also reported his pleasure at the admission of women delegates to the convention. Women labored just as men did and also deserved equal opportunity in the workplace. Loguen took pleasure in telling his audience about the southern delegates to the convention, who said they saw progress among their people wherever they were given opportunities for betterment. "All they want is a fair chance in the race of life," he concluded. Loguen's report ended on a positive note as he informed his audience that a committee had been appointed to visit President Ulysses Grant, who had succeeded Andrew Johnson in 1868, and that Grant "heartily concurred in their action in the interest of the laboring classes of the nation." The Syracuse meeting thus "broke up in joy, looking forward to the good time coming."[34]

Despite the optimism, Black laborers continued to be excluded from skilled professions throughout the northern states, and their pay remained depressed. They continued to agitate for change. In August 1870, Loguen traveled to the resort town of Saratoga Springs, New York, to participate in a state colored labor convention. Education was a central concern at this meeting. Delegates recognized that it was one of the "chief instrumentalities for making remunerative the labor of the working classes." In addition, they advocated the continued expansion of freedmen's savings banks, the establishment of a labor bureau, the formation of Black labor unions, and support for the Republican Party—all items that emphasized Black solidarity and self-help. Following the meeting, the New York Colored Labor Bureau was created to assist skilled Black workers in finding employment. Noting that "many who were masters of various mechanical arts were forced to act as waiters in hotels and restaurants," the bureau would help "do away with this state of things" by providing a registry that would allow it to help match skilled workers with "employment suited to their capacity and requirements."[35]

In January 1871, Loguen served as a senior vice president of the proceedings of the National Colored Labor Convention in Washington, DC. Delegates voted to petition Congress for a commission, made up of leading abolitionists, to assess the material condition of the freedpeople and to "propose a plan of cooperation that will assist freedmen in securing landed property, engaging in manufactures, and securing education."[36]

———

Even as Loguen worked for the education and economic interests of Black Americans during the Reconstruction years, he did not let up on his agitation for Black political equality. The pursuit of equal access to the franchise concerned Loguen his whole career, for he recognized that the vote was necessary to encourage and protect Black interests at both the state and national levels. Loguen's quest for equal access to the vote in New York continued through the Civil War and into the Reconstruction Era, but it broadened from his earlier antebellum efforts in New York as he began to concentrate on a national strategy, agitating for the federal government to ensure equal rights in all states following emancipation.

In October 1864, Loguen had hosted a National Colored Convention meeting at the Wesleyan Methodist church in Syracuse dedicated to the issue of Black civil rights. His friend Frederick Douglass presided, and southern as well as northern states sent delegates, making it a truly national affair. At it, attendees from eighteen states produced a "Declaration of Wrongs and Rights" that comprehensively described the inequities the American Black population had endured throughout the nation's history. The declaration demanded not only guarantees of freedom, as the federal government considered proposals for the Thirteenth Amendment ending slavery, but also the means to elevate Black people and encourage full political equality. The declaration pointed out that Black Americans had proved worthy of these rights through their dedication to the nation from the days of the American Revolution through the Civil War, where they did their part to save the Union. They were loyal citizens and deserved to be treated as such.[37]

The meeting was a milestone in the Colored Conventions Movement, notable for both the breadth of its attendance and its creation of the National Equal Rights League, which began coordinating efforts to promote equal rights on a national scale. Loguen served on its executive bureau, working alongside men like Frederick Douglass, John Mercer Langston, and Henry Highland Garnet to agitate for social justice. The new organization served as an umbrella for state equal rights leagues that quickly spread throughout the United States during the years following the Civil War. Active branches were created in northern as well as southern states, and they became important vehicles for Black support for the Republican Party, which had earned member loyalty through its emancipatory efforts. Black men wanted more than freedom, however, and they pushed the party to guarantee their rights to citizenship and all its privileges.[38]

The National Equal Rights League also took on issues such as segregation in public transportation, which had become increasingly common. Just a month before the convention, for example, Loguen and two fellow Black ministers had been denied seats on streetcars during a visit to Philadelphia. Delegates also argued for eliminating obstacles for Black teachers to participate in public education and debated the question of women's suffrage. On the latter issue, some feared that focusing on women's rights would damage the chances of achieving protections for universal Black male suffrage, while others insisted that a truly egalitarian nation would not circumscribe the vote based on sex. Loguen remained in the camp that advocated for women's rights. In the end, the convention made no explicit statement regarding votes for women, but it implicitly supported the idea that all disenfranchised groups should have a political voice.[39]

Loguen remained outspoken about the need for equal access to suffrage for Black Americans in part because he recognized the power of a united Black vote to enact change. He thus pushed for Black voters to support the Republican Party. Through Black solidarity, it could become a vehicle for their interests. Encouraging unity of action, he gave speeches emphasizing the "duties of colored people in working out their political salvation." In 1866, he offered a prayer and an address at the New York Colored Men's State Convention in which he reminded those attending that the state's propertied Black men had "something more than words to offer for the cause—they have votes." He expressed the hope that they would use those votes to "aid in completely burying the Copperheads in the ensuing election." He chaired another convention in Utica in 1868 and spoke on the need to pursue "impartial suffrage in the Empire State" and agitate for Republican candidates, encouraging "the bringing out of every colored voter for Grant and Colfax (for the presidency and vice-presidency), Griswold (for governor of New York) and Freedom." The convention responded by creating a permanent committee that would "appoint canvasses for different sections of the state and urge adoption of a constitutional provision prohibiting political disabilities on account of race or color." Loguen was made the committee president.[40]

The convention delegates also encouraged connections with Black groups elsewhere in the nation. At the Utica meeting, Loguen presented a letter from a sister colored convention that had been held in Macon, Georgia. "We have dedicated ourselves to the success of the issues at stake, and the Empire State of the South joins hands with the Empire State of the North in battling for universal rights," wrote the southerners. The final act of the Utica convention was a call for Black voters throughout the nation to support the Republican Party "with which we shall ally ourselves so long as it continues to battle for righteousness and justice."[41]

The Republican Party could gather strength from Black voters, but first, racial restrictions on the franchise had to be removed. After the ratification of the Thirteenth Amendment in December 1865, members of the National Equal Rights League and participants in the Colored Conventions Movement worked closely with white abolitionists and sympathetic politicians to push for additional amendments to remove such restrictions and protect their rights as citizens. They organized rallies, meetings, and petitions to urge Congress to legislate on their behalf, and they lobbied state legislatures to ratify the Fourteenth and Fifteenth Amendments after Congress responded to their demands. Finally, after much struggle, the vagaries of Reconstruction Era politics solidified into tangible change. In 1868, the Fourteenth Amendment was adopted, guaranteeing Black citizenship rights and equal protection under the law. In 1870, the Fifteenth Amendment prohibited racial discrimination in accessing the vote.

These amendments proved important not just for those formerly enslaved in the South but for the Black population in Loguen's home of New York. In 1869, state voters had been presented with yet another proposal to eliminate the property restrictions placed on Black suffrage, and again, a majority of New York voters rejected it at the polls. Only with the ratification of the Fifteenth Amendment in 1870 did equal suffrage come to the state.

It came to other states as well. In 1870, Loguen presided over the Kentucky Conference proceedings of the AME Zion Church, remarking on "the changed condition of the colored race." His words at the conference reflected his mission for the next few years, for he believed the elevation of the condition of his people hinged on their new legal status as citizens with equal rights, including the right to suffrage. He urged all his brethren to work together and "maintain friendly relations and kindly feelings one to another" so that they could unite on behalf of their interests. In characteristic style, he ended his speech with a quip: reflecting on the ill treatment he had once received in Indianapolis, "he hoped that now the colored man was a citizen, that he would at least be able to get his dinner in that town."[42]

Loguen went from exclusion from restaurants to meeting with major government officials within the year. In July 1871, in his capacity as bishop, he attended a meeting of the Philadelphia Conference of the AME Zion Church. Professor Howard Day was a guest speaker, and during the meeting, Day led the attendees to the state governor's office to pay their respects. When they arrived, Day told Republican governor John W. Geary that they had come to thank Geary, who had supported free state settlers as the third territorial governor in Kansas between 1856 and 1857 and had also served as a Union general during the Civil War. Day introduced Bishop Loguen and the other members of the conference to the governor, who shook hands with each of them. Geary praised them all for their work "to elevate and educate those who have so long been deprived of their right liberty," and Loguen thanked him on behalf of the conference. As the entourage took leave of the governor and walked through the capitol back to their church, they ran into a well-known Democratic congressman in the lobby. Day introduced him to Loguen, and the two men held a lengthy conversation about churches until Loguen was called away. A newspaper report, entitled "Our National Progress," made much of the exchange, expressing gratification that the representative "did not seem to be any more afraid of a colored man, nay, of twenty of them—than the twenty were of him." It concluded that "the Democratic abuse of colored men had been one of the inexplicable farces which that Party, for effect, enacts over and over again."[43]

For his own part, Loguen was determined to counter such farces. During an extended tour of the southern states in late 1871, Loguen emphasized the need for the freedpeople to remain politically informed. Once again, he connected his work in the South to an issue he had dwelt on in the long struggle for justice at home. As he traveled, he promoted the circulation of the *New National Era*, a newspaper that Frederick Douglass edited in Washington, DC, beginning in 1870, with the assistance of his son—and Loguen's son-in-law—Lewis Douglass. Loguen felt that the *New National Era* was essential reading for all Black voters. "Published at the centre of political influence, enjoying the confidence of Republican leaders, it cannot fail to be a useful and desirable medium through which to reach that element in the south upon which depends the safety and strength of the Republican party in that section."[44]

Loguen was optimistic about racial progress after the passage of the Reconstruction Amendments, but even as he saw change happening around him, Loguen was aware of widespread violence in the South as many white southerners resisted the transformations of Reconstruction. After the ratification of the Fifteenth Amendment, southern resistance was particularly strong, and in 1871, President Grant signed the Ku Klux Klan Act, which empowered the federal government to counter white terrorism and protect Black civil rights with force. During Loguen's trip south, the region nevertheless remained in disarray, and as he traveled through North Carolina, South Carolina, Georgia, and Alabama, Loguen felt "on strange ground." Even so, he strove to maintain an optimistic outlook. Citing the arrest of members of white racial terrorists in the Ku Klux Klan, he noted a "feeling of confidence and joy among the colored people." He hoped their "rapid progress in intelligence and industry" would be unimpeded.[45]

Back home in New York a few months later, Loguen spoke for nearly an hour at a meeting in Jamestown, reporting to his audience on his recent trip through the Deep South. He described the violence perpetrated by the Ku Klux Klan in the region, noting that three southern clergymen in his denomination had been murdered in the past year and that "many Republicans white and black" had been "horribly mutilated and scourged." Ex-Confederates would vote for Greeley, he said; thus, "the blacks will all go for Grant," for "they have learned by instinct to love what their old masters hate, and hate what their old masters love." He urged his audience to do the same. A presidential election was on the horizon, and Loguen vigorously campaigned for a Republican win, encouraging his fellow Black voters to "stand united for Grant and Wilson." On November 5, 1872, the two Republicans were easily reelected, carrying thirty-one of the thirty-seven states.[46]

Loguen's approach to party politics was aligned with his philosophy on education and economic uplift. In all of these areas, he emphasized the duties of Black reformers to take responsibility for the Black community's welfare and to cultivate Black solidarity in their demands for racial justice. These duties drove his own life's work—first at the local level in New York and then more broadly in the nation. Loguen did not, however, eschew cooperation with white reformers. He worked with white abolitionists in New York to raise money for schools and provide aid to freedom seekers; he sought jobs for young Black New Yorkers with white employers; he joined with white reformers such as Gerrit Smith in his land scheme and in the political antislavery parties that emerged throughout the North; and he participated in a movement to encourage white and Black laborers to unite to further working-class interests. Loguen's ultimate goal was a society where all Americans were fully equal and the distinctions of race, class, or sex did not affect one's position. Because of the realities of nineteenth-century American racism, however, Loguen realized that Black Americans had to take charge of their own education, economic efforts, and political organization to truly meet the needs of the Black community. Loguen's experiences as both a fugitive from slavery and someone who had dedicated his life to aiding other members of his race in freedom had taught him these lessons. Although white philanthropists had contributed to his varied efforts, members of the northern Black community had taken the lead in the work to promote legal and political racial equality in the North. He had experienced the power of this Black network in antebellum New York as he worked with colleagues in the AME Zion Church, the colored conventions, antislavery political parties, missionary societies, and the Underground Railroad. Loguen's core belief after the Civil War was that Black people should continue to direct the exertions for uplift and equality across the nation, for their education and experience had prepared them for the task of nurturing Black community institutions and political solidarity. Loguen's ultimate goal, however, was not the creation of Black institutions. It was for Black Americans to rouse their community to action to promote their integration into the larger polity, economy, and intellectual landscape of the United States on an equal basis.

EPILOGUE

WITH THE PASSAGE of the Reconstruction Amendments, Black reformers were optimistic about the future. Slavery was abolished, and the US Constitution guaranteed equal rights and suffrage. Loguen and others realized that much work remained as violent reactions to change spread through the South; even so, in the summer of 1872, the nation seemed to be entering a new chapter. For Loguen, this was especially true. One of the era's developments was a surge of interest in emigration westward following the completion of the transcontinental railroad in 1869, and the AME Zion Church was no exception. Even as the church worked to expand its network into the South, its leaders sought to nurture a stronger presence in the Far West as the population of the region multiplied. In July 1872, Zion leadership appointed Loguen as bishop to a new Sixth District for California and the Pacific Coast. His experience made him the ideal candidate for growing the church in the West.[1]

Loguen accepted his new assignment, but he never made the journey west. Following his southern tour of 1871, Loguen had again fallen ill with tuberculosis. Once more, Loguen recovered from his ailment, and he resumed his work at home. Soon after his appointment to the Pacific Coast, however, his symptoms reappeared. Loguen died of tuberculosis on September 30, 1872, in Saratoga Springs, New York, where he had gone to seek rehabilitation in one of its healing spas before departing for California. He was sixty-three years old. After his death, his body was transported back to Syracuse and buried alongside his wife, Caroline, at Oakwood Cemetery.[2]

An obituary notice rarely does justice to the accomplishments of a lifetime, but the *Syracuse Journal*'s announcement of Loguen's passing tried. It paid tribute to his work in the AME Zion Church, his participation in the Jerry Rescue, his Underground Railroad operation, and his exertions on behalf of the freedmen following the war. It noted his prediction that slavery "must go down in blood," his commitment to a war of emancipation, and his encouragement of education among Black Americans. The obituary said of Loguen that he had "a commanding influence among his people" as "his somewhat rough but sympathetic eloquence always told upon his audience." And it noted how important the larger network of community support had been to him: "Affable and courteous in manner, he really formed acquaintances, and his devotion to his work gained him many warm personal friends, not only at home but throughout the whole country." Among the "most ardent" were those who worked with him to end the injustices of slavery. "His strong resolution was key to his success, for when once engaged he knew no such word as fail. Indomitable perseverance was a leading trait of his character."[3]

Loguen's funeral was held at the First Methodist Episcopal Church in Syracuse. "And so closed the mission of this great man who rose from a poor slave to the highest rank of the church," one report on the occasion proclaimed. The funeral was crowded with friends, family, and colleagues—Black and white—who mourned their loss and testified to Loguen's influence. One member of the large body of Zion clergy present at the funeral summed up the general sentiments of the occasion: "A man had fallen who had not only done much for his race, but for humanity at large."[4]

Loguen departed life at the apex of hope and optimism concerning the future of Black rights during the postbellum era—during what W. E. B. Du Bois called "the brief moment in the sun" that came before Black Americans "moved back again toward slavery." He never had to witness the devolution of the Black condition that came when the violent reaction to Reconstruction led to a return of white supremacist governments in the southern states, a process that began in earnest in 1873. Neither did he have to witness the turning away from the needs of Black Americans in the nation at large, as its leaders privileged sectional reconciliation over racial justice. His children would, however.[5]

Loguen's work was cut short, but he left behind a legacy in his offspring, who were raised in households that emphasized education, self-help, and a commitment to the needs of their larger community. They became educators, artists, musicians, politicians, healers, and reformers.

Loguen's eldest, Helen Amelia, was a dedicated teacher who married into the nation's most prominent Black activist family. She settled in Washington, DC, with her husband, Lewis Douglass, who worked in a government printing office and edited the *New National Era*.[6]

Loguen's daughter Sarah Marinda acquired her medical degree from Syracuse University Medical School in 1876 and became one of the first Black women physicians in the nation. She practiced pediatrics and obstetrics in women's hospitals in Philadelphia and New England before marrying Charles Fraser, a pharmacist from Puerto Plata, San Domingo, the present-day Dominican Republic. Frederick Douglass, whose youngest son served in the San Domingo consulate during the 1870s, facilitated Sarah's introduction to her husband-to-be. Sarah continued her practice in Puerto Plata until Fraser's death, after which she moved with her only child, daughter Gregoria, to Washington, DC. After her return to the United States in the 1890s, Sarah found that the racial environment of the nation had changed. Segregation had become rampant, and it was difficult to purchase an adequate medical office to reestablish her practice. Sarah also could not find what she deemed to be a suitable school for her daughter; the best ones were designated as "whites only." She therefore sent Gregoria to a boarding school in Paris. When Gregoria returned to the United States, she studied at Howard University and later became the first Black person to study at the Music Conservatory at Syracuse University. She became a well-known concert pianist and music teacher and, happily, left a record of the Loguen family's past in her unpublished biography of her mother, which is currently housed at Howard University.[7]

Loguen's third daughter, Mary Catherine, married a barber, Theodore Cromwell, in 1877, and the couple had three children, including a son, Jermain, who was an artist and prize fighter, and a daughter, Amelia, who became a teacher at the Tuskegee Institute. Loguen's youngest, Cora Juliette, also married a barber, Eugene Foster, and had one child, Leon, who was a photographer, first for a newspaper in Chicago and later in his own studio. Less is known about Loguen's son Jermain William, who died at the relatively young age of thirty-three.[8]

The child who most closely followed Loguen's footsteps was his eldest son, Gerrit Smith Loguen. Gerrit held leadership positions in the Colored Conventions Movement and participated in party politics. He was the first Black elections inspector in New York State and also served for a time as the recorder of deeds in Washington, DC. He was a talented vocalist but was best known as a crayon artist who created portraits of prominent members of the antislavery movement, opening galleries in both Syracuse and New York City. Gerrit married a schoolteacher, Louise Matthews, who eventually became the first woman embalmer in the city of Syracuse. Together they had four children, one of whom was William James, a talented tenor and crayon artist like his father.[9]

Like his own father, Gerrit did not shy away from protesting injustice, and like his father, he often ran up against white racism as he did so. A few years after the war, he was denied admission to a Syracuse ice rink. Gerrit complained to the directors of the rink about the violation of his civil rights. This led to a change in policy, but it wasn't exactly a victory. The rink opened admission to Black patrons, but only between the hours of four and six in the morning. Later, Gerrit's son James would encounter similar difficulties. In 1901, James was denied entrance to the plunge pool at the Le Moyne Bath House in Syracuse. Still a minor at the time, James filed a complaint, and his father, as his guardian, sued the Onondaga Lake Improvement Company, which ran the bathhouse. Nothing seems to have come of the suit; the company refuted the charge of discrimination, asserting that admission was denied due to overcrowding rather than the boy's race. Gerrit thus met with little success in these battles. Still, his father would have been proud.[10]

In October 1884, Frederick Douglass, who outlived many of his former antislavery colleagues, gave a speech at a celebration of the thirty-third anniversary of the Jerry Rescue. He outlined the disappointments of the nation's Black citizens in the aftermath of Reconstruction. They suffered from racial hatred, inequalities in their treatment by the American justice system, efforts to bar them from political expression, and violent attacks based on false charges of rape and other crimes. The purpose of his address, however, was to celebrate the anniversary of the Jerry Rescue, which he characterized as his generation's Boston Tea Party. Despite present-day difficulties, Douglass acknowledged the progress that had been made since the "dark and troubled" days when slavery corrupted the nation and he and his colleagues protested the hunting of fugitives. The work of Loguen and all the other men who participated in the Jerry Rescue had been important to the larger work for Black rights. Douglass said he considered his alliance with such men "with expressible satisfaction," for, he said, "it is something to have lived in the same world with them, and to have been deemed worthy to be a coworker with them; to have seen their noble faces; and to have felt the manly grip of their honest hands." Their work should not be forgotten. While the Black man considered his future, Douglass asserted, he must also keep his eye on the past, for "memory was given to man for some wise purpose."[11]

Douglass spent the last years of his life raging against the nation's abandonment of racial justice and the editing of slavery out of the nation's history in the rush to sectional reunion. Black men and women were sacrificed at the altar of reconciliation, and the promise of the Reconstruction Amendments faded as they went unenforced. It would not be until the later part of the twentieth century, after the Civil Rights Movement, that mainstream histories would begin to acknowledge the role that the inequities of slavery played in shaping our nation or the importance of Black men and women as leaders in the fight for racial justice. And it would not be until the twenty-first century that historians would begin to understand the richness of that fight.[12]

Thankfully, most Americans now see Frederick Douglass as one of the important figures of the American past. Still, however, most are unaware of men such as Jermain Wesley Loguen who worked alongside him. The general public has been immersed in a sort of "Great Man" version of Black history from which we need to break free. Understanding the lives of men like Loguen, who did not rise to Douglass's iconic status but who nevertheless worked as energetically—in Loguen's case, by focusing largely on a grass-roots form of activism—is an important first step in doing so.

Loguen has garnered more attention in recent years than in the decades after his death, especially in his adopted town of Syracuse, where interest in the Underground Railroad has encouraged public historians to highlight his significance in the town's history. Although his provision of material aid for fugitives and his collaboration with others who worked on their behalf in upstate New York—including those more famous than himself such as Douglass, Gerrit Smith, Samuel J. May, Harriet Tubman, and John Brown—are central to his story, Loguen's activism was more expansive than his involvement with the Underground Railroad, for he was not only interested in aiding freedom seekers in their flight but dedicated to attacking the oppression from which fugitives fled and to creating a society that provided opportunity and equality into which they could settle. In doing this work, Loguen focused on local communities throughout upstate New York and Canada before the Civil War, and after emancipation he expanded his endeavors to aid freedpeople in the South and promote equal rights on a national scale. His story counters the traditional history of the struggle for Black rights that silos off an antebellum effort focused on abolition from the postemancipation movement for Black uplift and equality. Loguen's life contributes, as many biographies of Black reformers do, to the historian's effort to emphasize the broad and enduring nature of our nation's Black freedom struggle. Further, Loguen's story also shows how his status as a "defiant fugitive" from slavery was central to his work throughout his life, leading him to consistently emphasize the special duty of Black Americans who had secured freedom in the free North to join the struggle.

Because the multidimensional nature of Loguen's activism has largely been overlooked, his full significance to the national battle for Black equality has not duly been recognized. His story illuminates the important networks of reform that existed among free Black communities in the North during the nineteenth century and the centrality of this northern grassroots activism in the movement for racial justice in the United States. It clarifies the alliances Black activists made with white reformers and the tensions and accomplishments that grew out of these relationships. In addition, it reveals the way that those who worked with fugitives led lives that politicized private spaces, for as they invited freedom seekers into their homes and went out into communities of freedpeople, they defied unjust American laws and challenged existing hierarchies.

Loguen, as a defiant fugitive, led an inherently political life. As we continue to come to terms with the injustices of the nation's past, we need his example to see how political our own lives are—and to have a model for defiance in our own time.

A NOTE ON SOURCES

In presenting my narrative, I owe a great debt to those who laid the groundwork for telling Loguen's story before me. This is especially true of Carol Hunter, who wrote the only full-length biographical study of Loguen before this one, her published dissertation, *To Set the Captives Free: Reverend Jermain Wesley Loguen and the Struggle for Freedom in Central New York* (Garland, 1993). After that volume went out of print, Hunter self-published the unrevised work in 2013 (Hyrax). Hunter's lucid and well-researched book is a useful starting place for an understanding of Loguen and his life, but it is organized thematically, is aimed at a scholarly audience, and has had limited reach. It leaves gaps, many of which I have been able to fill due to the wider accessibility of source material through electronic resources as well as the ability to look at Loguen's life within the context of more recent works on the African American experience. More targeted published works on Loguen have included Milton C. Sernett's article "'A Citizen of No Mean City': Jermain W. Loguen and the Antislavery Reputation of Syracuse" (1987), which emphasizes his role within the Syracuse abolitionist network, and several articles by Paul Minifee on Loguen's rhetoric. The story of Loguen's defiance of the Fugitive Slave Law shines through in my own book, *The Jerry Rescue* (Oxford University Press, 2014), and his escape from slavery and Underground Railroad work is highlighted in Fergus Bordowich's book, *Bound for Canaan: The Epic Story of the Underground Railroad* (Amistad, 2005).[1]

Loguen left no cache of papers behind, but one can find his letters and speeches, reports of his actions, and information on the many causes in which he participated printed in various nineteenth-century newspapers. Much of my research, therefore, consisted of studying a wide array of these papers for mentions of Loguen and the movements with which he involved himself. Thanks to the many digital databases now available, newspapers can now be easily accessed and searched. The letters, meeting reports, and editorials found in them provide an archive unto themselves, since Americans of the period used newspapers as vehicles to present a variety of types of documents to the public. Searching through them for evidence of Loguen enabled me to effectively flesh out the contours of his story after his escape from enslavement. I relied on a number of databases in accessing this material, including newspapers.com, fultonhistory.com, Accessible Archives, Black Abolitionist Papers, Gale Primary Sources, and Proquest Historical Newspapers, among others. Future researchers will also benefit from an edited collection of news articles on Loguen, published in 2021 by Robert Djed Snead.[2]

Other types of archival material on Loguen can be found at the Onondaga Historical Association, the Arents Library at Syracuse University, the Antislavery Collection at the Boston Public Library, the Moorland-Spingarn Research Center at Howard University, the Tennessee Historical Society and Archives, and in the records of AME Zion Church and the American Missionary Association. The collected digital materials on nineteenth-century Black organizing gathered by the Colored Conventions Project at coloredconventions.org were useful in shedding light on Loguen's role in northern Black politics, as were items included in the Black Abolitionist Papers Database. Aspects of Loguen's story also appear in published and unpublished sources that focus on the activities of his many colleagues.

In telling Loguen's story—especially that of his early years in slavery, his escape, and his participation in the Jerry Rescue—I have relied heavily on Loguen's recollections as presented in his narrative, *The Rev. J. W. Loguen, as a Slave and as a Freeman.* Over the years, there has been scholarly controversy over the book's authorship. Some early historians characterized the work as a biography rather than one written by Loguen himself. Supporting this belief was the creative choice to write the narrative in the third person rather than the more traditional choice of first person. For some, doubts about authorship led to doubts about authenticity. The first chapter of Carol Hunter's biography of Loguen, however, asserts the veracity of the narrative, pointing out—correctly—that details included in the work are consistent with those in other sources in Tennessee and New York archives. Hunter argues that Loguen's colleague John Thomas was likely the author of the narrative, basing the work on interviews with Loguen. More recently, however, the editor of the critical edition of Loguen's narrative, Jennifer A. Williamson, contends that the book was written by Loguen himself, with John Thomas playing an editorial role. Pointing out Loguen's fluency in his speeches and letters throughout his life, she questions why he would rely on Thomas to write for him, and she cites a letter from Thomas to Gerrit Smith that references his editorial role. I agree with Williamson's interpretation. Thomas's obituary, in fact, states that he served as Loguen's editor, adding weight to that determination. No matter how heavily his story may have been edited by Thomas, however, the account is unquestionably Loguen's own, and the narrative proved to be an invaluable source that provided a window into Loguen's interior world during his time in slavery and early years of freedom.[3]

Another source that helped me to personalize Loguen's story was the unpublished biography of his daughter, Sarah Marinda Loguen Fraser, written by her own daughter, Gregoria Fraser Goins. The manuscript, entitled "Miss Doc" and available at the Moorland-Spingarn Research Center at Howard University, is based largely on Sarah's memories and Loguen family lore, and it provides a unique view of many of the family's activities presented in other sources. I treated this material cautiously as I used it, acknowledging that the details I mentioned are based on family memories as they appear in the manuscript. Like Loguen's narrative, the substance of Goins's work is generally consistent with that in sources found elsewhere. When in doubt of the veracity of the material presented in either source, I chose not to use it.[4]

My approach to these sources has been to synthesize the information provided within them to create a narrative of Loguen's life, taking care to contextualize his contributions by connecting them to the larger historical issues surrounding the effort to provide aid to fugitives and freedpeople and promote racial justice for all Black Americans. Throughout the Notes, I include citations of relevant secondary materials on the issues addressed, but they are far from comprehensive, for the literature on African American history is rich. Interested readers will find no lack of material if they wish to research these topics further.

NOTES

Introduction

1. J. W. Loguen, *The Rev. J. W. Loguen, as a Slave and as a Freeman: A Narrative of Real Life,* ed. Jennifer A. Williamson (Syracuse: Syracuse University Press, 2016), 301–2. This is a critical edition of the narrative, originally published in Syracuse in 1859. Subsequent references are to this edition.

2. The *Weekly Anglo-African* gave him the title Underground Railroad King, and other newspapers followed suit. See, e.g., *Weekly Anglo-African* (New York), December 10, 1859, January 7, May 5, November 24, 1860; *National Anti-Slavery Standard* (New York), March 11, 1865; *Harrisburg (PA) Telegraph,* December 19, 1868; *New National Era,* October 3, 1872; *Chicago Evening Post,* October 9, 1872; and *Little Rock (AR) Daily Republican,* October 10, 1872. See also Loguen, *Narrative,* 252–57.

3. Loguen, *Narrative,* 261.

4. Loguen, *Narrative,* 302–3.

5. *Syracuse Journal,* March 26, 31, 1860; *Syracuse Daily Courier and Union,* March 26, 1860; *Weekly Anglo-African* (New York), April 7, 1860; *Liberator* (Boston), April 27, 1860; *Anti-Slavery Bugle* (New Lisbon, OH), April 7, 1860; *National Standard,* May 5, 1860; Loguen, *Narrative,* 301–3.

6. *Frederick Douglass' Paper* (Rochester), April 14, 1854.

7. Broad works that highlight the complexity of nineteenth-century Black activism include Benjamin Quarles, *Black Abolitionists* (New York: Oxford University Press, 1969); Patrick Rael, *Black Identity and Black Protest in the Antebellum North* (Chapel Hill: University of North Carolina Press, 2002); Manisha Sinha, *The Slave's Cause: A History of Abolition* (New Haven: Yale University Press, 2017); and Van Gosse, *The First Reconstruction: Black Politics in America from the Revolu-*

tion to the Civil War (Chapel Hill: University of North Carolina Press, 2021). Studies centered on the importance of the Fugitive Slave Law include R. J. M. Blackett, *The Captive's Quest for Freedom: Fugitive Slaves, the 1850 Fugitive Slave Law, and the Politics of Slavery* (New York: Cambridge University Press, 2018); Andrew Delbanco, *The War Before the War: Fugitive Slaves and the Struggle for America's Soul from the Revolution to the Civil War* (New York: Penguin Press, 2018); and John L. Brooke, *There Is a North: Fugitive Slaves, Political Crisis, and Cultural Transformation in the Coming of the Civil War* (Amherst: University of Massachusetts Press, 2019).

CHAPTER 1. Slavery

1. *Syracuse Journal*, April 20, 1866; J. W. Loguen, *The Rev. J. W. Loguen, as a Slave and as a Freeman: A Narrative of Real Life*, ed. Jennifer A. Williamson (Syracuse: Syracuse University Press, 2016), 31. Although she is more commonly referred to as "Cherry" in the historical record, I have chosen to refer to Loguen's mother by her given name, Jane, rather than the name forced on her by her enslavers throughout this work.

2. James Olney, "'I Was Born': Slave Narratives, Their Status as Autobiography and as Literature," *Callaloo* 20 (Winter 1984): 46–73.

3. bell hooks, "Homeplace (a Site of Resistance)," in *Yearning: Race, Gender, and Cultural Politics* (Boston: South End Press, 1990), 41–49.

4. Loguen, *Narrative*, 32.

5. Loguen, *Narrative*, 32–33.

6. Virginia Gooch Watson, *History of the Logue Homes in West Wilson County, Tennessee*, 1986, Tennessee State Library and Archives, Nashville, 4–5; Loguen, *Narrative*, 33. The creek is called Mansker Creek in present-day Tennessee.

7. Loguen, *Narrative*, 31–33.

8. Matthew Salifia, *Slavery's Borderland: Freedom and Bondage Along the Ohio River* (Philadelphia: University of Pennsylvania Press, 2013); Emil Pocock, "Slavery and Freedom in the Early Republic: Robert Patterson's Slaves in Kentucky and Ohio, 1804–1919," *Ohio Valley History* 6, no. 1 (2006): 3–26.

9. Carol Wilson, *Freedom at Risk: The Kidnapping of Free Blacks in America, 1780–1865* (Lexington: University Press of Kentucky, 1994), 10–39; Loguen, *Narrative*, 32.

10. Loguen, *Narrative*, 35.

11. Jane Gray Buchannan, *John Logue of North Carolina—History and Hypothesis: Logue and Related Families of Delaware, Maryland, Pennsylvania, Virginia, and Tennessee*, 1980, Tennessee State Library and Archives, Nashville, 1–4, 10; Watson, *Logue Homes*, 1–3. In 1799, the Sugg's Creek land would become part of

Wilson County. Mansker's Creek is the present-day dividing line of Davidson and Sumner Counties.

12. Watson, *Logue Homes*, 2–3.

13. Loguen, *Narrative*, 38.

14. Loguen, *Narrative*, 37.

15. Loguen, *Narrative*, 35–36.

16. Loguen, *Narrative*, 34, 38.

17. Loguen, *Narrative*, 41.

18. Loguen, *Narrative*, 40–45.

19. Loguen, *Narrative*, 50–53; Watson, *Logue Homes*, 4. Records indicate that Elinor sold twenty acres of the Mansker's Creek property to Zachariah Betts, confirming his status as a neighbor to the Logues.

20. Watson, *Logue Homes*, 9.

21. Loguen, *Narrative*, 47–49.

22. Loguen, *Narrative*, 48.

23. Loguen, *Narrative*, 56–57.

24. Loguen, *Narrative*, 57, 60–64.

25. Loguen, *Narrative*, 64.

26. Watson, *Logue Homes*, 4–9.

27. Loguen, *Narrative*, 38.

28. Loguen, *Narrative*, 81. Loguen's narrative mistakenly refers to this creek as the Little Tombigbee River, which is a much larger navigable river in Alabama and parts of Mississippi. Today, there exists a Logue Cemetery near Bigby Creek, which was on land formerly owned by the Logues, indicating that this is the waterway Loguen referenced.

29. Loguen, *Narrative*, 82–83.

30. Loguen, *Narrative*, 81–82, 86–87.

31. Loguen, *Narrative*, 84.

32. Loguen, *Narrative*, 84.

33. On the Second Great Awakening, see Nathan O. Hatch, *The Democratization of American Christianity* (New Haven: Yale University Press, 1991); and John B. Boles, *The Great Revival: Beginnings of the Bible Belt* (Lexington: University of Kentucky Press, 1972).

34. On the spread of evangelism in the South, see Christine Leigh Heyrman, *Southern Cross: The Beginnings of the Bible Belt* (New York: Alfred A. Knopf, 1997).

35. Russel E. Richey, *Early American Methodism* (Bloomington: Indiana University Press, 1991), 82.

36. Loguen, *Narrative*, 89–91.

37. On the practice of slave mortgaging, see Bonnie Martin, "Slavery's In-

visible Engine: Mortgaging Human Property," *Journal of Southern History* 76, no. 4 (2010): 817–66.

38. Loguen, *Narrative,* 91–92.

39. Loguen, *Narrative,* 93–97.

40. Loguen, *Narrative,* 98–107.

CHAPTER 2. Freedom

1. J. W. Loguen, *The Rev. J. W. Loguen, as a Slave and as a Freeman: A Narrative of Real Life,* ed. Jennifer A. Williamson (Syracuse: Syracuse University Press, 2016), 114–16.

2. Loguen, *Narrative,* 107–9, 118–20.

3. Carl R. Osthaus, "The Work Ethic of the Plain Folk: Labor and Religion in the Old South," *Journal of Southern History* 70, no. 4 (2004): 745–82; Daniel T. Rodgers, *The Work Ethic in Industrial America, 1850–1920* (Chicago: University of Chicago Press, 1974), 248–94.

4. Loguen, *Narrative,* 120–21.

5. Loguen, *Narrative,* 133–40.

6. Loguen, *Narrative,* 130–32.

7. Loguen, *Narrative,* 133–34.

8. Loguen, *Narrative,* 144–51.

9. Loguen, *Narrative,* 161–62.

10. John Hope Franklin and Loren Schweninger, *Runaway Slaves: Rebels on the Plantation* (New York: Oxford University Press, 1999), 23–24.

11. Loguen, *Narrative,* 165–67, 177. On relations between poor white southerners and the enslaved, see Keri Leigh Merritt, *Masterless Men: Poor Whites and Slavery in the Antebellum South* (New York: Cambridge University Press, 2017).

12. Loguen, *Narrative,* 176.

13. Franklin and Schweninger, *Runaway Slaves,* 98–102.

14. Loguen, *Narrative,* 180.

15. Loguen, *Narrative,* 181; *Springfield (MA) Daily Republican,* May 14, 1860.

16. Loguen, *Narrative,* 181–82.

17. Loguen, *Narrative,* 184.

18. Loguen, *Narrative,* 192–95.

19. Loguen, *Narrative,* 202.

20. Loguen, *Narrative,* 202–5.

21. Loguen, *Narrative,* 205–6.

22. Loguen, *Narrative,* 207–10. In the narrative, Loguen refers to the town they were directed to as Corridon.

23. Eber Pettit, *Sketches in the History of the Underground Railroad* (1867; repr., Westfield, NY: Chautauqua Regional Press, 1999); Levi Coffin, *Reminiscences* (Cincinnati, OH: Western Tract Society, 1876); Wilbur H. Siebert, *The Underground Railroad from Slavery to Freedom* (1898; repr., New York: Dover, 2006). Mainstream historians generally accepted the view of an Underground Railroad formed primarily of white Quakers until the publication of Larry Gara's influential work *The Liberty Line: The Legend of the Underground Railroad* (Lexington: University of Kentucky Press, 1961).

24. Loguen, *Narrative*, 11–12.

25. Carol Hunter, *To Set the Captives Free: Reverend Jermain Wesley Loguen and the Struggle for Freedom in Central New York, 1835–1872* (Arlington, VA: Hyrax, 2013), 49; "Oswald Wright," State Historical Markers, Indiana Historical Bureau, https://www.in.gov/history/state-historical-markers/find-a-marker/oswell-wright/; J. Blaine Hudson, *Encyclopedia of the Underground Railroad* (Jefferson, NC: McFarland, 2006), s.v. "Bell-Wright Affair (1857)."

26. Stanley Harrold, *Border War: Fighting over Slavery Before the Civil War* (Chapel Hill: University of North Carolina Press, 2010), 1–16, 18.

27. Loguen, *Narrative*, 211–12. Loguen refers to this man as Mr. Overrals in the narrative. On Overall's Corydon connection, see Nicole Poletika, "James Overall: Indiana Free Person of Color and the 'Natural Rights of Man,'" *Untold Indiana*, Indiana Historical Bureau, April 1, 2020, https://blog.history.in.gov/james-overall-indiana-free-person-of-color-and-the-natural-rights-of-man/.

28. Loguen, *Narrative*, 213–16.

29. Loguen, *Narrative*, 217–18. On Black Underground Railroad activism, see Cheryl Janifer La Roche, *Free Black Communities and the Underground Railroad: The Geography of Resistance* (Urbana: University of Illinois Press, 2014); and Xenia Cord, *Black Rural Settlements in Indiana Before 1860* (Indianapolis: Indiana Historical Society, 1993).

30. Loguen, *Narrative*, 217.

31. Loguen, *Narrative*, 220.

32. Loguen, *Narrative*, 220; Poletika, "James Overall." See also annotations for "James Overall," State Historical Markers, Indiana Historical Bureau, https://www.in.gov/history/state-historical-markers/find-a-marker/find-historical-markers-by-county/indiana-historical-markers-by-county/james-overall/.

33. Loguen, *Narrative*, 220.

34. James H. Madison, *Hoosiers: A New History of Indiana* (Bloomington: Indiana University Press, 2014), 48–61, 109–10; "A Joint Resolution, Asking the Aid of the General Government for the American Colonization Society," *Indiana*

State Sentinel (Indianapolis), February 17, 1848. On the early Black population of Indiana, see also Emma Lou Thornborough, *The Negro in Indiana Before 1900* (Bloomington: Indiana University Press, 1993).

35. Loguen, *Narrative,* 220–22.

36. Loguen, *Narrative,* 223–28.

37. Loguen, *Narrative,* 229.

38. Loguen to Frederick Douglass, Syracuse, May 8, 1856, printed in *Frederick Douglass' Paper* (Rochester), May 23, 1856; Loguen, *Narrative,* 230.

39. Loguen to Douglass, May 8, 1856; Loguen, *Narrative,* 230.

CHAPTER 3. Mission

1. J. W. Loguen, *The Rev. J. W. Loguen, as a Slave and as a Freeman: A Narrative of Real Life,* ed. Jennifer A. Williamson (Syracuse: Syracuse University Press, 2016), 231–32.

2. For more on early Rochester, see William F. Peck, *Semi-Centennial History of the City of Rochester* (Syracuse: D. Mason, 1884), 90–127. A good history of the Erie Canal is Carol Sheriff, *The Artificial River* (New York: Hill and Wang, 1996). On Black mobility between Rochester and St. Catherines, see dann j. Broyld, *Borderland Blacks: Two Cities in the Niagara Region During the Final Decades of Slavery* (Baton Rouge: Louisiana State University Press, 2022).

3. Diane Shaw, *City Building on the Eastern Frontier: Sorting the New Nineteenth-Century City* (Baltimore: Johns Hopkins University Press, 2004), 71–76, 142.

4. Loguen, *Narrative,* 232.

5. Loguen, *Narrative,* 235.

6. Loguen, *Narrative,* 235.

7. Milton C. Sernett, *Abolition's Axe: Beriah Green, Oneida Institute, and the Black Freedom Struggle* (Syracuse: Syracuse University Press, 1986), 22–28, 58–59; Loguen, *Narrative,* 238.

8. Loguen, *Narrative,* 237–41.

9. *Colored American* (New York), August 25, 1838.

10. *Utica (NY) Observer,* February 17, 1985, 1659.pdf, *Fulton History,* https://fultonhistory.com/Fulton.html; William Charles Larkin, "The Black Preacher as Educator from 1787 to 1909" (PhD diss., University of Massachusetts, 1979), 42–44; Loguen, *Narrative,* 238–39.

11. Gregoria Fraser Goins, "Miss Doc," manuscript (biography of Sarah Loguen Fraser), 2, Gregoria Fraser Goins Papers, Howard University, Moorland-Spingarn Research Center; Loguen, *Narrative,* 240–41. The Loguens had eight children in total, but only six survived to adulthood.

12. Douglas H. Shephard, "Selected Persons of Color in Chautauqua County NY, 1850–1855," 2017, Chautauqua County, NY, https://chqgov.com; Loguen, *Narrative*, 240–41.

13. Loguen, *Narrative*, 242, 251.

14. Dennis J. Connors, *Crossroads in Time: An Illustrated History of Syracuse* (Syracuse: Syracuse University Press, 2006), 7–48; Milton C. Sernett, "'A Citizen of No Mean City': Jermain W. Loguen and the Antislavery Reputation of Syracuse," *Courier* 22, no. 2 (1987): 39; Carol Hunter, *To Set the Captives Free: Reverend Jermain Wesley Loguen and the Struggle for Freedom in Central New York, 1835–1872* (Arlington, VA: Hyrax, 2013), 165; *Syracuse Standard*, October 12, 1854.

15. *Colored American* (New York), May 15, 1841.

16. Loguen, *Narrative*, 373; Sernett, *Abolition's Axe*, 35; "AME Zion Church," *The Freedom Trail in Central New York, Uncovering the Freedom Trail in Syracuse and Onondaga County*, Preservation Association of Central New York, https://pacny.net/freedom_trail/AMEZION.htm.

17. On the politics of Black education in New York, see Carleton Mabee, *Black Education in New York State from Colonial to Modern Times* (Syracuse: Syracuse University Press, 1979); Loguen, *Narrative*, 353; Hunter, *To Set the Captives Free*, 62; and Russell W. Irvine and Donna Zani Dunkerton, "The Noyes Academy, 1834–35: The Road to the Oberlin Collegiate Institute and the Higher Education of African Americans in the Nineteenth Century," *Western Journal of Black Studies* 22, no. 4 (1998): 260–73.

18. William J. Walls, *The African Methodist Episcopal Zion Church* (Charlotte, NC: Zion, 1974), 28.

19. Walls, *Zion Church*, 32–39.

20. Walls, *Zion Church*, 50; Israel Daniel Rupp, comp., *The Religious Denominations in the United States* (Philadelphia: Charles De Silver, 1861), 417; Hunter, *To Set the Captives Free*, 180–81.

21. This conference is now the Western New York Conference.

22. Loguen, *Narrative*, 251. See also Thomas James, *Life of Rev. Thomas James, by Himself* (Rochester: Post Express, 1886), at *Documenting the South*, https://docsouth.unc.edu/neh/jamesth/jamesth.html.

23. Milton C. Sernett, "On Freedom's Threshold: The African American Presence in Central New York, 1760–1940," *Afro-Americans in New York Life and History* 19, no. 1 (1995): 25; *Syracuse Standard*, April 12, 26, 1851.

24. Loguen, *Narrative*, 242; "Minutes of the Annual Conference of the Wesleyan Methodist Episcopal Zion Church in America," January 1, 1842, May 20, 1843, African American Historical Serials Collection; *Syracuse Journal*, October

4, 1872; Sernett, "'Citizen of No Mean City,'" 36. Loguen asserts that he became a deacon in 1843, but he is listed as a "traveling preacher" admitted "on trial" in both the 1842 and 1843 minutes of the AME Zion Conference.

25. Andre Minifee, "Roots of Black Rhetoric: African Methodist Episcopal Zion's Pioneering Preacher-Politicians" (PhD diss., University of Texas, 2008); William Charles Larkin, "The Black Preacher as Educator from 1787 to 1909" (PhD diss., University of Massachusetts, 2014). On the Black church, see Henry Louis Gates Jr., *The Black Church: This Is Our Story, This Is Our Song* (New York: Penguin, 2021).

26. Alan M. Kraut and Phyllis F. Field, "Politics versus Principles: The Partisan Response to 'Bible Politics' in New York State," *Civil War History* 25, no. 2 (1979): 101–4.

27. An excellent edited collection on the Colored Conventions Movement is P. Gabrielle Foreman, Jim Casey, and Sarah Lynn Patterson, eds., *The Colored Conventions Movement: Black Organizing in the Nineteenth Century* (Chapel Hill: University of North Carolina Press, 2021). See also the Colored Conventions Project's digital collection of documents and essays produced by the editors of this collection at https://coloredconventions.org.

28. *Frederick Douglass' Paper* (Rochester), March 17, 1854; Loguen, *Narrative*, 252.

29. Loguen, *Narrative*, 254.

30. Loguen, *Narrative*, 254–55.

31. On Black abolitionists and violent resistance, see Kellie Carter Jackson, *Force and Freedom: Black Abolitionists and the Politics of Violence* (Philadelphia: University of Pennsylvania Press, 2019).

32. *Frederick Douglass' Paper* (Rochester), March 17, 1854; Loguen, *Narrative*, 255.

33. "The Meeting That Launched a Movement: The First National Convention," Colored Conventions Project Digital Records, https://coloredconventions.org/first-convention/; P. Gabrielle Foreman, "Black Organizing, Print Advocacy, and Collective Authorship: The Long History of the Colored Conventions Movement," in Foreman, Casey, and Patterson, *Colored Conventions Movement*, 23. See also Manisha Sinha, *The Slave's Cause: A History of Abolition* (New Haven: Yale University Press, 2017), a synthesis of the scholarship that recenters the discussion of abolition around the actions of Black Americans.

34. *Colored American* (New York), June 6, 1840; *Minutes of the State Convention of Colored Citizens, Held at Albany, on the 18th, 19th, and 20th of August 1840* (New York: Piercy and Reed Printers, 1840), available at Colored Conventions Project

Digital Records, https://omeka.coloredconventions.org/items/show/1071; Hunter, *To Set the Captives Free,* 87–91.

35. *Minutes of the State Convention of Colored Citizens, 1840;* Charles H. Wesley, "The Participation of Negroes in Anti-Slavery Political Parties," *Journal of Negro History* 29, no. 1 (1944): 32–74.

36. *Frederick Douglass' Paper* (Rochester), March 17, 1854; Vernon L. Volpe, "The Liberty Party and Polk's Election, 1844," *Historian* 53, no. 4 (2007): 691–710.

37. *National Anti-Slavery Standard* (New York), September 11, 1845; clipping of meeting, October 8, 1845, in Perry, NY, Misc. Newspapers, 0585.pdf, *Fulton History,* https://fultonhistory.com/Fulton.html.

38. Kraut and Field, "Politics versus Principles," 107–9.

39. On Black abolitionists and citizenship, see Christopher James Bonner, *Remaking the Republic: Black Politics and the Creation of American Citizenship* (Philadelphia: University of Pennsylvania Press, 2020); Charles H. Wesley, "The Participation of Negroes in Antislavery Political Parties," *Journal of Negro History* 29, no. 1 (January 1944), 49–50; and Van Gosse, *The First Reconstruction: Black Politics in America from the Revolution to the Civil War* (Chapel Hill: University of North Carolina Press, 2021).

40. *New York Tribune,* October 24, 1849; *Syracuse Journal,* October 22, 1849; Hunter, *To Set the Captives Free,* 164.

41. On the Smith Land program, see Amy Godine, *The Black Woods: Pursuing Racial Justice on the Adirondack Frontier* (Ithaca, NY: Cornell University Press, 2023); Lynne Feeley, "The Elevationists: Gerrit Smith, Black Agrarianism, and Land Reform in 1840s New York," *Environmental History* 24, no. 2 (2019): 307–26; Milton C. Sernett, *North Star Country: Upstate New York and the Crusade for African American Freedom* (Syracuse: Syracuse University Press, 2002), 197–202; and Daegan Miller, "At Home in the Great Northern Wilderness: African Americans and Freedom's Ecology in the Adirondacks, 1846–1859," *Environmental Humanities* 2, no. 1 (2013): 117–46.

42. Loguen to James McCune Smith, printed in *North Star* (Rochester), March 24, 1848.

43. Miller, "Great Northern Wilderness," 131–33.

44. Loguen to Smith, March 24, 1848.

45. Loguen to Smith, March 24, 1848.

46. Loguen, *Narrative,* 255–56.

47. On the AMA, see Joyce Hollyday, *On the Heels of Freedom: The American Missionary Association's Bold Campaign to Educate Minds, Open Hearts, and Heal the Soul of a Divided Nation* (Chestnut Ridge, NY: Crossroad, 2005), 16–22; Clara

Merritt De Boer, "The Role of Afro-Americans in the Origin and Work of the American Missionary Association, 1839–1877" (PhD diss., Rutgers University, 1973), 1–84; "American Missionary Association: Historical Note," Amistad Research Center, http://amistadresearchcenter.tulane.edu/.

48. Samuel Ringgold Ward to George Whipple, Cortlandville, NY, December 10, 1849; Loguen to Ovid Miner, Syracuse, January 24, 1850; Miner to Whipple, January 26, April 13, 1850; Charles Wheaton and Abner Bates to Whipple, February 15, 1850; American Missionary Association, *Fourth Annual Report of the American Missionary Association,* 1848, 33–34, all in AMA Archives, Amistad Research Center, Tulane University; De Boer, "Role of Afro-Americans," 200; Hunter, *To Set the Captives Free,* 192.

49. Loguen to Whipple, July 3, 1850, AMA Archives.

50. Loguen to Whipple, July 3, August 14, 1850, AMA Archives.

51. Miner to Whipple, Syracuse, April 13, 1850, January 8, February 5, July 24, 1851; Statement of the Treasurer, April 1851; Report of the Committee (Lewis Tappan, S. S. Jocelyn, Charles B. Ray, Thomas Ritter), November 27, 1850, all in AMA Archives; Hunter, *To Set the Captives Free,* 195.

52. Loguen, *Narrative,* 261; Miner to Whipple, December 8, 1850, Syracuse; AMA Treasurer's Balance, February 28, 1851; Treasurer's Report, March 1851, all in AMA Archives; De Boer, "Role of Afro-Americans," 200–201.

CHAPTER 4. Resistance

1. Portions of the discussion of Loguen's rejection of self-purchase are in Angela F. Murphy, "'My Freedom I Derived from God': Jermain Wesley Loguen's Rejection of Freedom Purchase," *Afro-Americans in New York Life and History* 48, no. 1 (2024): 15–30.

2. Public Letter of J. Thomas, Rev. S. R. Ward, and L. S. Pomeroy, Cortlandville, NY, July 28, 1846, *Steuben Advocate* (Bath, NY), n.d., 0567.pdf, *Fulton History*, https://fultonhistory.com/Fulton.html; *Syracuse Standard,* March 15, 1854; J. W. Loguen, *The Rev. J. W. Loguen, as a Slave and as a Freeman: A Narrative of Real Life,* ed. Jennifer A. Williamson (Syracuse: Syracuse University Press, 2016), 257. On Goodwin, see "Life Sketches of the Members of the Assembly of New York, 1867," in folder "Loguen, Rev. Jermain W. (Biography and Family)," Onondaga Historical Association, Syracuse.

3. Loguen, *Narrative,* 258–59.

4. Loguen, *Narrative,* 261.

5. *Liberator* (Boston), February 19, 1847; Henry Clarke Wright and Frederick Douglass, *Letter to Frederick Douglass with His Reply* (1846), 1–3, Samuel J. May Anti-Slavery Collection, Cornell University; Margaret M. R. Kellow, "Conflicting

Imperatives: Black and White American Abolitionists Debate Slave Redemption," in *Buying Freedom: The Ethics and Economics of Slave Redemption,* ed. Kwame Anthony Appiah and Martin Bunzl (Princeton, NJ: Princeton University Press, 2007), 204; Hannah Rose Murray, "'The Birthplace of *Your* Liberty': Purchasing Frederick Douglass's Freedom in 1846," *New North Star* 2 (2020): 63–65; John Stauffer, "Frederick Douglass and the Politics of Slave Redemption," in Appiah and Bunzl, *Buying Freedom,* 213–21.

6. William Wells Brown, *Narrative of William W. Brown, an American Slave, Written by Himself* (London: Charles Gilpin, 1849), ix; *Voice of the Fugitive* (Canada), November 5, 1851; *North Star* (Rochester), July 13, 1849.

7. *Liberator* (Boston), January 15, March 5, 1847; Kellow, "Conflicting Imperatives," 205–6; Stauffer, "Douglass and Slave Redemption," 214–15; Henry Mayer, *All on Fire: William Lloyd Garrison and the Abolition of Slavery* (New York: W. W. Norton, 2008), 372; Murray, "Birthplace," 63–64.

8. Israel Daniel Rupp, comp., *The Religious Denominations in the United States* (Philadelphia: Charles De Silver, 1861), 417; Loguen, *Narrative,* 264–65; Carol Hunter, *To Set the Captives Free: Reverend Jermain Wesley Loguen and the Struggle for Freedom in Central New York, 1835–1872* (Arlington, VA: Hyrax, 2013), 178–208; Andre Minifee, "Roots of Black Rhetoric: African Methodist Episcopal Zion's Pioneering Preacher-Politicians" (PhD diss., University of Texas, 2008), 8–9, 35.

9. Junius Rodriguez, ed., *Encyclopedia of Emancipation and Abolition in the Transatlantic World* (Armonk, NY: Sharpe Reference), s.v. "The Fugitive Slave Act, 1793"; Loguen, *Narrative,* 261.

10. *North Star* (Rochester), September 5, 1850.

11. Loguen to George Whipple, March 21, 1851, Syracuse, AMA Archives, Amistad Research Center, Tulane University.

12. Loguen, *Narrative,* 261.

13. Milton C. Sernett, *North Star Country: Upstate New York and the Crusade for African American Freedom* (Syracuse: Syracuse University Press, 2002), 44; Eva Marie Hardin, *Syracuse and the Underground Railroad* (Syracuse: Erie Canal Museum, 1989), 2–3; Esther C. Loucks, "The Anti-Slavery Movement in Syracuse from 1839–1851" (MA thesis, Syracuse University, 1934). For discussions of specific antislavery leaders active in Syracuse, see Ronald Burke, *Samuel Ringgold Ward, Christian Abolitionist* (New York: Garland, 1995); R. J. M. Blackett, *Samuel Ringgold Ward: A Life of Struggle* (New Haven: Yale University Press, 2023); Ralph V. Harlow, *Gerrit Smith: Philanthropist and Reformer* (New York: Henry Holt, 1939); and Donald Yacavone, *Samuel Joseph May and the Dilemmas of the Liberal Persuasion, 1797–1871* (Philadelphia: Temple University Press, 1991). See also personal

accounts in Samuel J. May, *Some Recollections of Our Anti-Slavery Conflict* (New York, 1968); and Samuel Ringgold Ward, *Autobiography of a Fugitive Negro* (New York: Arno Press, 1968).

14. Sernett, *North Star Country,* 77–102.

15. Loguen, *Narrative,* 366–68.

16. *Syracuse Standard,* September 27, 1850. On flight, see Fred Landon, "Negro Migration to Canada After 1850," *Journal of Negro History* 5, no. 1 (1920): 26–27; see also Angela F. Murphy, "'It Outlaws Me, and I Outlaw It!': Resistance to the Fugitive Slave Law in Syracuse, New York," *Afro-Americans in New York Life and History* 28, no. 1 (2004): 44.

17. May, *Recollections,* 350; Loguen, *Narrative,* 358–59, 364; *Syracuse Star,* October 5, 1850; Murphy, "It Outlaws Me," 45; Jayme Sokolow, "The Jerry McHenry Rescue and the Growth of Northern Antislavery Sentiment During the 1850s," *Journal of American Studies* 16, no. 3 (1982): 443; Donald Bluestone, "A Brief Study of Antislavery Activities in Syracuse and New York State," 1960, typescript, Onondaga Historical Association.

18. *Impartial Citizen* (Syracuse), October 5, 1850.

19. Loguen, *Narrative,* 264–65.

20. May, *Recollections,* 352; *Syracuse Standard,* October 7, 1850; Gurney S. Strong, *Early Landmarks of Syracuse* (Syracuse: Times Publishing, 1891), 274.

21. *Syracuse Standard,* October 14, 1850, January 8, 1851; *New York Tribune,* January 11, 1851; *Liberator* (Boston), January 24, 1851.

22. *Congressional Globe,* 31st Cong., 1st Sess., March 7, 1850. On the Compromise of 1850 debates, see Fergus M. Bordewich, *America's Great Debate: Henry Clay, Stephen A. Douglas, and the Compromise That Preserved the Union* (New York: Simon and Schuster, 2012); and John C. Waugh, *On the Brink of Civil War: The Compromise of 1850 and How It Changed the Course of American History* (New York: Rowman and Littlefield, 2003).

23. Daniel Webster, *Writings and Speeches of Daniel Webster,* vol. 17 (Boston: Little, Brown, 1903), 419–20; *Syracuse Star,* May 28, 1851; *New York Tribune,* May 28, 1851.

24. Loguen, *Narrative,* 114–15; Joseph Johnson to Whipple, June 24, 1851, AMA Archives. No records indicate that the Logues attempted to make any transaction concerning Loguen in 1851, although he had gained enough prominence by this time that it is certainly possible. See the discussion in Hunter, *To Set the Captives Free,* 115.

25. *Frederick Douglass' Paper* (Rochester), August 21, 1851.

26. Loguen, *Narrative,* 268–69; *Syracuse Standard,* October 7, 1851.

27. Loguen, *Narrative,* 268–69. See also "Parrish B. Johnson's Recollec-

tions," in *The Jerry Rescue: October 1, 1851,* ed. Franklin H. Chase (Syracuse: Onondaga Historical Association, 1924).

28. Loguen, *Narrative,* 268–69.

29. Loguen, *Narrative,* 270–71.

30. Loguen, *Narrative,* 270–71, 274; May, *Recollections,* 145, 376; "Merrick Reminiscences, 1893," in Chase, *Jerry Rescue.*

31. Loguen, *Narrative,* 272–74; May, *Recollections,* 377; Loguen, *Narrative,* 274; May, *Recollections,* 377; Carlton Mabee, *Black Freedom: Nonviolent Abolitionists from 1830 to the Civil War* (New York: McMillan, 1970), 307; "Merrick Reminiscences, 1893."

32. Sernett, *North Star Country,* 138.

33. *Syracuse Standard,* October 20, 1851; *Frederick Douglass' Paper,* February 11, 1853; Sernett, *North Star Country,* 144; *Liberator* (Boston), May 14, 1852.

34. Loguen, *Narrative,* 275–76; "Merrick Reminiscences, 1893."

35. *Frederick Douglass' Paper,* February 11, 1853; Loguen, *Narrative,* 282–83; "Mrs. Lucy Watson's Statement, 1894," in Chase, *Jerry Rescue,* 43–44; Ella B. Moffet, "Jerry's Rescue—The Story," *Syracuse Herald,* November 1, 1898, 44.

36. Loguen, *Narrative,* 282–83.

CHAPTER 5. Aid

1. J. W. Loguen, *The Rev. J. W. Loguen, as a Slave and as a Freeman: A Narrative of Real Life,* ed. Jennifer A. Williamson (Syracuse: Syracuse University Press, 2016), 284.

2. *National Anti-Slavery Standard* (New York), November 13, 1851; "Merrick Reminiscences," in *The Jerry Rescue: October 1, 1851,* ed. Franklin H. Chase (Syracuse: Onondaga Historical Association, 1924), 33. On the rescue's aftermath, see Angela F. Murphy, *The Jerry Rescue: The Fugitive Slave Law, Northern Rights, and the American Sectional Crisis* (New York: Oxford University Press, 2014), 124–45; and Angela F. Murphy, "'It Outlaws Me, and I Outlaw It!': Resistance to the Fugitive Slave Law in Syracuse, New York," *Afro-Americans in New York Life and History* 28, no. 1 (2004): 55–61.

3. Loguen, *Narrative,* 283–84.

4. Hiram Wilson to George Whipple, November 5, 1851, AMA Archives, Amistad Research Center, Tulane University; Loguen to J. R. Johnson, December 18, 1851, printed in *Frederick Douglass' Paper* (Rochester), January 8, 1852; Fred Landon, "The Anti-Slavery Society of Canada," *Journal of Negro History* 4, no. 1 (1919): 33–40.

5. Loguen, *Narrative,* 442; Earl E. Sperry, *The Jerry Rescue: October 1, 1851,* ed. Franklin H. Chase (Syracuse: Onondaga Historical Association, 1924), 27;

Loguen to James Lawrence, October 30, 1851, printed in *Frederick Douglass' Paper* (Rochester), November 27, 1851; "Testimony Before Judge Conkling in Auburn," *Syracuse Standard,* October 18, 20, 1851.

6. Loguen to Lawrence, October 30, 1851.

7. Webster-Ashburton Treaty, art. 10 (1841); Robin W. Winks, *The Blacks in Canada: A History,* 2nd ed. (Montreal: McGill-Queen's University Press, 1997), 168–77; dann j. Broyld, *Borderland Blacks: Two Cities in the Niagara Region During the Final Decades of Slavery* (Baton Rouge: Louisiana State University Press, 2022), 41–43; *Frederick Douglass' Paper,* November 27, 1851.

8. Gregoria Fraser Goins, "Miss Doc," manuscript (biography of Sarah Loguen Fraser), 11, Gregoria Fraser Goins Papers, Howard University, Moorland-Spingarn Research Center.

9. Loguen to Johnson, December 18, 1851.

10. Loguen to Washington Hunt, December 2, 1851, printed in *Frederick Douglass' Paper* (Rochester), April 8, 1852; *Liberator* (Boston), May 14, 1852.

11. Loguen to John Thomas, printed in *Frederick Douglass' Paper* (Rochester), February 5, 1852.

12. "The Trial of Henry W. Allen, US Deputy Marshal, for Kidnapping," 10, 38, Gerrit Smith Broadside and Pamphlet Collection, Syracuse University Library, Special Collections Research Center; *Frederick Douglass' Paper* (Rochester), December 25, 1851.

13. "Trial of Henry W. Allen," 96.

14. *Frederick Douglass' Paper* (Rochester), February 5, 1852.

15. John Anderson to Loguen, printed in *Frederick Douglass' Paper* (Rochester), May 6, 1852.

16. Goins, "Miss Doc," 13; Larry Gara, *The Liberty Line: The Legend of the Underground Railroad* (Lexington: University of Kentucky Press, 1961), 145.

17. *Syracuse Standard,* January 19, 1859, June 28, 1860; Eber M. Petit in Milton C. Sernett, *North Star Country: Upstate New York and the Crusade for African American Freedom* (Syracuse: Syracuse University Press, 2002), 174; "Merrick Reminiscences"; William Still, *The Underground Railroad* (Philadelphia: Porter and Coates, 1872), 127; "Parish B. Johnson's Recollections," in Chase, *Jerry Rescue;* Samuel J. May, *Some Recollections of Our Anti-Slavery Conflict* (New York, 1968), 292.

18. *Syracuse Standard,* June 28, 29, 1852.

19. Milton C. Sernett, "'A Citizen of No Mean City': Jermain W. Loguen and the Antislavery Reputation of Syracuse," *Courier* 22, no. 2 (1987): 45; Loguen to H. Bibb, August 13, 1852, printed in *Voice of the Fugitive* (Canada), September 9, 1852; Loguen to Frederick Douglass, August 5, 1853, printed in *Frederick Douglass'*

Paper (Rochester), August 12, 1853; Loguen to Nathan Randall Chapman, January 17, 1852, Chapman Family Papers, Arents Research Library, Syracuse.

20. Accounts of the incident can be found in *New York Tribune,* October 5, 1852; *New York Herald,* October 6, 1852; *Syracuse Standard,* October 6, 1852; *Syracuse Journal,* October 6, 1852; *Syracuse Star,* October 6, 1852; *Buffalo Morning Express,* October 7, 1852; *Albany Argus,* October 7, 1852; *Weekly Wisconsin* (Milwaukee), October 13, 1862; *Liberator* (Boston), October 15, 1852; and *Frederick Douglass' Paper* (Rochester), October 15, 1862.

21. *Syracuse Journal,* March 9, 1867; Goins, "Miss Doc," 13.

22. Goins, "Miss Doc," 13–14.

23. Letter dated October 7, 1852, in *Religious Recorder* (Syracuse), October 14, 1852, 0322.pdf, *Fulton History,* https://fultonhistory.com/Fulton.html; *Frederick Douglass' Paper* (Rochester), October 15, 1852.

24. *Syracuse Star,* October 6, 1852; *Weekly Wisconsin* (Milwaukee), October 13, 1852.

25. *Carson League* (Syracuse), December 2, 1852; *Religious Recorder* (Syracuse), December 2, 1852; *Liberator* (Boston), December 3, 1852; *Frederick Douglass' Paper* (Rochester), December 24, 1852; *Syracuse Journal,* October 1, 1872; Goins, "Miss Doc," 13; *Frederick Douglass' Paper* (Rochester), December 31, 1852.

26. Murphy, *Jerry Rescue,* 140–41.

27. *Carson League* (Syracuse), December 2, 1852; *Religious Recorder* (Syracuse), December 2, 1852.

28. *Syracuse Evening Chronicle,* July 9, 1855; *Frederick Douglass' Paper* (Rochester), July 20, 1855.

29. *Syracuse Standard,* September 3, 1855; *Syracuse Evening Chronicle,* September 12, 13, 1855; *Syracuse Journal* quoted in *Buffalo Morning Express,* September 5, 1855.

30. *Syracuse Standard,* January 25, 1854.

31. Loguen, *Narrative,* 240–41; Carol Hunter, *To Set the Captives Free: Reverend Jermain Wesley Loguen and the Struggle for Freedom in Central New York, 1835–1872* (Arlington, VA: Hyrax, 2013), 59–60; Wendy J. W. Straight and Douglas H. Shephard, eds., "The Underground Railroad in Chautauqua County," 2013, Chautauqua County, NY, https://chqgov.com/.

32. *Syracuse Standard,* January 1, 1855; Goins, "Miss Doc," 11.

33. *Syracuse Journal,* September 7, 1867.

34. Julie Roy Jeffrey, "Permeable Boundaries: Abolitionist Women and Separate Spheres," *Journal of the Early Republic* 21, no. 1 (2001): 79–93; James Oliver Horton, "Freedom's Yoke: Gender Conventions Among Antebellum Free Blacks," *Feminist Studies* 12, no. 1 (1986): 51–76; Martha Jones, *All Bound Up Together: The*

Woman Question in African American Public Culture, 1830–1900 (Chapel Hill: University of North Carolina Press, 2007).

35. bell hooks, "Homeplace (a Site of Resistance)," in *Yearning: Race, Gender, and Cultural Politics* (Boston: South End Press, 1990), 42–44.

36. Portions of the discussion of the Loguen family's operation are in Angela F. Murphy, "Politicizing the Home: The Loguen Family's Underground Railroad," *Journal of the Early Republic* 45, no. 3 (Fall 2025).

37. Goins, "Miss Doc," 2–3.

38. Goins, "Miss Doc," 2–3, 14.

39. Goins, "Miss Doc," 24. See William J. Switala, *Underground Railroad in New York and New Jersey* (Mechanicsburg, PA: Stackpole Books, 2006), 109–18, for a description of the Underground Railroad Routes of Central New York; Hunter, *To Set the Captives Free,* 138–39.

40. *Frederick Douglass' Paper* (Rochester), August 24, 1855.

41. *Syracuse Standard,* November 28, 1857.

42. Goins, "Miss Doc," 55; *National Anti-Slavery Standard* (New York), May 29, 1858. I thank Douglas Egerton for directing my attention to the Higginson speech.

43. *Douglass' Monthly,* May 1859; *Syracuse Standard,* December 19, 1854, May 31, 1855; *Syracuse Post Standard,* March 28, 1964; Sernett, *North Star Country,* 178; Goins, "Miss Doc," 55. On Tubman's work with Loguen, see Sernett, *North Star Country,* 190; and Kate Clifford Larson, "Racing for Freedom: Harriet Tubman's Underground Railroad Network Through New York," *Afro-Americans in New York Life and History* 31, no. 1 (2012): 16–17. On Sarah Loguen Fraser's career as a doctor, see E. v. d. Luft, "Sarah Loguen Fraser, MD (1850–1933): The Fourth African-American Woman Physician," *Journal of the National Medical Association* 92, no. 3 (2000): 149–53.

44. Goins, "Miss Doc," 55; *Syracuse Standard,* December 12, 1854, July 19, 1856, June 28, 1860; Loguen, *Narrative,* 295; Hunter, *To Set the Captives Free,* 154–55.

45. *Syracuse Standard,* September 27, December 19, 1854, December 13, May 31, 1855, June 11, 18, 1857; *Frederick Douglass' Paper* (Rochester), April 6, June 8, 1855; Sernett, *North Star Country,* 176; Jennifer A. Williamson, "Critical Introduction," in Loguen, *Narrative,* 3.

46. *Syracuse Standard,* July 8, 1858.

47. *Syracuse Standard,* December 13, 1856.

48. *Syracuse Standard,* December 13, 1856; Still, *Underground Railroad,* 517.

49. *Douglass' Monthly,* 1859; Still, *Underground Railroad,* 127, 154, 158, 221, 426, 517. On Still, see William C. Kashatus, *William Still: The Underground Railroad and the Angel at Philadelphia* (Notre Dame, IN: University of Notre Dame Press,

2021); and Andrew K. Diemer, *Vigilance: The Life of William Still, Father of the Underground Railroad* (New York: Alfred A. Knopf, 2022).

CHAPTER 6. Alms

1. Eric Foner, *Gateway to Freedom: The Hidden History of the Underground Railroad* (New York: W. W. Norton, 2016), 21; Andrew K. Diemer, "The Business of the Road: William Still, the Vigilance Committee, and the Management of the Underground Railroad," *Journal of the Early Republic* 42, no. 1 (2022): 83–113.

2. John Hope Frankin and Evelyn Brooks Higginbotham, *From Slavery to Freedom: A History of Negro Americans*, 9th ed. (New York: McGraw-Hill, 2011), 199–203; Foner, *Gateway to Freedom*, 20–21; Graham Russell Gao Hodges, *David Ruggles: A Radical Black Abolitionist and the Underground Railroad in New York City* (Chapel Hill: University of North Carolina Press, 2010), 4; Diemer, "Business of the Road," 87; Fergus Bordewich, *Bound for Canaan: The Underground Railroad and the War for the Soul of America* (New York: Amistad, 2005), 236–47.

3. Diemer, "Business of the Road," 87–107.

4. *Auburn (NY) Daily Advertiser*, May 1, 1857, April 16, 1858; *Syracuse Courier*, January 30, 1860.

5. *National Anti-Slavery Standard* (New York), October 10, November 21, 28, 1857; *Syracuse Standard*, September 28, 1857; *Syracuse Journal*, September 30, 1857; *Liberator* (Boston), October 16, 1857.

6. *Frederick Douglass' Paper* (Rochester), June 23, 1854, April 6, November 9, 1855.

7. *National Anti-Slavery Standard* (New York), November 29, 1856.

8. Loguen's exchange of correspondence with this minister, Hiram Mattison, was originally published in the *Jefferson County (NY) News* and *Syracuse Journal*, after which the letters were issued in pamphlet form as *Correspondence Between Rev. H. Mattison and Rev. J. W. Loguen in the Duty of Ministers to Allow Contributions in the Churches in the Aid of Fugitive Slaves and the Obligations of Civil Government and the Higher Law* (Syracuse: J. E. Masters, 1857). The pamphlet can be found at the Moorland-Spingarn Research Center at Howard University, and selections from it are available in the Black Abolitionist Papers database at https://www.proquest.com/bap.

9. Report on Mattison letter originally published in the *Jefferson County (NY) News*, reprinted in *Syracuse Journal*, August 12, 1856.

10. Loguen to Mattison, August 13, 1856, printed in *Syracuse Journal*, August 14, 1856; *Correspondence Between Mattison and Loguen*, 9–13.

11. Mattison to Loguen, August 25, 1856, in *Correspondence Between Mattison and Loguen*, 13–21.

12. Loguen to Mattison, October 2, 1856, November 6, 1856, in *Correspondence Between Mattison and Loguen,* 22–26, 33–40.

13. *Correspondence Between Mattison and Loguen;* Carol Hunter, *To Set the Captives Free: Reverend Jermain Wesley Loguen and the Struggle for Freedom in Central New York, 1835–1872* (Arlington, VA: Hyrax, 2013), 199.

14. *Syracuse Daily Courier and Union,* February 16, 1857.

15. *Syracuse Daily Courier and Union,* April 9, 1857.

16. *Syracuse Standard,* January 21, 22, 1857; Hunter, *To Set the Captives Free,* 148–49.

17. *Syracuse Standard,* January 15, 1858, January 22, 1859; *Syracuse Daily Courier and Union,* June 17, 1858.

18. Loguen to Mattison, October 2, 1856, in *Correspondence Between Mattison and Loguen,* 25–26.

19. *Syracuse Standard,* March 11, 1857, November 30, 1860; Loguen to Gerrit Smith, March 23, 1859, Gerrit Smith Papers, Special Collections Research Center, Syracuse University.

20. *National Anti-Slavery Standard* (New York), November 29, 1856; *Syracuse Journal,* January 24, 28, 1860; *Syracuse Courier,* January 26, 30, 31, 1860; *New York Herald,* January 31, 1860; *Plattsburgh (NY) Republican,* February 11, 1860. Brown's society was unaffiliated with the legitimate African Aid Society founded in Great Britain in 1860 to promote development and voluntary Black emigration to Africa.

21. *Auburn (NY) Daily Advertiser,* April 16, May 1, 1857; *Liberator* (Boston), January 7, 1858; *Syracuse Journal,* January 24, 28, 1860.

22. William Brown to Loguen, August 14, 1858, Anti-Slavery Collection, Boston Public Library; Hunter, *To Set the Captives Free,* 147–48.

23. *Syracuse Daily Courier and Union,* April 9, 1857, September 8, 1858.

24. *Syracuse Daily Courier and Union,* March 14, 1859.

25. *Syracuse Journal,* January 24, 28, 1860; *Syracuse Courier,* January 26, 30, 31, 1860; *New York Herald,* January 31, 1860; *Plattsburgh (NY) Republican,* February 11, 1860.

26. *Weekly Anglo-African* (New York), February 18, 1860.

27. *Syracuse Standard,* December 1, 1860.

28. *Syracuse Standard,* March 6, 1858, January 1, 1849, January 6, 1860; Loguen to Smith, March 23, 1859; Benjamin Quarles, *Black Abolitionists* (New York: Oxford University Press, 1969), 157–59; Samuel J. May, *Some Recollections of Our Anti-Slavery Conflict* (New York, 1968), 303; Milton C. Sernett, "'A Citizen of No Mean City': Jermain W. Loguen and the Antislavery Reputation of Syracuse," *Courier* 22, no. 2 (1987), 47–48.

29. Loguen to Smith, March 23, 1859.

30. *Syracuse Journal,* March 22, October 15, November 5, 1859; *Liberator* (Boston), October 28, 1859.

31. *Syracuse Standard,* September 30, 1859; *Syracuse Journal,* October 11, 1859, January 31, 1860; Jennifer A. Williamson, "Critical Introduction," in J. W. Loguen, *The Rev. J. W. Loguen, as a Slave and as a Freeman: A Narrative of Real Life,* ed. Williamson (Syracuse: Syracuse University Press, 2016), 6–16.

32. *Weekly Anglo-African* (New York), January 28, 1860; Williamson, "Critical Introduction," 14.

33. *Syracuse Journal,* November 23, 1860; *Oneida (NY) Sachem,* March 29, 1860.

CHAPTER 7. Uplift

1. J. W. Loguen, *The Rev. J. W. Loguen, as a Slave and as a Freeman: A Narrative of Real Life,* ed. Jennifer A. Williamson (Syracuse: Syracuse University Press, 2016), 261; *Frederick Douglass' Paper* (Rochester), August 21, 1851.

2. *Voice of the Fugitive* (Canada), November 5, 1851.

3. *Syracuse Journal,* March 21, 1853.

4. R. J. M. Blackett, *The Captive's Quest for Freedom: Fugitive Slaves, the 1850 Fugitive Slave Law, and the Politics of Slavery* (New York: Cambridge University Press, 2018), 88–94; *Syracuse Standard,* March 14, 1853; *Religious Recorder* (Syracuse), March 17, 1853; *Frederick Douglass' Paper* (Rochester), March 25, 1853.

5. *Syracuse Standard,* March 14, 1853; *Frederick Douglass' Paper* (Rochester), March 25, 1853.

6. *Syracuse Standard,* March 21, 1853; *Syracuse Evening Chronicle,* March 21, 1853; *Liberator* (Boston), April 15, 1853.

7. *Frederick Douglass' Paper* (Rochester), February 3, 1854; *Provincial Freeman* (Canada), March 25, 1854; Howard H. Bell, "Expressions of Negro Militancy in the North, 1840–1860," *Journal of Negro History* 45, no. 1 (1960): 16–20.

8. *Frederick Douglass' Paper* (Rochester), February 3, 1854.

9. *Liberator* (Boston), August 26, 1859.

10. *Syracuse Evening Chronicle,* November 24, 1853; *Frederick Douglass' Paper* (Rochester), January 14, 1854; *Syracuse Journal,* August 16, 1856.

11. Michael F. Hembree, "The Question of 'Begging': Fugitive Slave Relief in Canada, 1830–1865," *Civil War History* 37, no. 4 (1991): 318–20.

12. *Provincial Freeman* (Canada), November 3, 1855, March 22, April 5, May 10, 1856, January 10, 1857.

13. *Frederick Douglass' Paper* (Rochester), January 14, 1854; *Syracuse Standard,* June 5, 1856.

14. *Frederick Douglass' Paper* (Rochester), January 8, February 12, 1852; *National Anti-Slavery Standard* (New York), March 4, 1852.

15. *Frederick Douglass' Paper* (Rochester), January 14, 1854.

16. *Provincial Freeman* (Canada), May 24, 26, 1856.

17. *Syracuse Standard,* June 6, 1856; Hembree, "Question of 'Begging,'" 320–21; Alexander Lovell Murray, "Canada and the Anglo-American Anti-Slavery Movement: A Study in International Philanthropy" (PhD diss., University of Pennsylvania, 1960), 391–99; Willie J. Harrell Jr., "'Thanks Be to God That I Am Elected to Canada': The Formulation of the Black Canadian Jeremiad," *Journal of Canadian Studies* 42, no. 3 (2008): 68; dann j. Broyld, "The Power of Proximity: Frederick Douglass and His Transnational Relations with British Canada, 1847–1861," *Afro-Americans in New York Life and History* 41, no. 2 (2020): 3–25.

18. *Provincial Freeman* (Canada), May 24, 1856.

19. *Syracuse Journal,* May 23, 1856.

20. *Frederick Douglass' Paper* (Rochester), February 17, December 4, 1854, January 5, 8, April 6, September 11, November 9, December 14, 1855.

21. *Syracuse Journal,* December 28, 1855; *National Anti-Slavery Standard* (New York), April 5, 1855.

22. *Frederick Douglass' Paper* (Rochester), March 1, 1850.

23. From the *Wesleyan* in *Frederick Douglass' Paper* (Rochester), March 23, 1855; *Liberator* (Boston), March 30, 1855.

24. *Syracuse Journal,* October 15, 1860.

25. *Northern Star and Freeman's Advocate,* March 17, 1842; *Syracuse Standard,* August 29, 1855.

26. *Frederick Douglass' Paper* (Rochester), September 2, 1853; Carol Hunter, *To Set the Captives Free: Reverend Jermain Wesley Loguen and the Struggle for Freedom in Central New York, 1835–1872* (Arlington, VA: Hyrax, 2013), 143.

27. *Voice of the Fugitive* (Canada), July 1, 1852.

28. *Voice of the Fugitive* (Canada), September 9, 1852; R. J. M. Blackett, *Samuel Ringgold Ward: A Life of Struggle* (New Haven: Yale University Press, 2023), 64–65.

29. *Frederick Douglass' Paper* (Rochester), June 10, 1852.

30. *Weekly Anglo-African* (New York), June 16, 1860, September 28, 1861; *Christian Recorder* (Philadelphia), May 16, 1863.

31. "Proceedings of the Colored National Convention, Held in Rochester, July 6th, 7th, and 8th, 1853," *Frederick Douglass' Paper* (Rochester), September 2, 1853.

32. "Colored National Convention, Rochester," 3–11.

33. "Colored National Convention, Rochester," 18–26.

34. *Frederick Douglass' Paper* (Rochester), August 12, 1853.

35. *Frederick Douglass' Paper* (Rochester), February 3, 1854.

36. *Syracuse Evening Chronicle*, December 3, 1851; *Frederick Douglass' Paper* (Rochester), February 3, 1854.

37. *New York Tribune*, August 11, 1854; *Frederick Douglass' Paper* (Rochester), March 31, 1854; August 25, 1854.

38. *Frederick Douglass' Paper* (Rochester), March 30, 1855.

39. *Syracuse Standard*, September 6, 1855; *Frederick Douglass' Paper* (Rochester), September 14, 1855; "Colored Men's State Convention of New York, Troy, September 4, 1855," *Frederick Douglass' Paper* (Rochester), July 7, 1855; *Weekly Anglo-African* (New York), October 15, 1859, March 31, 1860; Howard Holman Bell, "Some Reform Interests of the Negro During the 1850s as Reflected in State Conventions," *Phylon* 21, no. 2 (1960): 175–78; Hunter, *To Set the Captives Free*, 95–96.

CHAPTER 8. Reckoning

1. J. W. Loguen, *The Rev. J. W. Loguen, as a Slave and as a Freeman: A Narrative of Real Life*, ed. Jennifer A. Williamson (Syracuse: Syracuse University Press, 2016), 296.

2. *Liberator* (Boston), September 24, 1852; Angela F. Murphy, *The Jerry Rescue: The Fugitive Slave Law, Northern Rights, and the American Sectional Crisis* (New York: Oxford University Press, 2014), 148–57.

3. Loguen to William Lloyd Garrison, April 28, 1854, and Response from the Editor of the *Liberator*, May 5, 1854, in *Mind of the Negro as Reflected in Letters Written During the Crisis, 1800–1860*, ed. Carter G. Woodson (Lancaster, PA: Lancaster Press, 1926), 267–68.

4. On Anthony Burns, see Earl M. Maltz, *Fugitive Slave on Trial: The Anthony Burns Case and Abolitionist Outrage* (Lawrence: University Press of Kansas, 2010); and Albert J. Von Frank, *The Trials of Anthony Burns: Freedom and Slavery in Emerson's Boston* (Cambridge, MA: Harvard University Press, 1998).

5. On the Kansas-Nebraska controversy, see Nicole Etcheson, *Bleeding Kansas: Contested Liberty in the Civil War Era* (Lawrence: University Press of Kansas, 2004).

6. *Frederick Douglass' Paper* (Rochester), April 14, 1854; *Syracuse Evening Chronicle*, July 9, 1855.

7. *Syracuse Journal*, October 2, 1854; *Albany Evening Journal*, October 2, 1854; *New York Daily Tribune*, October 12, 1854.

8. *Frederick Douglass' Paper* (Rochester), September 25, 1855; *Liberator* (Boston), October 12, 1855.

9. *Frederick Douglass' Paper* (Rochester), October 12, 1855.

10. *Syracuse Standard,* August 23, 1856.

11. *Anti-Slavery Bugle* (New Libson, OH), November 15, 1856.

12. On abolitionist third parties, see Corey M. Brooks, *Liberty Power: Anti-Slavery Third Parties and the Transformation of American Politics* (Chicago: University of Chicago Press, 2016).

13. *Syracuse Journal,* September 29, 1854; *Frederick Douglass' Paper* (Rochester), July 6, 1855.

14. On the Radical Abolitionist Party, see John Stauffer, *The Black Hearts of Men: Radical Abolitionists and the Transformation of Race* (Cambridge, MA: Harvard University Press, 2002); and Kellie Carter Jackson, *Force and Freedom: Black Abolitionists and the Politics of Violence* (Philadelphia: University of Pennsylvania Press, 2019), 445–80.

15. *Syracuse Daily Journal,* July 24, 1856.

16. *Frederick Douglass' Paper* (Rochester), November 9, 1855.

17. *Liberator* (Boston), October 23, 1857; *New York Herald,* September 5, 1859.

18. Franklin Benjamin Sanborn, *Recollections of Seventy Years* (Boston: R. G. Badger, 1909), 154.

19. On John Brown, see David S. Reynolds, *John Brown, Abolitionist* (New York: Penguin Random House, 2005); Jackson, *Force and Freedom,* 106–34.

20. *Frederick Douglass' Paper* (Rochester), August 26, 1853; Benjamin Quarles, *"Allies for Freedom" and "Blacks and John Brown"* (Boston: Da Capo Press, 2001).

21. *Proceedings of the Convention of Radical Political Abolitionists, Held at Syracuse, NY* (Ithaca, NY, 1855), 59, 62, Samuel J. May Antislavery Pamphlet Collection, Cornell University Library.

22. Frederick Douglass, *The Life and Times of Frederick Douglass* (New York: Library of America, 1996), 715; John Brown to Loguen, May 17, 1859, printed in *Syracuse Journal,* February 18, 1860; Wendell Phillips Garrison, "The Preludes of Harpers Ferry, II.—John Brown, Guerrilla," *Andover Review,* January 1891, 55.

23. *National Intelligencer* (Washington, DC), November 3, 1859; Robin W. Winks, *The Blacks in Canada: A History,* 2nd ed. (Montreal: McGill-Queen's University Press, 1997), 268.

24. Loguen to Brown, May 6, 1858, John Brown Collection, Kansas State Historical Society, Topeka, available online at https://www.kansasmemory.gov/item/4840; Quarles, *"Allies for Freedom,"* 49.

25. Jackson, *Force and Freedom,* 119.

26. Gregoria Fraser Goins, "Miss Doc," manuscript (biography of Sarah Loguen Fraser), 42, Gregoria Fraser Goins Papers, Howard University, Moorland-Spingarn Research Center.

27. *Syracuse Journal,* February 28, 1860.

28. *Douglass' Monthly,* October 1860.

29. The *Liberator* dedicated an issue to the antiabolitionist conflict in Syracuse, presenting a collection of articles that reported on the crisis. See *Liberator* (Boston), February 15, 1861.

30. *Liberator* (Boston), February 15, 1861.

31. *Liberator* (Boston), February 15, 1861.

32. *Syracuse Journal,* April 23, 1861.

33. *Pine and Palm* (Boston), June 15, 1861. On the Black emancipationist view of the war, see David W. Blight, "They Knew What Time It Was: African-Americans and the Coming of the Civil War," in *Why the Civil War Came,* ed. Gabor S. Boritt (New York: Oxford University Press, 1996), 51–78.

34. *Syracuse Standard,* April 14, September 7, 1861; *Jordan (NY) Transcript Courier,* May 7, 1861; *Syracuse Journal,* April 23, May 11, 1861.

35. *Syracuse Standard,* September 7, 1861.

36. *Weekly Anglo-African* (New York), September 29, 1861, April 5, 1862.

37. *Syracuse Journal,* January 2, March 27, 1863; *Syracuse Standard,* April 3, 1863.

38. *Principia* (New York), July 30, 1863.

39. *Weekly Anglo-African* (New York), September 5, 1863; *Rochester Evening Express,* September 12, 1864.

CHAPTER 9. Reconstruction

1. *Weekly Anglo-African* (New York), September 5, 1863.

2. *Principia* (New York), December 24, 1863; *American Freedmen's Friend Society, Thursday, May 28, 1863,* printed circular, in Abraham Lincoln Papers at the Library of Congress, Series 1, *General Correspondence, 1833 to 1916,* https://www.loc.gov/item/mal2371300/.

3. Steven Hahn, *A Nation Under Our Feet: Black Political Struggles in the Rural South from Slavery to the Great Migration* (Cambridge, MA: Harvard University Press, 2005), 73–74.

4. "Mr. Loguen's Visit to Virginia," *American Missionary* 8, no. 7 (1864): 175–76.

5. "Mr. Loguen's Visit," 75–76.

6. William J. Walls, *The African Methodist Episcopal Zion Church* (Charlotte, NC: Zion, 1974), 185; J. W. Hood, *One Hundred Years of the African Methodist Episcopal Zion Church; or, The Centennial of African Methodism* (New York: A.M.E. Zion Book Concern, 1895), 17, 180–81.

7. *Syracuse Journal,* November 11, 1864; *Christian Recorder* (Philadelphia), October 28, 1865; *Little Falls (NY) Journal Courier,* January 25, 1866.

8. *Syracuse Journal,* March 9, 11, July 13, 1867.

9. *Syracuse Journal,* May 15, 1865.

10. "Endorsement of a Runaway Slave to Return to Tennessee to Search for His Family," April 20, 1865, in "Documents Relating to the 1860s," Gilder Lehrman Collection, 1860–1945, Gilder Lehrman Institute of American History, New York.

11. *Syracuse Journal,* June 23, 1865; *Ogdensburg (NY) Daily Journal,* July 1, 1865.

12. *Syracuse Journal,* June 23, July 1, 1865.

13. *Syracuse Journal,* June 23, July 1, 1865.

14. *Weekly Anglo-African* (New York), July 22, 1865; *Christian Recorder* (Philadelphia), August 12, 1865; *Syracuse Standard,* July 27, 1865; *Rochester Evening Express,* August 29, 31, 1865; *Lockport (NY) Daily Journal-Courier,* September 2, 1865.

15. *Syracuse Standard,* July 27, 1865.

16. *Weekly Anglo-African* (New York), July 22, 1865; *Christian Recorder* (Philadelphia), August 12, 1865.

17. *Weekly Anglo-African* (New York), July 22, 1865; *Christian Recorder* (Philadelphia), August 12, 1865.

18. *Christian Recorder* (Philadelphia), August 12, 1865; *Syracuse Journal,* April 20, 1866.

19. *Weekly Anglo-African* (New York), July 22, 1865; Gregoria Fraser Goins, "Miss Doc," manuscript (biography of Sarah Loguen Fraser), 51–59, Gregoria Fraser Goins Papers, Howard University, Moorland-Spingarn Research Center; *Syracuse Journal,* August 19, 1867.

20. Goins, "Miss Doc," 58–59.

21. Goins, "Miss Doc," 51; *Syracuse Journal,* October 8, 1869; *Christian Recorder* (Philadelphia), October 23, 1869; letters of Lewis H. Douglass to H. Amelia Loguen in *The Mind of the Negro as Reflected in Letters Written During the Crisis, 1800–1860,* ed. Carter G. Woodson (Washington, DC: Association for the Study of Negro Life and History, 1926), 540–44. Additional correspondence between the two can be found in Celeste-Marie Bernier and Andrew Taylor, eds., *If I Survive: Frederick Douglass and Family in the Walter O. Evans Collection* (Edinburgh: Edinburgh University Press, 2018), 43–112.

22. Goins, "Miss Doc," 51; *Syracuse Journal,* October 8, 1869; *Christian Recorder* (Philadelphia), October 23, 1869. On the courtship of Lewis Douglass and Amelia Loguen, see also Douglas R. Egerton, *Thunder at the Gates: The Black Civil War Regiments That Redeemed America* (New York: Basic Books, 216), 78, 88, 159–60, 242, 330.

23. *Syracuse State League*, April 28, 1866; *Syracuse Standard*, July 7, 1871; *Woman's Journal*, July 29, 1871.

24. *Anglo-African Magazine* (New York), December 9, 1865; *Syracuse Journal*, March 5, 6, April 8, December 28, 1865.

25. *Mexico (NY) Independent*, April 5, 1866; *Syracuse Journal*, May 18, 1866, March 3, 11, 1867, July 13, 1867, July 1, 1869. On Black educational efforts in the South, see Hilary Green, *Educational Reconstruction: African American Schools in the Urban South, 1865–1890* (New York: Fordham University Press, 2016); and Heather Andrea Williams, *Self-Taught: African American Education in Slavery and Freedom* (Chapel Hill: University of North Carolina Press, 2005).

26. *Elevator* (San Francisco), August 4, 1845; National Lincoln Monument Association, *Celebration by the Colored People's Educational Monument Association in Memory of Abraham Lincoln* (Washington, DC: McGill and Witherow, 1865), Daniel Murray Pamphlet Collection and African American Pamphlet Collection, Library of Congress, https://www.loc.gov/item/12030032/.

27. *Frederick Douglass' Paper* (Rochester), June 8, 1855; *Syracuse Journal*, July 1, 1869.

28. Walls, *African Methodist Episcopal Zion Church*, 163; *The Methodist* (New York), June 27, 1868; *Syracuse Standard*, July 2, 1869; *Syracuse Journal*, December 23, 1870.

29. Peter C. Ripley, *Witness for Freedom: African American Voices on Race, Slavery, and Emancipation* (Chapel Hill: University of North Carolina Press, 1993), 26; *Syracuse Journal*, May 18, 1866, April 24, 1867, May 16, July 18, 1870; *Cortland (NY) Standard*, September 29, 1868; *Syracuse Courier*, April 30, 1870; *Christian Recorder* (Philadelphia), June 18, 1870; *Schoharie Union* (NY), May 2, 1867.

30. *Syracuse Standard*, July 2, 1869.

31. Walls, *African Methodist Episcopal Zion Church*, 163; *Syracuse Journal*, December 28, 1871.

32. *Syracuse Standard*, December 20, 24, 1869; *New Era* (Washington, DC), January 13, 1870; *Proceedings of the Colored National Labor Convention Held in Washington, D.C., . . . 1869* (Washington, DC: Office of the New Era, 1870), available at Colored Conventions Project Digital Records, https://omeka.coloredconventions.org/items/show/591.

33. *Proceedings of the Colored National Labor Convention.*

34. *Syracuse Standard*, December 24, 1869.

35. *New York Herald*, August 23, 1870; *National Standard* (New York), September 3, 17, 24, 1870.

36. *New National Era* (Washington, DC), January 19, 1871.

37. *Liberator* (Boston), September 9, 1864; Erik J. Chaput, "The Right Path:

The Civil Rights Movement and the 1864 Syracuse Black Convention," *Common-place—The Journal of Early American Life,* https://commonplace.online/article/right-path/.

38. Chaput, "Right Path."

39. *Syracuse Journal,* September 2, November 3, 1864.

40. *Syracuse Journal,* December 21, 1866; *New York Tribune,* October 17, 1866, October 8, 1868; *Utica (NY) Weekly Herald,* October 13, 1868.

41. *Utica (NY) Weekly Herald,* October 13, 1868.

42. *Syracuse Courier,* April 30, 1870; *Syracuse Journal,* May 16, July 18, 1870; *Christian Recorder* (Philadelphia), June 18, 1870; *Syracuse Standard,* June 2, 1870.

43. *Pacific Appeal* (San Francisco), July 1, 1871.

44. *New National Era* (Washington, DC), December 7, 1871.

45. *Syracuse Standard,* December 16, 1871.

46. *Jamestown (NY) Daily Journal,* July 25, 1872; *Little Rock (AR) Daily Republican,* October 10, 1872.

Epilogue

1. *Elevator* (San Francisco), July 20, 1872; William J. Walls, *The African Methodist Episcopal Zion Church* (Charlotte, NC: Zion, 1974), 199–200.

2. *Syracuse Journal,* October 2, 1872.

3. *Syracuse Journal,* October 1, 2, 1872.

4. *Ithaca (NY) Daily Journal,* October 5, 1872; *Syracuse Journal,* October 4, 1872.

5. W. E. B. Du Bois, *Black Reconstruction in America* (New York: Harcourt Brace, 1935), 30.

6. "The Loguen Family," *Negro History Bulletin* 10, no. 8 (1947): 171–74.

7. "Sarah Loguen Fraser, M.D., Class of 1876," SUNY HSC/Syracuse Medical Alumni Association, *Alumni Journal,* Summer 1998, 14; "Loguen Family," 171–74; "Sarah Loguen Fraser," *American National Biography Online,* http://www.anb.org/articles/13/13-02676.html; *Afro-American* (Washington, DC), June 6, 1964.

8. "Loguen Family," 173–74.

9. "Loguen Family," 173; *Syracuse Journal,* February 28, 1873; *Utica (NY) Daily Observer,* September 18, 1874; *Utica (NY) Morning Herald,* July 28, 1876; *Syracuse Standard,* April 22, 1887; *Syracuse Journal,* August 19, 1894; *Syracuse Evening Herald,* October 20, 1899; *New York Age,* September 20, 1906.

10. *Syracuse Standard,* January 24, 1886; *Syracuse Journal,* November 7, 1901. On northern Reconstruction Era segregation, see David E. Goldberg, *Retreats of Reconstruction: Race, Leisure, and the Politics of the New Jersey Shore, 1865–1920* (New York: Fordham University Press, 2016).

11. "Speech on the 33rd Anniversary of the Jerry Rescue, Rochester, NY, 1884," Frederick Douglass Papers at the Library of Congress, Speech, Article, and Book File, 1846–1894, https://www.loc.gov/item/mss1187900445/.

12. David W. Blight, "'For Something Beyond the Battlefield': Frederick Douglass and the Struggle for the Memory of the Civil War," *Journal of American History* 75, no. 4 (1989): 1156–78.

A Note on Sources

1. Paul Minifee, "Rhetoric of Doom and Redemption: Reverend Jermain Loguen's Jeremiadic Speech Against the Fugitive Slave Law of 1850," *Advances in the History of Rhetoric* 16, no. 1 (2013): 29–57; Paul Minifee, "Our World Wide Organ: Constitutive Rhetoric in Rev. Jermain W. Loguen's Letters to African American Newspapers," *Journal of Communication and Religion* 36, no. 3 (2013): 106–26.

2. Robert Djed Snead, ed., *Bishop J. W. Loguen: A Life Lived Loudly* (Rochester: Moon Water Products, 2021).

3. J. W. Loguen, *The Rev. J. W. Loguen, as a Slave and as a Freeman: A Narrative of Real Life*, ed. Jennifer A. Williamson (Syracuse: Syracuse University Press, 2016); Carol Hunter, *To Set the Captives Free: Reverend Jermain Wesley Loguen and the Struggle for Freedom in Central New York, 1835–1872* (Arlington, VA: Hyrax, 2013), 12–21; Jennifer A. Williamson, "Critical Introduction" to Loguen, *Narrative*, 6–15; *Syracuse State League*, April 28, 1866.

4. Gregoria Fraser Goins, "Miss Doc," manuscript (biography of Sarah Loguen Fraser), Gregoria Fraser Goins Papers, Howard University, Moorland-Spingarn Research Center.

ACKNOWLEDGMENTS

THIS BOOK would not have been possible without the incredible support and contributions from numerous individuals and institutions.

My heartfelt thanks go to the editors of the *Black Lives* series—David Blight, Jacqueline Goldsby, and Henry Louis Gates Jr.—for allowing Loguen's story to be included among its fabulous offerings. Special thanks go to David Blight, who made me aware of the series. I also want to thank senior editor at Yale University Press Jessie Kindig, who helped me see the book to completion. She was a joy to work with. Her prompt responses and invaluable suggestions for the manuscript improved it immensely. Thanks are also due to Erica Hanson, the production editor for the book, and to Laura Jones Dooley, who provided copy edits. This work also benefited from the suggestions of those who reviewed the manuscript for the press. Their insights brought clarity to the work and helped me think about aspects of Loguen's story in a fresh way.

I am deeply grateful to Richard Blackett, who took the time to read through an early draft and who provided critical suggestions for its improvement. He has listened to me talk about Loguen for a long time—since I first stumbled on his story in a graduate seminar almost a quarter century ago. I also extend my gratitude to

Leigh Fought and Douglas Egerton, who have shown interest in this project over the years and shared helpful documents and ideas that furthered my research.

Julie Mujic, Michael Becker, and Paul Quigly deserve a special mention. The weekly online sessions of our writing group have been a tremendous source of inspiration and motivation throughout the process of completing this biography. It truly would not be what it is, and likely would have taken much longer to complete, without those meetings. Thank you also to the Outreach Committee of the Society of Civil War Historians, chaired by Megan Bever, for organizing our group and others at the end of 2020 as a way to help members connect with one another in the midst of the Covid pandemic. This effort provided the four of us with a supportive writing community that has met consistently ever since.

Thank you to the Onondaga Historical Association for providing photographs of Jermain and Caroline Loguen for use in this book. I am also grateful to editors at the *Journal of the Early Republic* and *Afro-Americans in New York Life and History* for allowing me to integrate portions of articles submitted to those journals into my manuscript.

Appreciation also goes out to my home institution, Texas State University, whose Research Enhancement Program supported travel and research for this project and whose Faculty Senate granted a semester's developmental leave to begin the writing. I also benefited greatly from course releases and funds provided by the Ingram Family Professorship in History. Special thanks go to History Department Chair Jeff Helgeson, who accommodated this release time that allowed me to finish the biography.

Last, to friends and family who have heard me talk about this project over the years, read through chapters, and cheered me on with their enthusiasm—your support has been invaluable. Loguen's story is ultimately about family and community, and writing it was particularly poignant as I leaned on loved ones through the writing of this book. I lost my mother, Faye Batt, to Covid in 2023, and she was a constant presence in my thoughts as I considered Loguen's relationship with Jane. I am sorry that she did not get to read the book in its totality, for she also took special interest in Loguen's family relationships. I also appreciate the keen interest that my father, Murray Batt, showed in Loguen's story as he eagerly awaited chapter drafts as I wrote. Most special thanks go to my husband, Ned Murphy, who has always supported my work and the time it takes to complete it. As we visited Syracuse and walked the streets that Loguen walked, learning the details of his story, Ned became one of Loguen's biggest fans and urged me to do justice to the man as I shared that story with others. I hope I have done so.

INDEX